The Mathematics of Novelty:
Badiou's Minimalist Metaphysics

Anamnesis

Anamnesis means remembrance or reminiscence, the collection and recollection of what has been lost, forgotten, or effaced. It is therefore a matter of the very old, of what has made us who we are. But *anamnesis* is also a work that transforms its subject, always producing something new. To recollect the old, to produce the new: that is the task of *Anamnesis*.

a re.press series

The Mathematics of Novelty:
Badiou's Minimalist Metaphysics

Sam Gillespie

re.press Melbourne 2008

re.press

PO Box 75, Seddon, 3011, Melbourne, Australia
http://www.re-press.org

© re.press 2008

This work is 'Open Access', published under a creative commons license which means that you are free to copy, distribute, display, and perform the work as long as you clearly attribute the work to the authors, that you do not use this work for any commercial gain in any form whatsoever and that you in no way alter, transform or build on the work outside of its use in normal academic scholarship without express permission of the author (or their executors) *and* the publisher of this volume. For any reuse or distribution, you must make clear to others the license terms of this work. For more information see the details of the creative commons licence at this website:
http://creativecommons.org/licenses/by-nc-nd/2.5/

British Library Cataloguing-in-Publication Data
A catalogue record for this book is available from the British Library

Library of Congress Cataloguing-in-Publication Data
A catalogue record for this book is available from the Library of Congress

National Library of Australia Cataloguing-in-Publication Data

Gillespie, Sam, 1970- .
The mathematics of novelty : Badiou's minimalist metaphysics.

Bibliography.
Includes index.
ISBN 9780980305241 (pbk.).

1. Badiou, Alain. 2. Deleuze, Gilles, 1925-1995.
3.Ontology. 4. Materialism. 5. Metaphysics. 6. Philosophy.
7. Mathematics. I. Title. (Series : Anamnesis).

111

Designed and Typeset by *A&R*

This book is produced sustainably using plantation timber, and printed in the destination market on demand reducing wastage and excess transport.

for Nancy Gillespie

Contents

Acknowledgements ix
Abbreviations xi

1. Conditions of the New: Deleuze and Badiou 1
   I: Deleuzian Novelty 4
   II: Badiou's Novelty 7
   III: Paradoxes of the Whole 15
   IV: Overturning Assumptions 17
   V. Conclusion: Axiomatic 21

2. Nothing That Is 25
   I. Thinking and Being, They Are the Same 25
   II. Foreclosing the Void 29
   III. The Problem of Infinite Modes 33
   IV. Non-Causal Relations 37
   V. Conclusion: Enabling the Event 40

3. Approximately Infinite Universe 45
   I. Frege/Russell: Zero Exists 50
   II. Cantor: Infinity and Inconsistency 52
   II. Badiou: Mathematics is Ontology, the Void is the Name of Being 57
   IV. Towards the Situation 61
   V. Meta-structure: The State and its Excesses 62

4. Beyond Being: Badiou's Doctrine of Truth 71
   I. Contesting Truth 73
   II. Towards the Generic 77
   III. The Force is With You 82
   IV. Towards the Situation (Again) 85

5. Giving Form to Its Own Existence: Anxiety and the Subject of Truth 95
   I. Rudimentary Ontology: An Overview 98
   II. The Void: Subject or Being? 105
   III. Affect defined 117

6. From Reflection to Transformation: What is Philosophy? 125
   I. Beyond the World: Why Novelty? 139

Bibliography 151
Index 157

Acknowledgements

Bringing Sam Gillespie's remarkable manuscript *The Mathematics of Novelty* to publication has been the joint effort of Sam's partner Michael Mottram, Chris Gillespie and myself. We would like to thank Paul Ashton, Adam Bartlett and Justin Clemens from re.press for their much appreciated support of this project. Others who have offered invaluable assistance and support in seeing this project through are Keith Ansell-Pearson, Alain Badiou, Jason Barker, Bruno Besana, Oliver Feltham, Barbara Formis, Peter Hallward, Dominiek Hoens, Christopher Norris, Nina Power, and Alberto Toscano. We know that Sam wished to thank in particular Joan Copjec and Bill O'Hara. We trust that any others whose names should also be on this page will recognize themselves. Finally we would like to thank Brent Harris and Kaliman Gallery, Sydney, for the use of the cover image *Borrowed plumage #5 (double)*.

Modified portions of chapter 2 have appeared as 'Placing the Void: Badiou on Spinoza', *Angelaki*, vol. 6, no. 3, 2001 (this article can be found at http://www.informaworld.com). A part of chapter 5 appeared as 'Beyond Being: Badiou's Doctrine of Truth', *Communication and Cognition*, vol. 36, nos.1-2, 2003, while its complete version, 'Giving Form to its Own Existence: Anxiety and the Subject of Truth' appeared in *The Praxis of Alain Badiou*, Melbourne, re.press, 2006. We are grateful for the editors' permission to reprint this material.

Sigi Jöttkandt
Ghent, Belgium

Abbreviations

Works by Badiou have been abbreviated as follows:

BE	*Being and Event*, trans. Oliver Feltham, London, Continuum, 2005.
CB	*Deleuze: The Clamor of Being*, trans. Louise Burchill, Minneapolis, University of Minnesota Press, 2000.
CS	*Conditions*, Paris, Seuil, 1992.
CT	*Court traité d'ontologie transitoire*, Paris, Seuil, 1998.
EE	*L'être et l'événement*, Paris, Seuil, 1988.
Ethics	*Ethics: An Essay on the Understanding of Evil*, trans. Peter Hallward, London, Verso, 2001.
IT	*Infinite Thought: Truth and the Return to Philosophy*, ed. and trans. Justin Clemens and Oliver Feltham, London, Continuum, 2003
LM	*Logiques des mondes: L'être et l'événement 2*, Paris, Seuil, 2006.
MP	*Manifesto for Philosophy*, trans. Norman Madarasz, Albany, State University of New York Press, 1999.
NN	*Le Nombre et les nombres*, Paris, Seuil, 1990.
SP	*Saint Paul: The Foundation of Universalism*, trans.ß Ray Brassier, Stanford, Stanford University Press, 2003.
TS	*Théorie du sujet*, Paris, Seuil, 1982.
TW	*Theoretical Writings*, trans. Ray Brassier and Alberto Toscano, London, Continuum Books, 2004.

Except where otherwise noted, all translations from the French are Sam Gillespie's own with assistance by Oliver Feltham.

I

Conditions of the New: Deleuze and Badiou

Change is a constant of being. Although this remark sounds contradictory, its logic dominates any philosophical discussion of innovation. Change, as Aristotle wrote, has always existed. Without change, there could simply be no passage from one period to another. Organisms evolve, an artist creates, an individual wakes up one morning and joins a religious cult: these are just so many instances of being's innermost potential for variation and flux. If novelty is possible on the basis of pre-given conditions, philosophy's concern is to discover what these conditions are and have always been. Variation, innovation or the advent of the new can only ever be supposed from the outset: it simply isn't possible to think these fluctuations apart from the grip they have on all of being. But is philosophy's task one of discovering the conditions that enable change over the course of time (for which every innovation will have always already existed), or is change rather a matter of philosophical invention, assuming often unpredictable forms?

Gilles Deleuze writes that 'the aim of philosophy is not to rediscover the eternal or the universal, but to find the conditions under which something new is produced'.[1] Within its own terms, Deleuze's statement presents the reader with a choice: that between the eternal or universal, on one hand, and the variation of the new, on the other. If Deleuze unhesitatingly aligns his philosophy with the latter, it is because, in keeping with the tenets of his thought, the conditions for enabling the new affirm being's ability to differentiate itself as it appears in the world. While Hegel is traditionally taken as Deleuze's principal adversary, the primary target here is in fact a Platonism of eternal, unchanging forms, existing independently of a world that is continually in a state of change. Philosophy uncovers the conditions under which that change occurs. But it is not enough to say that philosophy simply describes the conditions under which being is multiply dispersed over the different lines, dimensions, or 'states' that are irreducible to

---

1. Gilles Deleuze and Claire Parnet, *Dialogues*, trans. Hugh Tomlinson and Barbara Habberjam, New York, Columbia, 1987, p. vii.

one another: it is from these irreducible differences that philosophy generates its own concepts. It is in this sense that the philosophy of Deleuze could be called creative. Being creative will have nothing to do with the general or abstract foundations for comprehending the world (which, for Deleuze, would entail that the world itself conform to the requirements of the abstract). Instead, Deleuzian concepts are created from a free act of the philosopher that operates alongside the concept's self-positing. Corresponding to the artist's or philosopher's subjective capacity to generate concepts is the concept's objective potential to exist.

> Creation and self-positing mutually imply each other because what is truly created from the living being to the work of art, thereby enjoys a self-positing of itself, or an auto-poetic characteristic by which it is recognized [...]. What depends on a free creative activity is also that which, independently and necessarily, posits itself in itself: the most subjective will be the most objective.[2]

For the Deleuzian, then, it would be absurd to look outside the tenets of the concept's self-manifestation for an explanation of cause, since such abstractions always operate externally to creation itself. Being is simply postulated for Deleuze, and this postulation is being's own creative activity: its objective status as given corresponds to the subjective activity of the philosopher. By extension, the question, 'what enables creation?' appears erroneous from the outset. Creation is tantamount to the positing of being. There is, thus, no need for an external, or subsidiary cause external to being to explain how it is created. And, not surprisingly, the conditions from which novelty derives will refuse the empty abstractions of the One, or the Whole: where the Deleuzian departs from is, of course, nothing other than pure multiplicity itself. 'The essential thing [...] is the noun multiplicity, which designates a set of lines or dimensions which are irreducible to one another. Every 'thing' is made up in this way'.[3] Innovation or difference simply follows from this presupposition of the inherent multiplicity and self-differentiation of being. For what at the level of being subsists as pure difference, appears in the world as actual differences that are manifest everywhere in various guises. The 'lines of flight' that should be familiar to even the most casual reader of Deleuze find their convergence not in a singular point, but in the various 'bifurcations' and 'divergences' they assume in the course of their own movement. Everywhere dispersed and stratified, being is the inherent constant through which the new cannot help but appear. And if this is the case, everything new has its origin in an appearing or expression of being's innermost potential.

If Deleuze is the great contemporary thinker of both novelty and multiplicity, he almost certainly finds his worthy rival in the figure of Alain Badiou. As Badiou's name increasingly circulates throughout the English-speaking acad-

---

2. Gilles Deleuze and Félix Guattari, *What is Philosophy?*, trans. Hugh Tomlinson and Graham Burchell, New York, Verso, 1994, p. 118.

3. Deleuze and Parnet, *Dialogues*, p. vii.

emy, and with publishers eager to distribute long-overdue translations of his writing, his theories can be referred to with a certain familiarity. Even the relatively small number of works available in English have immediately established him as a contentious and polemical writer whose position directly sets him apart from the majority of his contemporaries.[4] Nonetheless, Badiou shares with Deleuze the fundamental convictions that philosophy as a project is far from over, that being is inherently multiple and is irreducible to the tenets of language, that philosophical novelty proceeds from an event, and that, despite its different manifestations in the world, being in and of itself is inherently univocal. And yet, having said as much, we can just as readily produce a lengthy list detailing the manner in which their philosophical projects diverge. In place of the Deleuzian art of creating concepts adequate to being's capacity to appear everywhere in various guises, Badiou maintains that truths have their origin in the aleatory rarity of an event. Against the famous univocity of Deleuze (whereby being is said in '*in a single and same sense* of all the numerically distinct designators and expressors'[5]), Badiou will pose the mathematical empty set as the single term from which the most complex infinities are generated. Where we depart from, then, is not an assumption that being exists as a creative power, but rather that to think being, we need nothing more than a formal assertion that nothing—that is, the empty set or zero—exists. If the empty set is a pure formalization of being—having in itself no descriptive properties or content of any kind—then the being it formalizes is simply nothing, void. As Badiou puts it in *Being and Event*, 'the sole term from which ontology's compositions without concept are woven is inevitably the void'.[6]

It is not entirely controversial to link an inaugural existence of zero to the existence of infinite multiplicities: contemporary mathematics attests to the fact that zero and infinity are coextensive. And from the standpoint of both finite mathematics and experience, zero and infinity do not have tangible existences—they are purely inconsistent, they lack definitive form. But with regard to the question of novelty, it is somewhat more difficult to see how something new could derive from nothing. Nevertheless Badiou's unique thesis, as it will become apparent, is that it is from the inconsistency of the void that something new can appear within the realm of human experience as such: ruptures or breaks within knowledge that force us to redefine our general categories and standards of determination. These are Badiou's events. Events, in the most rudimentary of senses, are derived from the inconsistent domains of human experience, and while events as such may be rare, there is also an ontological guarantee that what Badiou calls 'historic' situations contain the potential for an event insofar as the inherent mul-

---

4. The most exemplary work in this respect would be Alain Badiou, *Manifesto for Philosophy*, trans. Norman Madarasz, Albany, State University of New York Press, 1999. Hereafter cited in the text as *MP*.

5. Gilles Deleuze, *Difference and Repetition*, trans. Paul Patton, New York, Columbia University Press, 1994, p. 35.

6. Alain Badiou, *L'être et l'événement*, Paris, Seuil, 1988, p. 70. Hereafter cited in the text as *EE*.

tiplicity of any situation escapes the grasp of consistent presentation.[7] Or rather, what is consistently presented in experience (and here we could refer to anything that could be classified, ordered, or regulated by language or intuition) cannot exhaust the ontological resources of inconsistency. It is this that allows for the possibility of an event.

I: Deleuzian Novelty

Whether novelty is conceived of in terms of the creation of concepts or art works that adequate to being's propensity to proliferate in the world (as for Deleuze), or if it is seen, rather, as the sporadic coming-to-be of a truth drawn from the margins of any situation (Badiou), the presupposed foundation for innovation in philosophy will extend from the criteria that both Deleuze and Badiou use to qualify multiplicity as such. It should be clear, at least in a general sense, that the question of multiplicity in Deleuze cannot be separated from being's capacity for differentiation in all of its manifestations. Multiplicity is comprised of lines and dimensions that are irreducible to one another. And if we are to follow at least one of Deleuze's arguments, the question of the manifestation of being qua difference is, in turn, inseparable from the question of the *repetition* of being as difference.

Very briefly, we could consider it from the perspective of the formation of a self. For what is a self if not a contraction of multiple tiny syntheses of differences into a broader synthesis of these differences *as habit*, which concerns 'not only the sensory-motor habits that we have (psychologically), but also, before these, the primary habits that we are; the thousands of passive syntheses of which we are organically composed'?[8] The composite parts that define an organism enter into differential relations with one another that eventually coalesce into an organized whole that assumes the form of a self. In *Difference and Repetition*, Deleuze draws upon Freud as an example. Taken from the point of view of the dominance that pleasure, as a principle, has over the entirety of psychic life, the question is not whether pleasure has its origin in the binding and release of excitation. Rather, if we are to believe Freud, the question concerns what it is that enables the various contractions and releases of excitation to form a principle of pleasure that has a hold on the sum total of psychic life.[9] The answer, writes Deleuze, resides in a larger synthesis that creates a self from the tiny, differential contractions which, prior to the formation of a habit, are simply chaotic multiples in general, un-

---

7. Badiou here distinguishes historic situations (which contain a site for an event) from natural situations (where no such site is present). The site of the event could be said to be presented in a historic situation, but its elements are not. It is thus a site 'on the edge of the void'. See *EE*, pp. 193-198.

8. Deleuze, *Difference and Repetition*, p. 74.

9. Perhaps more than any other reader of Freud, Deleuze has shown that *Beyond the Pleasure Principle* does not involve the competition of life and death 'instincts', but rather the determination of pleasure as a principle which inevitably instills its own beyond. See Deleuze, *Difference and Repetition*, p. 96. 'It is a question of knowing how pleasure ceases to be a process in order to become a principle, how it ceases to be a local process in order to assume the value of an empirical principle which tends to organise biopsychical life in the Id'.

bound excitation. The self, in such an instance, is the formation of an individual from such a synthesis *as habit*. To the contractions that appear as tiny instances of repeatable difference corresponds a larger contraction that fuses repetition with a contemplating mind. The repetition of differential relations (say, the conflict of various psychic faculties) forms a relation that is external to any one of the individual parts in that relation, and this externality is constitutive of a self.

From this general foray into the complexity of Deleuze's system, the question of novelty can be introduced. It is from the perspective of this contemplating mind that something new is derived: 'Habit *draws* something new from repetition—namely difference'.[10] Three pages later, Deleuze writes that 'the role of the imagination, or the mind which contemplates in its multiple and fragmented states, is to draw something new from repetition, to draw difference from it'.[11] The novelty derived from this is the individual that is formed from the repetition of these individual relations. Just as the subjective creation of a Deleuzian concept is linked to the auto-poetic character of self-positing, the contemplative self as habit can just as readily be correlated to the instantaneous unravelling of repetition in and of itself. And if the redistribution of particular differences corresponds to the generality of repetition as habit (whereby several registers of repetition can be opposed), the movement of repetition from the general to the singular, or from multiplicity to the individual, constitutes nothing less than a differentiation of what, from the perspective of repetition, is difference itself. It is from here that we can understand how Deleuzian being continually produces itself anew. For it is not enough to say that novelty is constituted by virtue of producing something new every time a repetition occurs—it is necessary that the new in repetition is drawn from a *totality* that is capable of recognizing the new *as new* (totality in this instance being the constitution of a self out of habit). Or rather: the contemplative soul is what poses the question of difference insofar as it draws its response from repetition.[12] If the process of differentiation can be traced in terms of lines, these lines move in two directions: one where the divergent lines actualize a whole, or virtual totality (say, the transcendental foundation of difference and repetition that makes the formation of individuals possible), and another where these digressions and divergences express the whole from their own individual perspective.[13] Differentiation, and hence novelty, is inseparable from a totality, thus returning the metaphysics of the whole full-circle to Deleuze's system.

Although Deleuze is conventionally read as the great thinker of the multiple, the 'metaphysics of the whole' is completely compatible with how Deleuze's philosophy accounts for change. For example, as we will see shortly with regard to the problem of movement, Deleuze freely writes that it 'expresses something

---

10. Deleuze, *Difference and Repetition*, p. 73.
11. Deleuze, *Difference and Repetition*, p. 76.
12. Deleuze, *Difference and Repetition*, p. 78.
13. The Bergsonian implications of this process of novelty with respect to a virtual totality is nowhere more clearly expressed than in pages 100-101 of Gilles Deleuze, *Bergsonism*, trans. Hugh Tomlinson and Barbara Habberjam, New York, Zone Books, 1991.

more profound, which is a change in duration or in the whole'.[14] Qualitative change, and thus the emergence of the new, occurs in and through the whole, rather than in any term or instant in which it is composed. Change, in other words, results from a process and is not given in the end result of what change produces.

The problem with this interpretation, however, occurs at the ontological level. For if the whole is ontologically given at the outset, the modifications that occur within the whole over time and space are also given, and this is what makes a philosophy of becoming problematic. For if the whole is indeed everything, anything new that comes to be produced would occur externally to the whole. From the perspective of the whole, nothing can be new if it always already is. On the other hand, it is just as true that the new proceeds from the whole.

This is a problem only if one overlooks the dimension of time through which the trajectory of the whole unfolds and changes. For Deleuze, as for Bergson, if the positing of the whole is said to give everything at once, it is time that *prevents* everything from being given at once. From within a classical framework, this would lead to contradictions: either the whole exists (insofar as its existence can be posited) or it does not (insofar as it is never given at once). If the former is true, then the whole should be giveable; if the latter is the case, the whole is not giveable. Deleuze sidesteps this opposition altogether: the whole is neither given nor giveable at the same time that it exists. That is to say: 'if the whole is not giveable, it is because it is the open, and because its nature is to change constantly, or to give rise to something new, in short, to endure'.[15]

So, if we re-examine this ontological status of change, we find that what is produced is not, at an ontological level, something more or additional to what already is, but rather something *new*. Thus the above conclusion that change is antithetical to the concept of a whole is plausible only insofar as we assume that the whole is numerically quantifiable—that is, insofar as we normally assume that the production of something new occurs on the basis of an ontological incompletion. Deleuze finds his way out of this quandary through his appeal to Spinozism: it is impossible that there could be anything outside the infinite productivity of substance, since infinity cannot be missing any parts.[16] But this doesn't mean that substance cannot be said to be open to modifications.

However, while it may not be paradoxical to derive change from a whole, it is still unresolved why it is through the whole that change is possible. Deleuze, as we will see, has very good reasons to believe this. For if the conditions for the emergence of the new presuppose multiplicity, it is because the trajectory of being presupposes a multiplicity of possible relations that allows for a great diversity in life. A 'Deleuzian' evolutionary theory, for example, would presuppose that an organism develops by

---

14. Gilles Deleuze, *Cinema 1: The Movement Image*, trans. Hugh Tomlinson and Barbara Habberjam, Minneapolis, University of Minnesota Press, 1986, p. 8.

15. Deleuze, *Cinema 1: The Movement Image*, p. 9.

16. See Book I, Proposition 8 of Benedictus de Spinoza, *The Collected Works of Spinoza*, ed. and trans. Edwin Curley, Princeton, Princeton University Press, 1985.

way of certain processes of integration and differentiation of cells into various formations that come to form organs. These organs coalesce to form organisms, and then relations between organisms in various ecological systems form communities. The organizing principle underneath such a development, however, is a general tendency of an organic multiplicity to organize and individuate itself according to various patterns and cycles of convergence and divergence. At a very simple level, cells converge with other cells to form tissues, and this convergence allows for the development of different (divergent) organs.[17] These differing organs then establish networks and relations of mutual functioning that could be said to define how a single organism is individuated. If we then place this organism in the world, it is evident that it, too, converges and diverges with other life forms (it preys upon other organisms while perhaps providing nourishment for other animals, etc). At an 'atomic' level, the multiplicity of cells presuppose a multiplicity of relations that is external to any single cell, and the relations that are formed at any single level of an organism's development presupposes, at another level, a greater plurality of relations between other organisms and their shared environment. It is from this plurality of relations that one could say there is a great possibility for change in variation in a theory of evolution, since every time this process is repeated, it always produces a difference or variation in a single species itself (since no two individuals in a species are exactly alike) at the same time that it allows for change and development in a single species as a whole (since the process of convergence and divergence within a multiplicity presupposes various modes of adaptivity that change a species over the course of time).

From this perspective, we can see how change is possible from the point of view of the whole. The possibility for variation is intrinsically at odds with any fixed notion of identity that is attributed to a singular organism. A philosophy grounded in becoming over being can never isolate a becoming in any singular instant, nor can a principle concerning the evolution of a species be attributed to any singular organism. As such, the open whole for Deleuze provides philosophy, art and science with the metaphysical foundation that orients them towards the new. This open whole has a temporal dimension as well. What allows for novelty is not so much the fact that the future is never given, but rather that the present, and hence the new, is perpetually woven out of the past which does not cease to transform itself.

II: Badiou's Novelty

On the basis of the above, Badiou is led to conclude that for Deleuze, 'the *thought* of the new plunges the latter into that part of it which is its virtual-past'.[18]

---

17. In his book on Deleuze and science, Manuel De Landa explains that the adhesion process that cells undergo in the development of organs depends less upon the spatial locations of the cells, but rather upon factors such as the 'local, adhesive interactions between cells (or between cells and their extra-cellular matrix during migration), interactions which are typically both nonlinear (small changes may lead to large consequences) and statistical'. See Manuel De Landa, *Intensive Science and Virtual Philosophy*, London, Continuum, 2002, p. 52.

18. Alain Badiou, *Deleuze: The Clamor of Being*, trans. Louise Burchill, Minneapolis, University of Minnesota Press, 2000, p. 91. Hereafter cited in the text as *CB*.

Significantly, and perhaps not surprisingly, this is not Badiou's own position. What Badiou cannot accept is the idea that something new can occur if it is a repetition of the whole of the past—for what is the new if not a complete break with what, either from an ontological or a worldly perspective, already is or has been? Absolute beginnings require an altogether different kind of theory, one that departs from the void.[19] If the present discussion has been almost exclusively devoted to Deleuze until now, it is because it serves as one theory of the new that is irreconcilably opposed to Badiou's. Novelty, for Badiou, does not have its origin in the determination of an already existing multiple that cannot help but appear everywhere as different or new. It extends from an aleatory point that only the rarity of an event reveals. 'All radical transformative action originates in a point which, from the interior of the situation, is an eventual site' (*EE*, p. 197). To be sure, any situation can contain this point (a situation, that is, could contain parts that are not accounted for by the regulative practices of its metastructure). In fact, ontology (being qua being), to which the rarity of the event can appear only as an aberration or disruption, is founded on the very same void as the site of the event. Unlike the pre-given, internally differentiated substance from which Deleuze extracts actual differences, Badiou's multiple is rigorously mathematical, with no underlying substance other than presentation itself. Thus, while being and the event must be distinguished from one another, even though they both depart from the void, one must also distinguish the ontological operation of subtraction (the presentative law of the situation) from the supplementation (which will be the plus-one, or *subtraction from subtraction*[20]) that the event alone inaugurates.

However economical its explanation of Badiou's system, the above exegesis offers us no foundation for understanding the void, the situation, or the event. Furthermore, even if we are to distinguish being from the event in order to grasp what is at stake in the present, there is at bottom a more fundamental differentiation in Badiou's system. At its foundation, Badiou divides the domain of experience into two distinct categories. On the one hand, there is the situation, which follows the lead of unified presentation (the 'count-as-one'); consistency (an order to the multiple terms that appear within it); and representation. The latter term can be said to supplement the situation at a distance in order to render the gap between consistency (that which comes to be presented or counted in the situation) and inconsistency (the void that escapes, or exceeds, the count for one) veritably null. It is from the position of the State of the situation that the representation of presentation occurs; the State of the situation is what structures the structure. 'The consistency of presentation demands in this way that all structures be *doubled* by a metastructure, which closes all fixation of the void' (*EE*, p. 109).

---

19. Badiou, *Deleuze: The Clamor of Being*, p. 91. 'As for myself [Badiou], however, I cannot bring myself to think that the new is a fold of the past, or that thinking can be reduced to philosophy or a single configuration of its act. This is why I conceptualize absolute beginnings (which requires a theory of the void) and singularities of thought that are incomparable in their constitutive gestures (which requires a theory—Cantorian, to be precise—of the plurality of the types of infinity)'.

20. I borrow this expression from Ray Brassier.

Presentation, in other words, would be an operation of the situation (consistent ontological positing), whereas representation would be an operation of the State (the organization and distribution of that consistent multiplicity into various sectors or subsets that come to be represented).

On the other hand, however, there is another register of human experience that exceeds the lawful consistency of situation and the State: the event. Events, for Badiou, are rare; nothing within the situation can guarantee when or how they will occur or what their effects will be. It is, however, from the fleeting appearance of an event that something anterior to the presentative immediacy of the known or discerned within the situation can appear. In and of themselves, events do not signal the advent of a truth; rather, they inaugurate subjects who intervene in a situation to the extent that these unique individuals remain faithful to an event by seeing its consequences through to a restructuring of the situation. As the coming-to-be of a truth, this restructuring is what determines that an event *has taken place* in the future anterior of the situation's temporality. Furthermore, by Badiou's definition, events are entirely procedural. Truth for Badiou is essentially an empty category:[21] in itself, it contains no content. Its 'materiality' is given through the hole it produces in knowledge. It is only through the action of a subject who is faithful to an event that truth can come to be spoken of in the situation, and truth per se is produced only if it avoids coinciding with what can be known or discerned.

Now, the unique inconsistency of truth as a singular category for philosophy is at odds with the particularity of the truth procedures that any rare subject, in any given situation, installs. This is perhaps the most striking criterion of Badiou's unique doctrine of truth: for philosophy, there is the empty category of Truth (with a capital T), and there are the local truths (plural, small t) produced in the situations that are unique to the conditions or generic procedures where these truths are effected. There are four such conditions for Badiou: art, science, politics, and love. The aim of philosophy (insofar as it is more than a mere amalgam of these four conditions) is to maintain a distance between these truths and Truth as such. No single condition can be determining for philosophical truth in and of itself. The various attempts at such a determination can be witnessed within philosophy's own history. For Descartes and Leibniz, philosophy was under the mathematical or scientific condition of truth; for Rousseau or Marx, it was to politics that philosophy was sutured; for Heidegger, art alone unveiled truth at the expense of a science reduced to technological nihilism. Finally, from Plato's *Symposium* to Lacan's *Encore*, the amorous procedure of two lovers sought to interrogate the indiscernibility of sexual difference on the basis of generic humanity.

It is by looking at Badiou's reinvigoration of truth as a concept that one can understand the manner in which his philosophy is ostensibly concerned with novelty as such: as procedures, events signal disruptions in the consistency[22] of

---

21. Bruce Fink, 'Alain Badiou', *UMBR(a)*, no. 1, 1996, p. 11.

22. Consistency, as used by Badiou, does not refer to logical consistency, but rather to the set theoretical definition of a well-ordered set.

any given situation and, to the extent that their effects can be measured or felt, the situations in which they occur will be fundamentally restructured. Badiou's events, then, are by no means ordinary, and are as far removed as possible from the Deleuzian maxim that any given thing, understood in its incorporeal materiality, can effectively be called an event. Very little of what happens in everyday science, art, politics, or love could be deemed an event as such. It is in this immediate respect that Badiou's philosophy seems radically severed from what is worldly. As he has recently written:

> The contemporary world is thus doubly hostile to truth procedures. This hostility betrays itself through nominal occlusions: where the name of a truth procedure should obtain, another, which represses it, holds sway. The name 'culture' comes to obliterate that of 'art'. The word 'technology' obliterates the word 'science'. The word 'management' obliterates the word politics. The word 'sexuality' obliterates love. The 'culture-technology-management-sexuality' system, which has the immense merit of being homogeneous to the market, and all of whose terms designate a category of commercial presentation, constitutes the modern nominal occlusion of the 'art-science-politics-love' system, which identifies truth procedures typologically. (*SP*, p. 12)[23]

Badiou's philosophy stands in complete contrast to a phenomenological inquiry into the lived foundations of human experience. The striking examples he gives of events institute subjective procedures that come to establish that there *will have been a truth* in the situation. In politics, there are political revolutions (of 1789 in France or 1917 in the Soviet Union). In science, there are Cantor's discoveries of the existence of indiscernible multiples and transfinite infinities that cannot be limited by our system of natural numbers. In art we have Schoenberg's retroactive invention of the twelve-note tonal scale through the advent of atonal or serial composition. And in the case of love, for which the teachings of Plato or Lacan prove exemplary, there are the two lovers who, in the progression of a relationship, adhere to the event of the declaration of love. There are other examples, of course, and there are other subjects who remain faithful to the consequences of an event, remaining in the situation to see its effects manifest in any given situation: Weber, Berg or Stockhaussen with respect to Schoenberg, Lacan with respect to Freud, Lenin to Marx, Zermelo, Von Neumann or Cohen with respect to Cantor, and the various political and cultural revolutions that follow in the wake of past events (such as May '68, the Chinese Cultural revolution, etc).

Despite the fact that it is always unique individuals who see the outcome of an event through to its transformation of a given situation, Badiou nonetheless firmly maintains that truth is universal, for everyone. The question at this point concerns the criteria of truth's universality: if truth is not decided from the standpoint of the situation (i.e., if it has no determination through knowledge or experience), then what parameters designate it as truth? This question returns to the original

---

23. Alain Badiou, *Saint Paul: The Foundation of Universalism*, trans. Ray Brassier, Stanford, Stanford University Press, 2003 (henceforth *SP*).

distinction made in Badiou's system: it is not being and the event that are initially opposed, but the event and the situation. From the standpoint of the situation, everything is consistently presented, counted as one. 'When in a situation, something is counted as one, this only signifies its belonging to a situation in the proper mode of the effects of its structure' (*EE*, p. 32). Events, in contrast, signal breaks in situations as such; they bring the void, with which any situation is sutured to being, to the fore. But if situations are sutured to being, and if being-qua-being is subtracted from presentation, a distinction proper to ontology itself is necessary. Prior to the distinction between the situation (consistency) and the event (pure chance), there is a more direct ontological distinction between being-qua-being (inconsistency) and the situation (where being, in subtracted form, can be presented according to the count-as-one). It is in this respect that Badiou's ontology is subtractive: inconsistency as such is subtracted from presentation. 'Structure is at the same time what obliges us to consider, through retroaction, that presentation is a multiple (inconsistent) and that which authorizes us, via anticipation, to compose the terms of the presentation as units of a multiple (consistent)' (*EE*, p. 33).

Inconsistency as pure being is, then, the retroactive effect of consistent presentation. And it is fairly well-known, if poorly understood, that Badiou views Cantorian set theory as the best means we have of formalizing the inherent inconsistency of being as such.[24] Now, Badiou maintains both that ontology can be a situation *and* that Cantor's discovery constituted an event whose effects led to the eventual restructuring of contemporary mathematics. Furthermore, if ontology is a situation, it is also the case that being-qua-being is inherently inconsistent in subtracted form—and thus exterior to any situation as such. So even if we could oppose being-qua-being to the situation, on the one hand, and the situation to the event, on the other, it seems unavoidable that the set-theoretical implications of Badiou's ontology play a decisive role in all three areas (being-qua-being, the situation, the event). What, exactly, is the relation between being-qua-being, the ontology of the situation, and the event, then, and what does this have to do with the new?

To simplify matters, if there are two primary theses in *Being and Event* as a whole (and thus in Badiou's project overall), they may be stated thus:

Mathematics is ontology. This is the already familiar argument Badiou offers at the outset of his project: mathematics, and in particular set theory, is what formalizes multiplicity in a manner that radically separates the question of being-qua-being from any criteria of actual existence.

Truth is essentially undecidable from the perspective of any consistently presented situation. As a process, it originates in an event which, through the action of a militant subject, comes to bore a hole in the knowledge of the situation. At this point, one can then

---

24. Consistency for Badiou seems analogous to a principle of well-ordering whereby a set can have every element presented. As defined by Lavine, 'in the *Grundlagen*, Cantor regarded the process of bringing a set into the form of a well-ordered set, thereby specifying a definite succession of the elements of the set, as giving a way of *counting* the members of a set. See Shaughan Lavine, *Understanding the Infinite*, Cambridge, Mass., Harvard University Press, 1994, p. 53.

speak of the action of the subject as constituting a generic procedure. Even if a truth procedure comes to produce a subset containing elements that, from the perspective of the situation, are simply indiscernible, the subject can nonetheless produce an investigation (or, more generally, an inquiry) into that indiscernible subset, such that the situation is forced to account for its existence and, in so doing, fundamentally reorganize itself.

Now, the advantages of set theory for approaching both ontology (qua Zermelo-Fraenkel's axiomatic) and truth (qua Cohen's generic procedure), are determined by what lies at its very foundation: inconsistency. What the uniform presentation of an ontological situation assumes as its foundation is a pure multiplicity underlying, and preceding, any act of presentation.[25] The name for this inconsistency will be the void. 'The void is the name of being—of inconsistency—according to a situation, such that the presentation gives us an unpresentable access or non-access to this access, in the mode of that which is not-one, nor composable of ones, and is thus only qualifiable in the situation as the errancy of nothing' (*EE*, p. 69). This would be inconsistency in regards to ontological presentation.

As regards gaining knowledge of inconsistency (in the example of mathematics, of the transfinite infinities that cannot be discerned from the perspective of a situation), Badiou utilizes Paul Cohen's generic procedures. If, for any situation, there will always be an excess of subsets of a situation over the elements of the situation itself, there will always be *some* multiplicity for which questions of consistency (principles of well-ordering) will be unknowable from the perspective of the situation. For some, such excesses could simply be viewed as exorbitant to the finite evaluations of the situation, hence unknowable and thus perpetually open to an endless proliferation of hermeneutic evaluations, metaphorical slippage, and so forth. Or, one could claim that insofar as such multiplicities cannot be experienced within finite intuition, they simply do not exist. Badiou opposes these two positions by opting instead for Cohen's generic procedure. The series of evaluations that comprise a generic procedure, while not directly presenting those inconsistent multiples as such, nonetheless forces some information about its elements. When assembled together, through a finite and rigorous procedure, these evaluations form a subset of the situation that will be called (by both Cohen and Badiou) *generic* precisely insofar as it avoids any correspondence with a determinant predicate (that is, with what can be directly proven in the situation). But insofar as these subsets can be said to exist independently of proof, any situation as such will have to be fundamentally restructured with respect to the effects of a generic evaluation:

> Cohen's demonstration that the existence of generic subsets is consistent is truly a modern proof that truths can exist irreducible to any encyclopaedic given. Cohen's theorem achieves, in the ontological radicality of the

---

25. 'The numbers that we manipulate are only a very small sample of the infinite prodigality of the being of number'. Alain Badiou, *Le Nombre et les nombres*, Paris, Seuil, 1990, p. 199. Hereafter cited in the text as *NN*.

matheme, the modernity that was opened by the Kantian distinction between thought and knowledge.[26]

It is only with respect to this crucial distinction of truth and knowledge that we can understand Badiou's concern with the new: he rigorously looks to terms outside any situation (outside the world, knowledge, opinion, etc.) for truth's criteria.

Between the poles of inconsistency as such and a generic procedure lies the situation, the site of symbolic mediation between pure inconsistency (the primary, ontological void) and innovation. The restructuring of any situation as it is forced to acknowledge the second void of truth (as a hole in knowledge) is the immanent determination that an event has occurred. It is not too difficult, at this point, to see what it is that enables the creation of something new: it would be the void as the name for ontological inconsistency that both founds a situation *and* enables a situation to always be restructured according to the ontological tenets of incompletion. For if it is true that inconsistency is subtracted from any situation as such, it is also true that presentation cannot deplete the wealth of multiplicity. Cantor has forced contemporary mathematics to acknowledge this.[27]

A discerning reader may have noticed that a theory of the void as a name for what cannot be consistently presented to human experience is not altogether different from the manner in which Deleuze qualifies his famous theory of the virtual. The virtual cannot be said to be readily available to immediate experience in and of itself: it requires a process of actualization. Deleuze even wrote in one of his last works that ontological chaos 'is a void that is not nothingness but a virtual, containing all possible particles and drawing out all possible forms, which spring up only in order to disappear immediately, without consistency or reference, without consequence'.[28] Extending from this, one could regard the Deleuzian project as an attempt to give a consistency to this inconsistency through the creation of concepts that adequate to the speed with which the virtual simultaneously moves and disappears, actualizing itself in the world that it simultaneously withdraws from. Art could be seen as performing a similar function in the creation of visual sensations, the correlate of concepts. Science, on the other hand, constructs a plane of reference with which the speed of the virtual, qua creation, could be regarded as frozen in functions and formalizations. But all three (philosophy, science, art) aim to make the inconsistent consist in some manner.

Aside from the obvious example of Deleuze's curt treatment of science, how exactly does this differ from Badiou? Don't both thinkers subscribe to thoughts of inconsistency from which philosophical innovation proceeds? The first distinction should be obvious: Deleuze uses the world as the criterion by which the new

---

26. Alain Badiou, *Conditions*, Paris, Seuil, 1992, p. 203. Hereafter cited in the text as *CS*.

27. Mary Tiles credits Cantor with separating the existence of true or false propositions from questions of their proof. This extended in part from Cantor's continuum hypothesis, from which Gödel's first incompleteness theorem and Cohen's generic procedure commence. See Mary Tiles, *The Philosophy of Set Theory: An Historical Introduction to Cantor's Paradise*, Oxford, Blackwell, 1989, p. 111.

28. Deleuze and Guattari, *What is Philosophy?*, p. 118.

is said to appear, insofar as the virtual actualizes itself in the world. By extension, this is the criterion by which Deleuze will then call the appearance of the things of the world, events. That the sky is blue, that an organism evolves, that Caesar crossed the Rubicon are for Deleuze nothing more than events exhibited in and through the world. This is a point that remained resolutely uniform throughout the entirety of Deleuze's writing: one question of his last great work was 'in what conditions does the objective world allow for a subjective production of novelty, that is, of creation?'[29] Deleuze's answer is unequivocal: it is found in the Leibnizian affirmation of this world as the best of all possible worlds.[30] The affirmation of this world is tantamount to its propensity for innovation. That Badiou, on the contrary, sees the contemporary world as hostile to truth places him (not surprisingly) directly at odds with Deleuze. Events are nothing if not radical breaks or ruptures with the worldly, regardless of how the latter is experienced (in the liberal-democratic consensus of opinion, identity politics, the phenomenological inquiry into human experience, the exchanges of global capital, etc.).

Second, Deleuze sees philosophy as that which creates concepts, whereas for Badiou, philosophy *creates nothing as such*—rather, it simply oversees the manner in which truths are generated in its four conditions. This has the obvious advantage of restricting any one of the categories of philosophy from having an exclusive hold on the question of truth. Furthermore, the fact that it creates nothing in itself is what allows philosophy to have an external point from which to separate the creation *of* truths from its criterion *as* truth. The fact that philosophy is neither the medium of creation (which belongs to its conditions), nor of ontological inconsistency (the site of truth's possibility), is what allows it to have a disinterested investment in the coming-to-be of a truth in any situation. In this respect, Bruce Fink is correct to assert that 'philosophy has a certain "sobering" effect on such discourses, a restricting or limiting power over them'.[31]

Finally, the void for Deleuze is one half of an ontological equation which finds its counterpart in the actualizations that express virtual intentionality, and retroactively generate the virtual qua expression.[32] Badiou emphatically differs on this point: inconsistency (the void) comes to be retroactively apprehended through an act of enumeration where everything is consistently presented as one. There is nothing that could be said to be philosophically challenging about this process of actualization and, in this respect, *Being and Event* does little to theorize

---

29. Gilles Deleuze, *The Fold: Leibniz and the Baroque*, trans. Tom Conley, Minneapolis, University of Minnesota Press, 1992, p. 79.

30. Deleuze, *The Fold: Leibniz and the Baroque*, p. 79. 'The best of all worlds is not the one that reproduces the eternal, but the one in which new creations are produced, the one endowed with a capacity for innovation or creativity: a teleological conversion of philosophy'.

31. Fink, 'Alain Badiou', p. 11. 'Discourses' in this respect are the four conditions of philosophy.

32. In a slightly more complex take on this point, Badiou notes 'That being is bereft of properties is an old thesis. However, Deleuze renews this thesis by arguing that being is the active neutralization of properties by the inseparable virtualisation of their actual division'. See, Alain Badiou, 'Of Life as a Name of Being, or, Deleuze's Vitalist Ontology', *Pli: Warwick Journal of Philosophy*, no. 10, 2000, p. 192.

the relation between being and its actualization or individuation. The advantages of set theory are that it allows us to think multiplicity in the most direct manner possible—through formalization. But what is of interest to philosophy (the means through which truths come to be implemented in various situations) comes with an ontological guarantee, insofar as events take their cue from the void of any situation—situations include elements that are not presented.[33] What this implies is that there is no direct movement from inconsistency to consistency, as would be the case in the Deleuzian ascending/descending movement from virtualization to actualization. Inconsistency is either made consistent through a purely external act (of counting) or it comes to the fore in any situation in the form of a rupture (the fleetingness of the event which subjective action alone makes possible).

III: Paradoxes of the Whole

One might regard Badiou's project, then, as a means of reclaiming the powers of the negative away from the positivity and pure productiveness of Deleuze's system. To be sure, Badiou is a thinker of force or action, but the genesis of this force finds its origin not in any vital energy as the possibility of existence, but rather in the internal impasses which render the conceptual closure of any situation impossible. Subjective action is what follows from this impossibility. Moreover, it is from the place of the void that the status of a number's being is measured.[34] No number is ever dignified through the positivity or immediacy of presentation, for which the negative exists only as expelled: 'One is tempted to refer all occurrences which present nothing, all marks for which the multiple-referent presents nothing, to the negative. But the truth is otherwise: it is precisely under that mark that being-qua-being comes to be thought' (*NN*, p. 199).

Consider the opposite tendency, towards the positive, in the famous responses to Zeno's paradoxes given first by Aristotle and later echoed by Bergson. To briefly recapitulate one paradox: if the movement of an arrow is divided into successive spatial instances (each one spanning the length of the arrow), the arrow could be said to be at rest at every moment: there is no one point at which the arrow is in motion. Hence, the paradox suggests, movement is impossible. Bergson's response follows that of Aristotle's *Physics*: it is not movement that is

---

33. Badiou is a bit ambiguous on this point. On one hand, he firmly maintains that 'at the heart of every situation, as the foundation of its being, there is a "situated" void, around which is organized the plenitude (or the stable multiples) of the situation in question'. Alain Badiou, *Ethics: An Essay on the Understanding of Evil*, trans. Peter Hallward, London, Verso, 2001, p. 68. It would seem that every situation could contain the possibility for an event insofar as an event 'names' the void of the situation. On the other hand, Badiou firmly maintains a distinction between historic and natural situations (in which events do not or cannot occur).

34. For example, '[...] the particular mode in which any situation-"being" is sutured to its being is not Presence (the blossoming of what is pro-posed at its limit) but pure subtraction, the unqualifiable void: in that form of being which is Number, this is said as "zero exists", or in a style more homogeneous to the ontological creation of Cantor: "there exists a set which has no element"'. *NN*, p. 75.

impossible, it is rather the human intellect that is incapable of grasping the 'qualitative change' that transpires throughout movement as a whole. Movement, for Bergson is an 'undivided fact' that abstract reasoning (which sets out to compose movement out of successive instances) fails to comprehend. The whole, in such a view, precedes the part. Or, as Bergson writes: 'we will content ourselves with observing that motion, as given to spontaneous perception, is a fact which is quite clear, and that the difficulties and contradictions pointed out by the Eleatic school concern far less the living movement itself than a dead and artificial reorganization of movement by the mind'.[35]

Yet an altogether different problem springs directly from Bergson's response. For such a position insists that movement must be given as a whole at the same time that the whole itself expresses change. The problem is that if the whole precedes the parts, the change that occurs throughout the course of a body's movement must also be given at the outset. Now, if the change that occurs over a temporal progression is always already given (that is, if space and time are already given as totalities, however infinite), then its status as change is in question.[36] If change is endemic to the whole, it is nonetheless only through abstract reasoning, which splits duration into temporally discrete instances, that change as such can be observed from one moment to the next—one would otherwise have a purely undifferentiated amalgam. Yet it is from this abstract reasoning that movement as such is impossible. Aristotle's answer to this impasse was to make change a constant of being: change has always existed and will always exist. From such a perspective, the only way to think novelty is as one moment isolated within a pre-given totality, a repetition of the whole of the past.

However, following Zeno's second paradox of Achilles and the tortoise, one can formulate another response to Zeno's paradox, one that directly concerns infinity. In a race between Achilles and a tortoise, and giving the tortoise a sufficient head-start, one could successively divide the difference separating Achilles from his opponent such that he will never catch up. Unlike the arrow paradox, the difficulty here extends from the fact that space and time can be divided infinitely: any one instant can always be divided anew, such that the tortoise will be one foot ahead of Achilles, then half a foot, and a quarter foot, and so forth. To simply respond that movement must be given as a whole at the outset amounts, then, to a denial of the actual infinity of spatial division. Aristotle's position suggested that the infinite parts of a continuum are only ever potential, not actual.[37] Yet if

---

35. Henri Bergson, *Matter and Memory*, trans. Nancy M. Paul and W. Scott Palmer, New York, Zone Books, 1990, p. 193.

36. Tiles suggests that the presupposition of a continuous whole poses problems for a philosophy of becoming. For it would follow from such a perspective that 'time too would have to be actually, not merely potentially, infinite and thus in some sense wholly actual even though not simultaneously present. It is from this point of view that the reality of time as associated with change and becoming is questionable'. Tiles, *The Philosophy of Set Theory: An Historical Introduction to Cantor's Paradise*, p. 30.

37. See Aristotle, *Physics*, trans. Robin Waterfield, Oxford, Oxford, 1996, p. 220. Aristotle maintains that 'continuous movement is movement over a continuum, and although there are infinitely many halves in any continuum, they are potential, not actual'.

a thought of multiplicity requires an actual infinity, then an altogether different solution is required.

The resolution involves the introduction of a limit into physical space. A principal reason why Zeno's second paradox remained a paradox for the Greeks is that zero was not admitted into their numerical system. Its existence was not applicable to geometrical objects, insofar as no squares had sides measuring zero units. But it is precisely the introduction of this limit into physical space that provides an answer to the paradox. As the physical movements that measure the space of Achilles' course are successively broken down into smaller units, they approach a limit: zero. It would be at this limit point that Achilles could be said to overtake the tortoise.[38] Now, if Zeno's paradox remained a paradox for the Greeks, it was because the infinity of the paradox could only be conceived *potentially* as movement broken down increasingly with no end in sight. What the potential infinity affirms is the finitude of the human situation as such.[39] One way in which an actual infinity could be affirmed would be through a notion of a pre-given infinite whole. Or conversely, one could introduce an infinite limit irreducible to finite units of space or time. This limit is heteronomous to experience as such, even while serving as the condition of movement's possibility.[40] If Deleuze consistently supports the former position, it is Badiou who emerges as a champion of the latter. Infinity requires a limit, and one which cannot be reduced to the finitude of physical space or natural numbers. Badiou's axiom of infinity posits just that: an ordinal limit that no finite succession ever reaches.

IV: Overturning Assumptions

However convenient the contrast it makes between the two thinkers, the above example presents a considerable set of problems. Assume, for the moment, that the distinction between continuous and discrete multiplicities could be neatly mapped onto the positions of Deleuze and Badiou respectively. It is evident that misinterpretations will occur. What we are assuming, for a thinker like Deleuze, is that if movement is indivisible, then so, too, is the space and time in which it occurs. This obviously runs in direct contrast to Bergson's (as well as Deleuze's) theory that time is what prevents everything from already being given. The prob-

---

38. Jacques Lacan attempted an explanation of this in his famous twentieth seminar. See Jacques Lacan, *On Feminine Sexuality: The Limits of Love and Knowledge - The Seminar of Jacques Lacan, Book XX, Encore*, Jacques-Alain Miller (ed.), trans. Bruce Fink, New York, Norton, 1998, p. 8. 'A number has a limit and it is to that extent that it is infinite. It is quite clear that Achilles can only pass the tortoise—he cannot catch up with it. He only catches up with it at infinity'. For a refutation of Bergson/Aristotle on this point from a Lacanian perspective, see the third chapter of Joan Copjec, *Read My Desire: Lacan Against the Historicists*, Cambridge, MIT Press, 1994, pp. 39-64.

39. Such an approach, for Badiou, would be inherently theological.

40. See Charles Seife, *Zero: The Biography of a Dangerous Idea*, New York, Penguin, 2000, p. 46. The Greeks 'didn't have the concept of a limit because they didn't believe in zero. The terms in the infinite series didn't have a limit or a destination; they seemed to get smaller and smaller without any particular end in sight'.

lem, of course, is that we have reduced the movement of an arrow to the space and time in which it occurs. Or rather, we have reduced a definition of movement and time to the addition of metrically divisible units. And this, of course, is *not* what a Bergsonian position upholds. The indivisibility of movement is simply the *intensive* trajectory of the arrow that produces qualitative change in the whole that is composed of the arrow, its target, and the space in-between. Movement is indivisible. Or rather, any division in movement produces a difference in kind.

A convenient, if simple, example that Manuel de Landa gives to describe an intensive property of an object is one that is not metrically divisible. While a litre of 90° water can be divided to produce two half-litres of water, the temperature of the water remains the same. Unlike volume, which is an extensive property of the water, temperature is intensive, and thus non-divisible. An intensive property cannot be divided without changing in kind. To divide water into units of hot and cold that produce, when mixed together, 90° water supposes that a difference in kind (in this case, hot and cold) must undergo a dynamic process of fusion in order to produce water that is consistently 90°. So the first conclusion is that what underlies any discrete, or extensive, property of an object is a dynamic, or intensive, process that produces it. To uncover this process appears, at first sight, the goal of Deleuze's system: uncovering the multiplicity of conditions under which transformation occurs. One immediately recognizes in this Bergson's famous example of mixing sugar in a glass of water. The change that occurs—the production of sugared water—cannot be reduced to the simple addition of parts; it is, rather, the process of transformation that occurs when they are mixed together to form something new that is philosophically significant for Deleuze.

But even this is inadequate to explain how Deleuze's ontology works. The example of the arrow has simply treated movement as a property of the object, rather than as a process that the arrow undergoes in its trajectory. If one accepts that relations for Deleuze are external to their terms (that is, the relation that the movement of the arrow holds with respect to the 'terms' that facilitate it), it is impossible to say that the whole out of which movement is comprised can, in turn, exhaust the possibility for change, since every whole that comprises a multiplicity presupposes a greater possibility for difference, change and variation.

Things do not look any easier when examined from the position of the discrete. We saw that the limit point zero, at which the successive division of spatial units breaks down, is the point at which movement could be said to be possible. At zero, there is a qualitative leap from one unit to the other. As an example, zero's convenience is that it cannot measure any spatial mass or temporal unit, and is thus irreducible to the spatial segments that, in Zeno's paradox, would deny the possibility of movement. But the reason it offers such a weak example is that the number zero is nonetheless used as a unit of measure: its content (the qualitative leap of movement) has simply been subtracted from experience, and delegated to some ineffable power of movement that escapes measurement.

The problems that occur with proposing a limit point to movement become just as evident. For we are assuming, in the first instance, that 'the void', as an ontological concept, has relevance insofar as it can measure and assess the brute physical fact of movement, and abstractly at best. However, for Badiou, there is no necessary reciprocity between the ontological register of set theory and what occurs in the physical world. Secondly, it should be just as clear to a reader of Deleuze that the concept of zero as a limit point to movement has a counterpart in the notion of a singularity. A singularity for Deleuze is what determines the *tendency* of a system, a point at which its possible form may be realized. In short, a singularity is a topical point in a multiplicity that does not determine one measurable unit among others, but rather defines a tendency of the ordinary points in that system such that they converge in an individuated, or completed, form. A singularity is thus defined by the *relations* it holds with other points or trajectories in a given system, rather than through any discrete properties that are unique to it. At the same time, however, it is constitutive of a system.[41]

Thus, the usefulness of the above example seems to be quite limited in its applicability for speaking either of Deleuze or Badiou, and certainly for contrasting them. If we consider the conditions under which the new occurs, there must therefore be *other* outlets of recognition. For me, the most pressing problem with the above example is that it conflates the question of novelty with physical movement, and then treats the goal of philosophy as a tool with which to measure or describe the effects, or end-products, of a process of novelty. Now, such a project is surely at odds with what either Deleuze or Badiou expect from philosophy. But it does become pertinent to ask what role philosophy plays with respect to the conditions under which the new can occur. To what extent does either thinker provide an adequate *foundation*, rather than a description, for the emergence of something new?

In order to answer this question, a certain delimitation of what can truly count as new is required. I began by mentioning change, but it is obvious that for a philosopher like Badiou, change and novelty are entirely separate affairs. Badiou is thus in some respects a less difficult thinker on this account than Deleuze, since for Badiou, novelty always occurs at one remove from any process or occurrence that would characterize the familiar world. For Badiou, a novelty is contingent upon a truth. In fact, unless I am mistaken, a novelty for Badiou *is* truth, and is furthermore always produced anterior to anything that can be known or discerned in a situation. For Deleuze, things are somewhat more difficult. Given that the *process* by which something new is produced is more important than its realization, the end-products of *any* intensive process could thus be said to enjoy an equally novel status. The process is what poses a problem, for which the solution is a residual effect, or actualization. This is true as long as the procedure undergoes differentiation (of the neutrality of being) and repetition (allowing for diversity in the actual). This follows from two general tendencies of his system: the univocity of being (which would entail that all beings are ontologically equal),

---

41. De Landa writes that 'singularities, by determining long-term tendencies, structure the possibilities which make up state space, and by extension, structure the possibilities open to the physical process modelled by a state space'. De Landa, *Intensive Science and Virtual Philosophy*, p. 16.

and his affirmation of the virtual (process) over the actual (end-product). The reason that Badiou's criteria for the new seem less problematic, then, is that it is a severely restricted definition of truth. For Deleuze, in contrast, if all events emanate from a dynamic process, then everything is of equal value from the perspective of novelty. Everything is new. Or rather, from the perspective of the virtual as power, there is no criteria by which any actual being could be said to be more unique than any other, since what truly matter are the means through which the new is engendered.

Both Deleuze and Badiou equally orient their philosophies around possible foundations from which novelty can occur. The obvious difference, however, concerns the extent to which that foundation merely supposes a process that already exists. If the virtual, for example, is a model for the way one accounts for change and variation in the physical world, its philosophical formulation seems to offer little more than a description of processes that exist independently of human action or thought. Yet, on the other hand, the virtual is said to provide creation in science, philosophy and art with the metaphysics that are proper to them, broadly understood as a propensity towards change and variation. It adds something to what already is, and thus ontologically supplements actual beings with the ground of their possibility. Thus, the creation of concepts, theorems and works of art will be assessed to the extent that they approximate their proper virtuality (their ability to be engendered and form links with other virtualities). In this sense, one could call the virtual a foundation.

But if the virtual is a *foundation* for Deleuze, it is directly at odds with what Deleuze sets as the proper *goal* of his philosophy, which is to affirm the *reality* of the virtual. That is, if the virtual is a foundation, it must be a foundation for something other than an affirmation of itself. One would be left with mere tautology by which the means of a philosophical project would be indistinguishable from its ends. Of course, in many respects, it is a foundation for other things, not least of which for actual beings and their proliferation. But a derivation of the actual from the virtual is not what Deleuze sets as the goal for his philosophy. In fact, he seeks the exact opposite: to uncover or approximate the virtuality that inheres beneath the creation of the new as it manifests itself in the actual. And if so, his philosophy turns full circle from the virtual as foundation to a philosophical methodology as a description of that virtuality. As for the new, it is never properly in question, since the capacity for creation is always already assumed.

Herein reside two crucial points at which Badiou's philosophy can be opposed to Deleuze. On the one hand, the affirmation of the reality of the virtual presupposes a circularity in methodology. If the virtual is to presuppose a foundation on which change in science can occur, it is also the end point for philosophy, science and art insofar as their respective capacities for creation have the virtual as their criterion. The validity of concepts, theorems, or works of art are not their truth or falsity, but rather their ability to approximate the virtual process by which philosophical, artistic and scientific phenomena are ontologically enabled. *It is in this sense that Deleuze's philosophy amounts to a description.*

Second, in the analysis of continuous and discrete multiplicities, I refuted the assumption that the ontological validity of the open whole means that everything is given all at once. But this doesn't mean that the risk of continuity escapes the picture. We affirmed above that when a multiplicity admits of greater possible lines of convergence and divergence, the propensity for diversity in the world increases as well. This, in part, is what allows for a non-teleological theory of evolution. This engendering of divergence creates a greater possibility for new relations and new forms of life in turn. Thus, the process that accounts for change and innovation in life is also what further enables its perpetuation, since an ontological multiplicity engenders more multiplicity, and thus a greater propensity for variation. The problem with this is not that it posits a circular foundation for innovation, but rather that it inscribes the new as a constant. Which is to say that, if Deleuze refuses continuity at an ontological level of a closed whole, it nonetheless appears in his philosophy under the banner of a principle that is endemic to life. Not only does this deny the absolutely sporadic character of chance that is essential for Badiou's definition of novelty, it furthermore denies the possibility of there being any difference between change, as a worldly phenomenon, and novelty as a transformation of the new.

The success with which Badiou effectively separates his philosophy from description is something that will be assessed in the following chapters. Simply contrasting him with Deleuze is obviously not enough to create an argument for the advantages of his system over those of Deleuze or, on another register of thought, Foucault. But the comparison between the two thinkers helps delimit a set of questions that can uniquely qualify Badiou's approach to the question of the new. The first question would be entirely concomitant with Deleuze's own method; the second, not at all. In the two chapters that follow, I will first present an exposition of Badiou's ontology and indicate to what extent it meets the criteria of multiplicity. I will then account for the possible emergence first of an event, and second of a truth procedure. Given that both chapters are grounded in questions of ontological multiplicity, comparisons with Deleuze will be inevitable.

The second problematic will concern Badiou's reinvigoration of the category of truth. As a philosophical category, truth is not something Deleuze had much time for. Truth is classically seen as eternal and unchanging, and as such is antithetical to the principles according to which the new occurs. To further interrogate Badiou's own take on truth will take us away from the familiar set of oppositions that have thus far been outlined, and will therefore involve a further step beyond the ontological problem of multiplicity. Seeing in what manner the two sets of problems are in fact related is what will ultimately determine the uniqueness and strength of Badiou's own position.

V. Conclusion: Axiomatic

This introductory (and inevitably simplified) presentation of Badiou makes the chaotic complexity of Deleuze's own system appear simplicity itself. It is clear that one cannot simply proffer terms that are specific to Badiou's own system (situation, event, state, subtraction, etc.) without a fairly lengthy analysis of what that system is. Thus, to make a foray into what will be the more challenging task of making a coherence out of Badiou's system, I will take an 'axiomatic shortcut' of sorts, presenting what the explicit, underlying theses that a Badiouian conception of the new will require.

1. [*There exists an empty set.* The empty set or void set is the proper name of being. Thus this 'there exists' is marked $\emptyset$ which as void is the name of being qua being. Therefore the empty set under the rule of subsets implies $\{\emptyset\}$ also exists. Thus we have $\{\emptyset,\{\emptyset\}\}$. 'Our reference point will be the existent figure of the Two; that is, the multiple $\{\emptyset,\{\emptyset\}\}$, whose elements are the void and its singleton'. (*EE*, p. 170) The name of the void marks the assertion of the existence of the empty set. The presentation of this two is required.][42]

2. *The void and infinity are coextensive.* In breaking with any tradition that defines number, infinity, or being through worldly criteria (such as Greek geometry or Spinozist necessity), Badiou founds being on the pure presentation of the empty-set, or void: a set containing nothing beyond its own axiomatic positing as set. 'Contrary to all intuition, zero, or the void, is a natural ontological given. The void, suture to being of all language and all thought, is the point of nature where number anchors itself' (*NN*, p. 91). With the addition of the presentative law of the count-as-one, the system of ordinal numbers can be generated from the empty set, such that one is the set of the empty set, two is the set of the set of the empty set, and so forth. It is in the axiomatic as such that Badiou's break between ontology and lived experience is founded. But following the axiomatic of the void, from which numerical succession derives, is an axiom of infinity, which states that an ordinal limit exists, a number that cannot be directly preceded by any other ordinal. No succession of numbers will ever reach it; between it and the multiples that precede it, 'there is a total absence of mediation'. (*EE*, p. 178)

While this is a mathematical thesis,

3. *The challenge for thought will not be that of defining limits, but rather that of defining successors.* Or rather, even if the existence of limits poses a challenge at the level of being, at the level of thought, there is nothing more to think in the limit apart from what precedes it (*NN*, p. 105). Limit thought (of potential infinity, temporal finitude, linguistic restrictions) remains trapped within the constraints of philosophical passivity as such: 'Any genuine test for thought originates in the localizable necessity of a supplementary step, an unbeginnable beginning, which is neither soldered together by the infinite filling in of what precedes it, nor identical to its dissemination' (*NN*, p.

---

42. [Editor's Note: This is an editorial reconstruction as the author's manuscript is incomplete at this point. This axiom statement is reconstructed from the following sources: *NN*, Sections 10:18 & 11:5; and *EE*, Med 14.].

105).

Although it is not philosophy's ambition constantly to be questioning being, this is not to say that set theory safely puts the project of ontology aside. Being and event are not two mutually independent categories, one of which can freely be thought without the other. If events are what allow for innovation (innovation being the main focal point of this work), their existence depends upon the set-theoretical tenets of ontological incompletion. It will be necessary to conduct an in-depth assessment of Badiou's ontology in order to speak of events and the procedures they install. In what follows, I will shuttle between expositions of select parts of Badiou's system: his definition of ontology, truth and the event. This will mimic the general presentation of *Being and Event*, with the difference that my exposition of the event here follows a chapter on truth. This is because Badiou's doctrine of truth is closely tied to his ontology, whereas the event has an extraneous set of criteria that is not reducible to ontology. Readers familiar with Badiou's other writings will observe that almost no attention will be devoted to his political philosophy or writings on love or poetry and art. While books such as *Ethics*, *Saint Paul* and the *Deleuze* monograph will make appearances from time to time as a point of reference, they will do so only in reference to the outline of some rudimentary features of *Being and Event*. In this respect, mine is a selective reading of a philosopher along the lines of a given problematic. In doing so, I have chosen deliberately: I have not tackled the problem of novelty from a general philosophical perspective so as to gradually narrow the problem down to a set of criteria for which Badiou will provide the best possible fit. This is not my intention. Even in my comparisons between Badiou and Deleuze, which will appear throughout, there is no great intention to argue for the superiority of one thinker over another. At bottom, philosophy for Badiou rests upon a decision: one takes a path on point of conviction and sees its effects played out in the trajectory of one's actions. What I will effectively do in the following, then, is set up a problem—what are the conditions under which the new can occur?—and see its effects through in the form of a philosophy that is both resolutely classical (it maintains categories of ontology and truth) and radically innovative at the same time.

Much of the present work will be given over to clarifying the more difficult and ambitious parts of his project. These more expository parts will hopefully serve as a preamble to a wider discussion concerning innovation in philosophy at a time when many have declared it to be complete. Few have put as strong a case forward for the continuation of philosophy as Badiou, and few have done it in a manner that refuses any restriction of philosophy to the exclusive domains of language, ethics, aesthetics, politics or science. It is perhaps in this respect, more than any other, that Badiou's project is worthy of consideration in the English-speaking world, and if it is only now that his work is beginning to receive attention, this reception can be called nothing less than long overdue.

2

Nothing That Is

In the previous chapter, I indicated how Badiou's reader must accept a tautological equivalence between being and multiplicity in order to accept the assertion that mathematics is ontology. In other words, for Badiou, there is a meta-ontological equivalence between being and multiplicity even while there does not appear to be any meta-ontological criteria that enable us to say why being is multiplicity.

This is not entirely correct, however. If we assume that thought is capable of engendering new thoughts, and if philosophy can examine the conditions under which those new thoughts can be engendered in and through the production of truths, we must be able to accept that thought is multiple. There is a multiplicity of thoughts that already exist, and the project of thought, its propensity for truth, must certainly be able to continue if philosophy is to be seen as a fundamentally open and unending project. The step towards the meta-ontological assertion that mathematics is ontology is dependent on our ability to equate thought and being.

I. Thinking and Being, They Are the Same

Certainly what we have just said is consistent with a philosophical history ranging from Parmenides to Descartes' cogito and the beginning of Hegel's *Science of Logic*. All of these are thinkers Badiou has drawn upon in the presentation of his own system. Descartes and Hegel took different departures from their initial equivalence of thought and being, since, for Descartes, thought was only one particular instantiation of being, while for Hegel, the determination of being in and through thought, while certainly the result of a process, is inseparable from either thought or being themselves. In other words (and here Badiou and Hegel are very close), the fact that there is no meta-ontology means that there is no thought outside of thought, or no being outside of ontology. This is simple enough, but what is perhaps less obvious is the fact that the statement that *there is no being outside ontology* is itself a primary ontological assertion. For the purposes of asking what being is, there is nothing outside ontology, and the acknowledgment of this nothingness is for Badiou the minimal condition under which thought can think being. There are particular instantiations of thought, and there is also thought itself beyond its instantiations which, when thought, is nothing apart from this instantiation. Once thought thinks the conditions under which thought can occur, it instantiates particular instances of thought, thus making the possibility of a thought beyond its instantiations impossible. But on the other hand, it is just as readily assumed that thought is more than just the sum total of thoughts that exist. The void, then, is the name given to that excess that occurs when thought thinks itself.

Nevertheless, given that we are still operating at the level of ontology, it is not Hegel who will concern us in this chapter. I will focus instead upon one thinker who most closely resembles Badiou at a methodological level—Spinoza. Both Badiou and Spinoza depart from a rational determination of being, and both begin with an axiomatic system that posits being in and through the resources of thought itself. For each thinker, thought's ability to posit axioms of being is tantamount to an equivalence between thought and being. That is, Spinoza's *Ethics*, no less than Badiou's *Being and Event*, is not a description of being as much as it is a rational ontology that, as an ontology, departs from the minimal condition under which thought and being are the same. For Spinoza, this was simply the axiomatic postulation that it follows from the nature of substance to exist. And insofar as substance must necessarily exist, it does. The tautology of being (substance) and existence knows of no other determination apart from the axiom, just as, for Badiou, the empty-set axiom knows of no other determination apart from the supposition that a minimal thought of being-qua-being is a thought of nothing.

There is, however, a very important way in which Badiou differs from Spinoza, and this will be our focus here. In Badiou's reading of Spinoza (primarily of the *Ethics*), he will maintain that Spinoza cannot accept the void into his system. Instead, there are substance and modes. Undoubtedly, substance can produce itself, it can produce more than what there is, but, for Spinoza, the excess of the infinity of substance over and above its instantiation in modes does not result in the existence of a void. What is specific to thought, as an attribute of thought, is its particular instantiation in modes, on the one hand, and its instantiation in thought as an infinite mode (which, as infinite mode, allows for the continual generation of modes above and beyond what already is). The same relation holds for extension as an attribute of substance as well. Infinite modes, then, are what fill in the excess that is left between the denumerable instantiation of finite modes, on the one hand, and the infinite productivity of substance, on the other. There is no need for a void. But when interrogated by Badiou, infinite modes are precisely that—the empty names for the excess of inconsistency above and beyond the instantiation of being in and through particular modes. This is not necessarily to say that they do not exist; rather they exist as void. Badiou's question will be whether Spinoza has adequately thought either infinite modes or the conditions under which thought and being are truly infinite.

Spinoza is a useful figure here because he provides a common ground for engaging in a dialogue between Deleuze and Badiou. Spinoza is, notes Badiou, 'a point of intersection, but "his" Spinoza was (and still is) for me an unrecognizable creature' (*CB*, p. 1). Perhaps this unrecognizable character of Spinoza follows from the difference between the two thinkers' approaches to mathematics: Deleuze drew upon the continuity of geometry and differential calculus, while Badiou preferred the discretion of algebra and sets. In this sense, we can see why Badiou would regard counting, rather than expression, as causality in Spinoza's ethics. Things are caused insofar as they are counted, or discretely presented, rather than being infinitely expressed. But this is a cursory comparison, given that both thinkers clearly think multiplicity both through discrete operations, and through the continuous excess of what I would call unpresented being. What is important is not that they think it, but how they differ in thinking this multiplicity. Now, for Deleuze, there must be an equivalence between thought and being, given that thought is substance. His great supplement to Spinoza's system is the introduction of the concept of expression: thought expresses substance by thinking substance. Thus, thinking is not a reflection upon being as much as it is an engendering of being. If this is the case, expression is that through which substance is given, and from which an axiomatic demonstration follows as a rational, or purely logical consequence. The act of expression, then, is a foundation for Spinoza's ontology insofar as it is through the expression of substance in thought that one can produce the axioms that secure its existence in a rational framework. Expression produces rather than deduces substance, and this, of course, is consistent with the entire productive framework of Deleuze's entire philosophy, up to and including *A Thousand Plateaus*. 'There is no question of deducing Expression: rather it is expression that embeds deduction in the Absolute, renders proof the *direct manifestation* of absolutely infinite substance'.[1]

Proof for Deleuze renders visible the invisible or, rather, gives a determinate existence to something that inheres as a pure power or capacity to exist in and through expression. Thought is expression, and there is no need for there to be a void. Deleuzians are frequently frustrated by the postulation of the void, typically seeing it as an empty abstraction that deprives thought of its proper power. But for Badiou's interrogation of the foundations upon which thought is capable of producing truths (which, when all is said and done, is its productive power), thought is invariably void and this is its enabling condition. This is a result, for Badiou, of the purely minimal framework through which thought can occur: thought is not consciousness, or intentionality, or a rapport between faculties, any more than it is expression. There are particular thoughts that, like the material support of set theory itself, are subject to certain laws and formal groupings, even if, for a formalist, mathematics is nothing apart from the symbols that are

---

1. Gilles Deleuze, *Expressionism in Philosophy: Spinoza*, trans. Martin Joughin, New York, Zone Books, 1991, p. 22.

formally manipulated. But this 'is nothing' is precisely what enables thought. For Badiou, then, proof or axioms are both produced by thought at the same time that they are deduced, internally to thought, from the minimal conditions under which thought can think itself as a self-organizing multiplicity through set theory. Negation is not a denial of the capacity of thought as much as it is the fundamental condition under which thought is enabled.

If the void is the primary name of being for Badiou, it is because the multiplicity that presentation presents has no qualitative being in and of itself: multiplicity is not a constitutive determination of being at any sort of substantial level. It is rather the result of an impasse internal to formalization. The letters and symbols of mathematics are the material support of a thought of being: this would be their 'substantial level'—numbers are nothing apart from their instantiation as symbols. But these letters are themselves subject to formal laws of grouping and ordering that, internally to the operations of mathematics, do not exhaust the totality of multiplicity that there necessarily is. Presentation inscribes the existence of what cannot be directly presented. With regard to Spinoza, then, for whom infinity is a non-mathematical *quality* of substance, the existence of a void can only be introduced through the employment of an external determination of substance that modifies its proper content. For example, in a work predating the *Ethics* by over a decade, Spinoza postulated that 'it involves a contradiction that there should be a vacuum'.[2] The existence of a vacuum implies that there could be extension without corporeal substance. By virtue of the fact that Spinoza previously proposed that 'body and extension do not really differ', having extension without corporeal substance (or a body) would be tantamount to having extension without extension, a self-contradictory statement if ever there was one. Spinoza's refusal of a vacuum was thus necessary on two counts. In the first place, his geometrical method served as a model in which the rejection of a vacuum logically followed from the parameters of what was already outlined in an axiomatic system (that is, from what space, bodies, extension, substance—and the relations between them—precisely were). It was a model that contained its own criteria for verification, making recourse to any external term superfluous. Given this, it could secondly be said that the refusal of the void in Spinoza's philosophy logically extended from the fact that nothing external to a geometrical method was necessary to ensure its internal consistency. Like the monism of his substance, Spinoza's geometrical method was not a reflection upon being or the world, or any external object or domain, but rather a system in which creation was fully immanent to the created.

If one assumes that Spinoza is a thinker of multiplicity (a fairly uncontroversial conjecture), he is undoubtedly one who conceives it as a continuous whole that pre-exists any division into parts. Only abstractions from the intricate relatedness of multiplicity would allow multiplicity to be divided into discrete sections. And the fact that for Spinoza there is no vacuum in nature is the direct result of the indi-

---

2. Proposition 3 of Book II of Descartes' 'Principles of Philosophy', in Spinoza, *The Collected Works of Spinoza*, p. 268.

visibility of substance itself. To quote Spinoza fully on this count from the *Ethics*: 'Since therefore, there is no vacuum in Nature [...] but all its parts must concur that there is no vacuum, it follows also that they cannot be really distinguished, that is, that corporeal substance, insofar as it is a substance, cannot be divided'.[3] The key point is that it is precisely *as substance* that a whole cannot be divided into parts. Parts inhere in matter only insofar as matter can be seen as something that is 'affected in different ways, so that its parts are distinguished only modally, but not really' (*Spinoza's Ethics*, Bk I, prop. 15, p. 424). Like Deleuze and Bergson after him, Spinoza undoubtedly posits the actuality of infinity at the outset, such that parts are merely abstractions or divisions extracted from the density of the whole. Only from a perspective that deems corporeal substance to be a discrete whole composed of parts could it then be inferred that substance is finite, and thus separate from God. The logical absurdities that follow from this are amply given in the *Ethics*,[4] and I won't labour their implication in detail except to say that the problem that extends from thinking infinity through the summation of discrete (or finite) divisions would introduce the problem of a void, something that Spinoza refuses on both logical and ontological grounds (the void, in this case, being the empty beyond that the infinite addition of parts would be directed towards in the pursuit of infinity).

As Badiou thus sees it, Spinozan being (substance) is founded upon an exclusion of the void in a very specific manner. It is not simply that there is no vacuum in nature (which could merely expel a physically existing void); it is rather that everything that is substance (which would in fact be everything) falls under the logic of a unified presentation insofar as everything is either a finite mode (counted as one) or a singular substance (which is only ever *the* one as totality of what is). The only exceptions to these principles are found in infinite modes, something that Badiou will read as the reappearance of the void (*qua* inconsistency) into Spinoza's axiomatic. How successful Badiou is in his attempts will ultimately depend upon the manner in which the reader accepts Spinoza's initial positing of infinite modes. My brief allusions to Deleuze's interpretation of infinite modes should leave their legitimacy open to further questioning. For the present, however, what is important is the manner in which they exceed the principles of unified presentation that otherwise inform Spinoza's axiomatic.

II. Foreclosing the Void

Spinoza is one of the earliest thinkers to be introduced in the lineage of Badiou's *Being and Event* (with the exception of Plato and Aristotle), and the relative

---

3. Spinoza, *Ethics*, Book I, Proposition 15, in Spinoza, *The Collected Works of Spinoza*, p. 420. Hereafter cited in the text, with book and proposition numbers, as *Spinoza's Ethics*.

4. On one hand, if corporeal substance is infinite and divisible, it could be divided into two parts, which can either be infinite or finite. If both parts are finite, one would have an infinity composed of two finite parts. If both are infinite, one would have more than one infinity, which is absurd. Or one could be infinite, and the other finite, and thus it would be the case that infinity is missing a part, which is equally absurd. Either one must conclude that corporeal substance is finite, or that it is not divisible into parts. Spinoza clearly opted for the latter position.

economy of Badiou's analysis will lay the groundwork for the more difficult issues that bear upon the relations between Badiou and Deleuze. Badiou embarks upon his analysis of Spinoza not from the place most commentators usually begin (that is, singular substance), but rather with the multiplicity of singular things. It is a curious choice for Badiou, given that this is not necessarily the manner in which Spinoza organizes the *Ethics*.[5] But Badiou's unique stance on this is to complicate the way the unifying principle of substance—equivalent to the *cause* of singular things—can be derived from the multiplicity of what Deleuze calls extensive parts: 'In effect, a composition of individual multiples (*plura individua*) is one and the same thing if those individuals work toward their unique action—that is to say if they are simultaneously the cause of a unique effect' (*EE*, p. 129). Here we find a bizarre reversal of the principles one usually uses to understand Spinoza: how could an individual be the cause of an effect of unity, if unity itself (*qua* substance) was the underlying *cause* of singular things? For Badiou, this is not a problem of interpretation if we understand that the count-as-one (the individuation of singular modes from the multiplicity of substance) *is* causality. 'A combination of multiples is a one-multiple inasmuch as it is the one of a causal action' (*EE*, p. 129). This logic could just as easily be read backwards: the one as causal effect of the counting of multiples comes to be that which validates the one as cause of a singular thing.[6]

The most immediate objection to Badiou's equation of counting with causality is that, for Spinoza, number is only an external determination of an existing thing. Thus, for twenty men to exist in the world, the number twenty must 'necessarily be outside' the twenty men themselves (*Spinoza's Ethics*, Bk I, prop. 8, p. 415). Whatever exists as a number of individuals must have an external cause to exist. It is substance itself that determines that number—and thus the count itself. The problem with this, for Badiou, is that it is circular. Two principles of unity must be presupposed to make sense of this: one as the effect of the count, and another one as the supposition of that effect (the one of causality). But the latter, in order to be supported by principles anterior to the effects of the count, will define itself as the *effect of the effect*—that is, the effect of the count. If it was initially difficult to see what the count had to do with causality (insofar as the latter was not yet distinct from the unity of substance), Badiou's intentions should now be clear: what assures the consistency of the count is nothing other than the unity of God or substance itself, insofar as it is inseparable from the internal determination of substance as a singular situation. Herein lies the unique character of his monism: substance is both metastructure *and* structure insofar as substance posits both itself (*qua* metastructure, determination of the whole) and its singular modes. If no

---

5. Deleuze is not far from this approach when he writes that 'substance, by virtue of its power, exists only in its relation to modes'. It should be noted that for Deleuze, substance only exists as the *puissance* that enables the existence of modes. Deleuze, *Expressionism in Philosophy: Spinoza*, p. 95.

6. Again, even Deleuze is close to this interpretation when he writes that for Spinoza, '*to exist is to actually possess a very great number [plurimae] of parts*'. See Deleuze, *Expressionism in Philosophy: Spinoza*, p. 201.

term outside substance accounts for the manner in which it is both cause of itself and its singular modes (such a determination being endemic to substance itself), then Badiou will maintain that 'Spinoza's is the most radical ontological attempt ever at identifying structure and metastructure, [...] belonging and inclusion' (*EE*, p. 130).

The immediate consequence is that Spinoza's is a philosophy that 'forecloses the void *par excellence*' (*EE*, p. 130). While Badiou will go on to show that this foreclosure fails, I wish to stay for the moment with what is implicit in the conflation of what Badiou calls belonging and inclusion. If one maps these set-theoretical terms onto Spinozism, the fact that there is a perfect transitivity at work in Spinoza ensures that everything presented in substance is also represented (individuated) as singular modes, and everything individuated as a mode is presented as well (insofar as modes constitute substance). It is a fairly straightforward point of Spinoza's that the only things that exist are substance, on the one hand, and modifications of that substance—that is, modes—on the other (attributes only being expressions of essence).[7] Now, the latter clearly *belong* to the former, given Spinoza's axiom, in the first book of the *Ethics*, that '*Whatever is, is in God, and nothing can be or be conceived without God*' (*Spinoza's Ethics*: Bk 1, prop. 15, p. 420). For Badiou, the 'in' of the belonging to God is the universal relation for Spinoza—there is no other relation than belonging. 'If, in effect, you combine several things—several individuals, for example—according to the causal count-for-one (on the basis of the one of their effect), you never obtain but an other thing, that is to say, a mode that belongs to God' (*EE*, p. 130-1). Thus, if a collection of things themselves form a thing that does not qualitatively differ from any one of its parts, the counting of terms never amounts to anything excessive to substance, given that the count of terms is nothing other than the 'inexhaustible immanent productivity of substance itself' (*EE*, p. 131).

To frame the point Badiou is making, and to perhaps allude to what will only later become apparent, consider the manner in which Deleuze handled the problem of Spinoza's monism. It is clear that Deleuze privileged Spinoza over Descartes because substances in the latter were distinguished from each other only in distilled, mathematical terms—that is, only through abstracting from the substantial differences between the attributes of thought and extension are the primary differences between the two determined on a more elevated register of two substances (*res cogitans, res extensia*). But for Deleuze-Spinoza, this amounts to nothing more than a denial of difference as something that is *real*. Not only does Spinoza's monism successfully affirm actual multiplicity, it internally differentiates the singularities inherent to it without making recourse to an external criteria (e.g., number) for that differentiation. 'Detached from all numerical distinction, real distinction is carried into the absolute, and becomes capable of expressing difference within Being, so bringing about the restructuring of other

---

7. Deleuze, *Expressionism in Philosophy: Spinoza*, p. 95. '[Substance] has an absolutely infinite power of existence only by exercising in an infinity of things, in an infinity of ways or modes, the capacity to be affected corresponding to that power'.

distinctions'.[8]

If Deleuze's point is that the singularity of substance is precisely what allows for a real difference among attributes, this point is not lost on Badiou. For he clearly concludes that Spinoza does not fail to distinguish multiple 'situations'. The singularity of God is what allows him to be identified in an infinity of different manners, in attributes. 'Here we must distinguish between being-qua-being (the substantiality of substance), and what thought is able to conceive of as constituting the differentiable identity—Spinoza says: the essence—of being, which is plural' (*EE*, p. 131). Furthermore, Badiou makes the rather Deleuzian point that the multiplicity of situations (that is, the attributes of substance) is what upholds the unity of substance insofar as that unity, were it to be thought in only a single one of its attributes 'would have in this way difference external to itself, that is to say, it would be counted itself, which is impossible, since it *is* the supreme count' (*EE*, p. 131).

But despite the fact that an infinity of attributes exist, there are precisely only two attributes ('two countable situations') that can be experienced by humans: thought and extension. And the 'uniqueness' of a human is that even if he or she can inhabit two separate situations (mind and body, thought and extension), a human is also counted as one thing. For Badiou, this is the quintessential example of the subordination of statist excess (representation) to presentative immediacy. The mind and the body are *included* in a unified human being that does nothing more than *belong* to an ontological situation. Even if the mind and the body simultaneously belong to two separate situations or attributes, their inclusion in the singular mode of a human being ultimately subordinates their *inclusion* as human beings (subsets of modes) to their *belonging* to an ontological situation.

For Spinoza, however, given that modes that comprise the various affections of substance and its attributes belong to the ontological situation 'substance' (alongside the humans that belong to that situation), there is no need to produce a 'power-set' of all the various combinations of these thoughts and ideas (for example, the humans that these bodies and minds combine to make) since, in the first place, there is no place outside substance to posit such a set, and second, the plurality of substance pre-exists the division of substance into discrete parts, thus making the application of a numerical measure (or cardinality) to the multiplicity of substance absurd. In other words, the minds and bodies that are elements of substance (*qua* modes) together form a subset that just as legitimately belongs to substance themselves. Nothing exceeds presentation, either causally or ontologically.

The foreclosure of the void directly follows from this. The void neither belongs to an ontological situation (since it doesn't result in being counted as one), nor can it be included in the metastructure as causality or representation that is excessive to presentation, since metastructure for Spinoza is nothing other than causal counting, conceived this time as the immanent self-positing of substance

---

8. Deleuze, *Expressionism in Philosophy: Spinoza*, p. 39.

in and through itself. Substance, as cause of itself, is what guarantees that nothing exceeds it precisely insofar as it posits itself as one substance. As Deleuze notes, correctly I believe, to apply external causality to substance in and through the positing of more than one substance would force substance to 'operate outside the terms that legitimate and define it—to propose its operation in a sort of void, and quite indeterminately'.[9]

The fact that there is no vacuum in nature follows from the indivisibility of substance. A vacuum (or physically existing void) could only exist alongside a limitation of substance. But if substance is singularly indivisible, any limitation to substance could only occur through abstracting from the true nature of substance itself. Now, it will be in this disproportion between modes and substance, or the divisible and indivisible, that the question of the void itself will re-emerge. If God, or substance, is the *cause* of modes (insofar as 'modes can neither be nor be conceived without substance'), the question as to the measure between the count (substance, causality) and its result (effect of one, singular mode) necessarily reintroduces the void into Spinoza's system *qua* 'measurable non-rapport between its infinite origin and the finitude of the one-effect' (*EE*, p. 133). If only substance or modes exist, there will necessarily be an 'excess of the causal source' precisely insofar as the absolute infinite indivisibility of substance is not itself present *at the same level* as the effects it produces in the count of finite things. There will be a potential disruption in what would otherwise be seen as the complete immanence of Spinoza's system.

III. The Problem of Infinite Modes

The crux of the problem directs the reader to Propositions 21, 22 and 28 of the first book of the *Ethics*, where three points are established:

Everything that follows from the absolute nature of any of God's attributes must exist and be infinite. If an effect, or mode, directly results from the infinite nature of substance/God, it too must be infinite. These would be *immediate infinite modes*.

Everything that directly follows from an immediate infinite mode—that is, if it is modified by a mode that exists necessarily and is infinite—must also exist necessarily and be infinite. These are *mediate infinite modes*.

Any singular finite thing can neither exist nor produce an effect unless it is itself determined to exist and produce an effect by another singular finite thing which itself must be determined to exist by another singular finite thing, and so on to infinity.

The immediate implication of this, as has already been stated, is the complete disjunction between the finite and the infinite: one cannot directly ensue from the other, even if the recurrence of finite modes themselves create an infinite chain. 'The flaw between the infinite and the finite, where the danger of the

---

9. Deleuze, *Expressionism in Philosophy: Spinoza*, p. 32.

void lies, does not traverse the presentation of the finite' (*EE*, p. 134). Yet with regard to propositions 21 and 22, it is a question of modes that, by virtue of following either from substance or one of its attributes, are infinite. The question for Badiou (among others) is one of knowing the extent to which these infinite modes can be said to exist. What exactly are they? Drawing on a communication between Spinoza and a correspondent, Badiou proffers the following examples: in the order of thought, an immediate infinite mode would be 'absolutely infinite understanding', in the order of extension, 'movement and rest'. As for mediate infinite modes, he offers only one example in extension: 'the figure of the entire universe' (*EE*, p. 135).

The direct gap left in his system would evidently be the lack of a mediate infinite mode in thought. But this may be secondary to the actual problem Badiou finds in Spinoza's positing of infinite modes: it is not that a lack of one of them leaves a void in his system—infinite modes, as Juliette Simont notes, are themselves *void itself*.[10] I want to be very clear about what this problem is for Badiou. He is not simply dismantling Spinoza by locating a certain indeterminate nothingness in the circularity of his method. It is rather that infinite modes are posited to provide a leeway between the presentative immediacy of finite modes and the indivisible infinity of substance. Of course, a leeway for Badiou exists, but only through an operation of subtraction, which is obviously at odds with the immanent productivity of Spinozist substance. More specifically, with regard to infinite modes, one could certainly argue that the totality of the universe is composed of modes at the same time that it can be read (at least by Spinoza) as infinite. But there is a difference between a modal infinite *unity* established through 'summation *ad infinitum*' and the principle of unity that operates as the causality of modes in general. The former departs from modes to posit totality as one, whereas the latter would be inherent to the causal operations of substance (from which modes are produced). Why, then, is it legitimate to call infinite modes, modes at all? The totality of the figure of the entire universe, for example, while being an immanent production of substance, cannot be said to be presented as one in the same manner as a finite mode. It departs from the finite onto the infinite, which is the direct opposite of the manner in which infinite substance can be said to be the cause of finite modes. The question needs to be asked whether infinite modes are even presented at all since:

> [...] the principle of the All that is obtained by addition ad infinitum has nothing to do with the principle of the One through which substance guarantees the counting of all singular things in radical statist excess, which is nonetheless immanent. (*EE*, p. 135-6)

If it is true that all that exists is either a substance or a mode, it should be perfectly easy to test their existence. It pertains to the nature of substance to exist,

---

10. Juliette Simont, 'Le Pur et l'impur (Sur deux questions de l'histoire de la philosophie dans L'être et l'événement)', *Le Temps Modernes*, no. 526, 1990, pp. 27-60, p. 32. Simont sees Badiou's reading of Spinoza as an argument for infinite modes' lack of existence, which is not the case at all. Infinite modes for Badiou are simply not consistently presented in experience as modes.

whereas the existence of modes 'cannot be inferred from the definition of the thing'.[11] Modes, that is, exist *a posteriori*, through experience. Now, no single one of these modes can be given in experience: one cannot observe movement or rest directly (only things that move or are at rest), nor can the totality of extension be represented in experience. On the other hand, one cannot say that these modes *necessarily* exist outside experience, for they would thus be qualified as substance, not as modes. Or, as Badiou writes, 'at best, they will be the identifications of situations', that is, attributes (*EE*, p. 136).

We have thus reached an impasse. Infinite modes were introduced precisely in order to avoid having singular finite modes directly follow from infinite substance, since the void would emerge therein as the excess of causality over the singular thing which is simultaneously immanent to, but incommensurable with, the infinite indivisibility of substance. But if infinite modes make amends of sorts for this excess in that nothing finite can directly be caused by what is infinite, they are nothing more, for Badiou, than pure names whose existence cannot be proven. 'One needs to propose either that these modes exist, but are as inaccessible to thought as to experience, or that they don't exist' (*EE*, p. 136). If they do exist, they do so purely as a name designating a certain outside to experience: the name 'infinite mode'. If they don't exist, on the other hand, they directly create a void in the sense that they uphold infinity as such in the 'causal recurrence of the finite' (the totality of souls that comprise the universe as a whole, for example). This is an empty name as well: it is there 'to put forward what the [geometrical] proof requires, to be successively annulled in all finite experience where it served to found unity' (*EE*, p. 137).

For Badiou, Spinoza's 'lesson' is that if the void is excluded from presentation, it will necessarily re-emerge in the form of an empty name. Perhaps this is Badiou's own schematic take on Lacan's famous dictum of the 50's: 'what is foreclosed in the symbolic returns in the real'—the very deliberate use of the Lacanian term 'foreclosure' would suggest as much. 'Infinite mode' would thus name the return of the void as a name for what cannot be consistently presented in Spinoza's system. We can furthermore see how this initial foreclosure/exclusion was installed on three counts:

1. in the simple (almost axiomatic) proclamation of Spinoza in Book 1: 'the vacuum is not found in Nature'. As we have seen, this is a direct result of the indivisibility of nature at the level of its substantiality.
2. in a point derived from Deleuze's reading of Spinoza's monism: there is nothing outside the terms of substance that can distinguish it from another substance, and thus serve as the cause of that distinction, for to do so, in Deleuze's own terms, would 'propose its operation in a sort of void—and quite indeterminately'. This would be the foreclosure of the excess of metastructure (a term anterior to the immanent productivity of substance).

---

11. See Letter 10, Spinoza to Simon de Vries in Spinoza, *The Collected Works of Spinoza*, p. 196.

3. the void finally remains absent from the disjunctive relation between substance, as cause, and modes as effects. Ironically enough, this disjunction will be necessary for Spinoza if he is to avoid installing causality as excessive to presentation. That is, the infinite can only directly result in modes that are infinite if it is to avoid appearing as a cause that is incommensurable with its effects.

If the void simply marks the place of an unacknowledged excess of infinite substance over the finite modes of which it alone is the cause, this would, in the first place, follow from the fact that a direct correlation between infinite substance as cause, and finite modes as effects, has been established. Taken directly in this manner, infinite modes are void not simply because they have no existence that can be directly attested to in experience (and thus by the criteria of Spinoza's system); rather, they secure the empty name of what is not directly accounted for in Spinoza's causal operations. Deleuze, in contrast, found that movement and rest have a character that is particular to them alone, insofar as they are what allow for the unification of the extrinsic parts of a mode to form a complete whole. As he wrote:

> The attribute of Extension has an extensive modal quantity that actually divides into an infinity of simple bodies. These simple bodies are extrinsic parts which are only distinguished from one another, and which are only related to one another, through movement and rest. Movement and rest are precisely the form of extrinsic distinction and external relation between simple bodies. Simple bodies [...] are always grouped in infinite wholes, *each whole being defined by a certain relation of movement and rest.*[12]

From this it is evident that movement and rest, far from being singular modes among others, comprise relations that make the existence of finite modes possible. Or rather, movement and rest are what allow the infinite decomposable parts of a mode to determine a modal essence (which Deleuze characterizes, in terms too complex to outline here, as a *degree of intensity*). Now, Deleuze's take on this is that it is only by virtue of these relations that the extrinsic parts that comprise a mode come to have an existence (that is, in Badiou's terms, by virtue of *belonging*). 'They have no existence of their own, but existence is composed of them: to exist is to actually have an infinity of extensive parts'.[13] Conveniently side-stepping the problem of defining movement and rest as modes, Deleuze maintains that movement and rest are what allow for 'the conditions for modes to come into existence'.[14] If we follow this point to its conclusion, we must infer that their modal existence follows directly from their essence, given that the means by which they act upon the extensive parts of finite modes mirror the manner in which substance externally causes modes. Movement and rest could even be said to

---

12. Deleuze, *Expressionism in Philosophy: Spinoza*, p. 205.
13. Deleuze, *Expressionism in Philosophy: Spinoza*, p. 207.
14. Deleuze, *Expressionism in Philosophy: Spinoza*, p. 236.

constitute the essences of things that don't exist;[15] they thus comprise a relation which is analogous to causality insofar as they enable the existence of modes in general. But the relation in question is nonetheless a different sort of relation than causality, strictly speaking. Thus, to return to an earlier point, relations other than causality are needed if we are to account for the workings of Spinoza's system.

IV. Non-Causal Relations

In an article originally published in 1994,[16] Badiou acknowledged that Spinoza, not unlike Badiou himself, opts for an ontology founded upon the axiomatic of the decision. From this is derived the *more geometrico*, which 'is not a form of thought—it is the written trace of an originally thought decision'. What Badiou rejects, however, is that the 'there is' of the axiomatic decision, referring to the infinity of substance, or God, admits exclusively of causality as relation (*CT*, p. 74). In effect, Badiou admits that two other relations are necessary to maintain the coherence of Spinoza's system: *coupling* and, surprisingly, *inclusion* (*CT*, p. 75).

The crux of Badiou's conclusion encompasses a problem that was encountered earlier: the circularity of Spinoza's system. If we inquire as to the resources with which thought can have access to infinity, and if the intellect offers the means (or 'singular localization') with which divine infinity can be conceived (along with the 'there is' of pure positing itself), we are faced with what Badiou will call a 'torsion'. For the intellect is not only that through which one grasps divine infinity, it is also what attributes to substance its nature as an infinite thing conceived through itself.[17] The circularity is introduced as such:

> To think this torsion is to say: how can the Spinozist determination of the 'there is' return to its interior fold which is the intellect? Or, more simply, how can one think the being of the intellect, the 'there is some intellect', if rational access to the thought of being, or of the 'there is', is itself dependent upon the operations of the intellect? Or: the intellect operates, but what is the status of being of its operation? (*CT*, p. 78)

The difficulty is not peculiar to Badiou's interpretation. Following the lineage of Hegel's objections to Spinoza, Pierre Macherey has observed that the attribute thought, as an essence of substance, must precede the intellect as a mode if Spinoza's system is to have a logical order. Yet, as a mode, it is the intellect that perceives the attribute as constituting the essence of substance. If abstract reasoning supposes a circle, it does so by definition, not through any procedure of

---

15. Deleuze, *Expressionism in Philosophy: Spinoza*, p. 235.

16. Alain Badiou, 'L'ontologie implicite de Spinoza', in Myriam Revault d'Allones (ed.), *Spinoza: puissance et ontology*, Paris, Kimé, 1994. Reprinted in Alain Badiou, *Court traité d'ontologie transitoire*, Paris, Seuil, 1998. Hereafter cited in the text as *CT*.

17. See Spinoza's letter to Simon de Vries from March, 1663: 'By substance I understand what is in itself and is conceived through itself, i.e., whose concept does not involve the concept of another thing. I understand the same by attribute, except that it is called attribute in relation to the intellect, which attributes such and such a definite nature to substance'. Spinoza, *The Collected Works of Spinoza*, p. 195.

realization. Thus the circularity of Spinoza's logic explicates itself, for Macherey, through the fact that the definition of an attribute 'makes the nature of the attribute depend on the existence of this mode without which it would be not only incomprehensible, but even impossible'.[18]

The fact that this will foreshadow an acknowledgment of non-causal relations is what, in effect, allows Badiou to avoid the necessity of resolving the aforementioned enigma through placing the void. First, in acknowledging that the relation between an idea and its object is not directly causal, Badiou introduces another relation called *coupling*, whereby 'an idea of the intellect is always coupled with an object' (*CT*, p. 82). Or, by extension, 'a mode of thought is always coupled with another mode, which could be extension, or thought, or a whole other attribute entirely'.[19] Now, to conceive this as a coupling between two distinct attributes is one thing; clearly, this is how Spinoza's familiar definition of the mind as the idea of the body is usually received. But if one acknowledges the theorem that 'the order and connection of ideas is the same as the order and connection of things' (*Spinoza's Ethics*, Bk II, prop. 7, p. 451), how can one then account for the intellect being coupled with a mode of thought? Clearly, thoughts have connections with other thoughts in a way that is not isomorphic to the relations among extended modes. For the intellect, two infinite recurrences have to be posited to account for this particular relation: one of causality, and one of coupling. Thoughts can be said to be the cause of other thoughts (and even of God's essence) at the same time that they are coupled with thoughts and objects that have no causal bearing upon them. And unlike extension, the attribute of thought has a structure that is isomorphic to itself—insofar as *the idea of an idea is the object of an idea*. The connection between ideas and ideas of ideas is not isomorphic to the 'order and connection of things' in extension. Thus, the attribute thought, or the intellect, remains radically singular in Spinoza's system insofar as modes of thought can be coupled with other thoughts. As such, substance can think itself through the mode of thought.

Things are even more complex with regards to the finite intellect (human mind). Badiou immediately asks how the finite intellect 'can conceive itself as a modification or affection of the infinite intellect?' (*CT*, p. 84). If everything that follows from an infinite mode (the infinite intellect) is infinite, there is simply no way the finite intellect can directly ensue from the infinite. But neither is it the idea or object of the infinite intellect, as would be the case in a relation of coupling. A third relation is necessary, and Badiou is quick to name this relation, curiously enough, *inclusion*. 'Certainly', writes Badiou, 'the finite intellect is not an effect of infinite intellect, but, as Spinoza says, it is a part of it' (*CT*, p. 85). It hardly seems arbitrary that the word for part will be *partie*, French for subset. For the inclusive relation between the finite and infinite intellect (such that the finite

---

18. Pierre Macherey, 'The Problem of the Attributes', in Warren Montag and Ted Stolze (eds.), *The New Spinoza*, Minneapolis, University of Minnesota Press, 1997, pp. 65-96, p. 67.

19. This almost certainly bears resemblance to Deleuze's interpretation of parallelism in Spinoza. See Deleuze, *Expressionism in Philosophy: Spinoza*, pp. 99-111.

intellect is included in the infinite intellect) could, reciprocally, just as well be viewed in set-theoretical terms: the infinite intellect is the sum total, or collection (or power-set), of finite intellects, as Badiou keenly observes in quoting from book 5 of the *Ethics*: 'our Mind, insofar as it understands, is an eternal mode of thinking, which is determined by another eternal mode of thinking, and this again by another, and so on, to infinity; so that together, they all constitute God's eternal and infinite intellect' (*Spinoza's Ethics*, Bk V, prop. 40, p. 615). The uniqueness of inclusion is that it names what specifically constitutes the content of the infinite intellect (being the 'limit point for the finitudes it totalizes') *and*, simultaneously, the being of the finite intellect (a 'point of composition for its infinite summation' of the intellect) (*CT*, p. 85-6). More generally, inclusion alone is what accounts for the cyclic relation between the finite and the infinite intellect which causality, in its strict linear movement from substance to modes, cannot justify.

Now—cutting across Badiou's analysis of 'common notion' in Spinoza—we are in a position to see the manner in which these two extra relations, rather than opening Spinoza's ontology to its own meta-ontological grounds that exceed substance as such, effect a closure that is necessary to sort out the different determinations (the 'multiple and complex muddling') of the positing of substance. If Spinoza's system only admits the existence of singularities as the immanent effects of the postulation of substance, the criteria of assessing the truth of singular propositions can only be attributed to notions that are common to *all singularities*. If the relations between the human intellect (which is included in the infinite intellect) reintroduces coupling at the level of relations between an idea and its object (for example, the body), the singularity of such an assertion is traversed by what is common to all bodies. Badiou's unique contribution to the theory of common notions is that their commonality is no longer justified through what is singular to all bodies, but through the *geometrical method* itself, which—otherwise stated by Badiou—would entail that all truth is mathematical. This expression could be easily exchanged with another: all being is mathematical.

At the end of the essay that has just been recapitulated, we find a point that is resolutely singular for Badiou: Spinoza lacks anything that exceeds, or supplements, the presentation of being—a conception of the event (*CT*, p. 92). A theory of the void—that is, of something that remains on the fringe of any situation—is required for an event to occur. It seems rather abrupt for Badiou to introduce the category of the event within an analysis which, up to this point, has been exclusively concerned with the relations that sustain the consistency of Spinoza's ontology. The event, for Badiou, is not an ontological category, insofar as it is never posited or presented in a situation through any normative or regulative act of formalization: it is resolutely meta-ontological and, as such, cannot be reduced to an analysis of Spinoza. Unlike Deleuze, for whom an event is an expression of the world (whether understood as an expression of continuity or disruption),[20] Ba-

---

20. Badiou's interpretation of Spinoza departs significantly from that of Deleuze, for whom the geometrical method served precisely as a method of invention. As Deleuze writes, 'The geometrical method ceases to be a method of intellectual exposition; it is no longer a means of professorial presen-

diou's event is always detached from the world, from substance, and thus dependent upon something transitive to substance. Badiou's later analysis ultimately ends up assuming that the impossibility of an event in Spinozism is a consequence of the closed nature of substance. His conclusion is thus fully relevant to the analysis in *Being and Event*. Let us conclude, then, with a brief outline of the implications of this conclusion.

V. Conclusion: Enabling the Event

In outlining the principles of Badiou's ontology, I have emphasized the dual nature of presentation: while it comes to organize everything internal to the situation under the unifying principles of the count, it furthermore contains an operation of *unpresentation*, whereby the void names the ontological inconsistency that presentation cannot exhaust. Any situation can contain elements, or presented parts, that inhabit the margins of any situation, and are thus on the 'edge of the void'.[21] Only subjective action can bring the effects of the unpresented to bear upon any situation in order to fundamentally change it. Or rather, one could say that from the inconsistency of the void, subjective action re-decides the consistency of any situation. I have already emphasized how any situation contains an excess of subsets over elements, and thus always contains a profusion of trans-situational multiplicity for which questions of quantity are fundamentally undecidable on both ontological and epistemological grounds. To bring this undecidability of the inconsistent excess to bear upon the regulative principles of the situation thus extends from a local decision that an event has occurred. As Ray Brassier has succinctly put it, for Badiou, 'subjectivity originates in the event as that interruption of consistency through which the void's inconsistency is summoned to the surface of a situation'.[22]

The problem with this analysis for a reading of Spinoza is that nothing in Spinozism exceeds presentation. Not only is there no void in Spinoza, there is nothing external to the situation 'substance' for which questions of belonging or non-belonging, and thus decidability and undecidability, can even apply. The implications of this for the present discussion are crucial: if the regulative principles that determine the 'belonging to' of substance are everywhere immanent to sub-

---

tation but rather a method of *invention*. It becomes a method of vital and optical rectification. If man is somehow distorted, this torsion effect will be rectified by connecting it to its causes *more geometrico*'. Gilles Deleuze, *Spinoza: Practical Philosophy*, trans. Robert Hurley, San Francisco, City Lights, 1998, p. 13.

21. Badiou here distinguishes historic situations (which contain a site for an event) from natural situations (where no such site is present). The site of the event can be said to be presented in a historic situation, but its elements are not. It is thus a site 'on the edge of the void'. See *EE*, pp. 193-198. It seems that every situation contains the possibility for an event insofar as an event 'names' the void of the situation. On the other hand, as we saw, Badiou firmly maintains a distinction between historic and natural situations (in which events do not or cannot occur). See footnote 32, chapter 1.

22. Ray Brassier, 'Stellar Void or Cosmic Animal? Badiou and Deleuze', *Pli: Warwick Journal of Philosophy*, no. 10, 2000, p. 210.

stance, it becomes impossible to distinguish what is globally determined to exist and what can become a local site of intervention through the fleeting appearance of an event, which the void alone inaugurates.[23] On the contrary, for Spinoza, belonging is not an issue because substance cannot be determined by anything other than what belongs to it: non-belonging does not emerge as another relation that could have measurable effects for the determination of substance.

The three Spinozist relations that Badiou engages with (causality, inclusion, coupling) were introduced to resolve certain problems in Spinoza's ontology. With regard to causality, one should ask how it is that the principle of the unity of substance comes to engender modes through a unifying principle of causality. Is there not a certain circularity in this theory, if a principle of unity *as cause* is attributed to *the effects* of the appearance of modes? Of course, given that Deleuze views substance simply as a capacity to exist, the unity of substance is what allows for the best possible multiplicity, but it is less prudent to conclude that the modes (as liberated differences within multiplicity) come to deplete the univocal totality of substance. Second, does the problem of the intellect's ability to think itself not introduce another impasse into the framework of the *Ethics*: the need to account for something extrinsic to modes in order to think them properly? If coupling or inclusion successfully come to *describe* the manner in which thought can think itself, they do so at the expense of necessarily introducing another void into the operations of Spinoza's method: the void of the incommensurable disjunction between the continuous infinity of substance in itself (*qua* thought as attribute) and the discrete multiplicity of finite thoughts.

Indeed, this point illuminates the often unnoticed slippage Spinoza frequently makes between two types of infinities. On the one hand, there is the indivisible, infinite totality of substance that can only be divided into parts through extrinsic action. On the other hand, the figures of the entire universe, the commonality of all bodies, or even nature as totality, are multiples composed of discrete modes. On the one hand, positing the infinity of substance at the outset allows for an actual infinity, a means of thinking multiplicity beyond the successive addition of finite parts towards its impossible 'infinite' goal (for which the void would be the empty beyond of repetition). But, on the other hand, if we conceive the infinity of substance as its capacity to continually affect itself, it is only through the differential relations established by finite modes—that is, their continual generation— that we can truly have an ontology founded upon a principle of becoming (for which the void would be 'substance' as abstract totality of actual differences).[24] Clearly Deleuze aligned himself with the latter tradition when he wrote that 'what interested me most in Spinoza wasn't his Substance, but the composition of finite modes'.[25] If we accept the existence of both continuous and discrete mul-

---

23. See Badiou, *Deleuze: The Clamor of Being*, p. 91.
24. See Tiles, *The Philosophy of Set Theory: An Historical Introduction to Cantor's Paradise*, pp. 29-30.
25. Martin Joughin's introduction to Deleuze, *Expressionism in Philosophy: Spinoza*, p. 11. I thank Daniel Smith for bringing this quote to my attention. Deleuze continues, 'the hope of making substance turn on finite modes, or at least of seeing in substance a *plane of immanence* in which finite modes operate,

tiples in defining infinity, we have the best of both worlds. However, if one assumes the causal reciprocity between substance and modes, one is forced to account for what transpires in the causal movement from the finite to the infinite, the movement of thought as it thinks itself above and beyond the immediacy of presentation. And for an effective decision to ensue from this process, an act of subtraction (or negation) is required. Foreclosed from Spinoza's system, the void becomes the necessary precondition not only for thinking multiplicity, but also for thinking itself. The price paid for its foreclosure is a philosophy that can only take recourse in a descriptive affirmation of what always already is.

---

already appears in this book'.

3

Approximately Infinite Universe

If the decline of determinism in twentieth-century physics offered a certain freedom from the strictures of regulative laws, its effects were certainly not felt socially. This, at least, is Ian Hacking's argument in *The Taming of Chance*.[1] Progress in the sciences opened the way for an analysis of the world that no longer abided by necessity, but if these developments relinquished determination in favour of the more or less haphazard probability of chance, this was accompanied in turn by a proliferation of statistics and figures that could best predict—and by extension, regulate—human behaviour and economic development. In fact, if progress in physics had little immediate impact upon society in general, its indirect effects were everywhere to be seen. Hacking writes:

> What has the avalanche of printed numbers to do with my chief topic, the erosion of determinism? One answer is immediate. Determinism was subverted by laws of chance. To believe there were such laws one needed law-like statistical regularities in large populations [...]. Statistical laws that look like brute, irreducible facts were first found in human affairs, but they could be noticed only after social phenomena had been enumerated, tabulated and made public. That role was well served by the avalanche of printed numbers at the start of the nineteenth century.[2]

The greater the chance, the greater the social control these numbers exerted upon society.[3] For any reader of Hacking (or Foucault), these numbers were not simply neutral; they were there to account for what was left by the departure of determinism. And this was nothing less than a need to regulate human behaviour through numbers that thwarted the haphazard occurrence of the decline of determinism. Figures were produced that could enumerate and classify humans according to standards of normative behaviour (figures of disease, crime, suicide, marriage, pathology, etc.) in order to assess risk, regulate crime, manage health

---

1. Ian Hacking, *The Taming of Chance*, Cambridge, Cambridge University Press, 1990.
2. Hacking, *The Taming of Chance*, p. 3.
3. 'The more the indeterminism, the more the control'. Hacking, *The Taming of Chance*, p. 2.

care, distribute information, and so on. Knowledge and decisions were regulated by very specific laws of numbers that were hardly impartial with regards to either their content or effects; rather, they were *descriptive* of a state of social affairs. 'One can ask: who had more effect on class consciousness, Marx or the authors of the official reports which created the classifications into which people came to recognize themselves? These are examples of questions about what I call "making up people"'.[4] If Hacking is to be believed, numbers do more than merely describe or reflect social conditions; they are *constitutive* of the standards of normativity and deviance from which methods of social control extend.

None of Hacking's argument should be very surprising. It echoes the standard tenets of contemporary historicism whereby attention is no longer given to the linear progression of events, but rather to any network of relations that sustains a given historical system. I myself find it fairly convincing, and it's not for nothing that Hacking's sentiments are consistent with those given by Badiou in a book written in 1990 (the same year as the publication of the *Taming of Chance*). In *Le Nombre et les nombres*, Badiou argues that numbers regulate and organize our daily lives: 'we live in the time of the despotism of numbers' (*NN*, p. 11). Politics, the human sciences (history, sociology, medicine), mass communications, economics, human relations (as in the American custom of stating how much money one makes) all fall under the law of the count insofar as individuals are counted, money is exchanged, culture is consumed, communities are defined, and so forth. It is thus not simply for the mathematician that numbers matter: numbers, in a sense, are for everyone: 'they serve, in the strict sense, for everything, they norm the Whole' (*NN*, p. 11).

And yet, given the hold that numbers have on the course of our daily lives, it is surprising to find that, for Badiou, 'we do not have any recent, active idea of what a number is' (*NN*, p. 14). Not unlike Hacking's statistics (which are always more than mere numbers in and of themselves), numbers can be defined socially through the uses to which they distribute and regulate people in what I would call a process of *particularization*. This is to say that the numbers in question are not simple abstractions: they mean very little outside the categories they measure or assess.

None of this is, properly speaking, ontological, and will thus be of little use for us if we are to understand Badiou's fundamental assertion that mathematics is ontology. As Badiou defined it at the end of *Le Nombre et les nombres*, a number 'is neither the trait of a concept, an operatory fiction, an empirical given, nor a constitutive or transcendental category, nor a syntax or language game, nor an abstraction of our idea of order. A number is *a form of being*' (*NN*, p. 261). Rather than describing, counting, or regulating things or concepts that already exist, Badiou's numbers are formalized determinations of being itself. However, unlike an ontological realist who would assert that numbers themselves exist as ideal entities independently of the mind that thinks them, Badiou's thought is aligned

---

4. Hacking, *The Taming of Chance*, p. 3.

with mathematical formalism.[5] For Badiou's formalism, numbers are given to thought through the symbols, manipulations and rules that lie at the foundation of set theory.[6] But whereas some formalists may argue that numbers are nothing apart from the characters that designate them (such that $x+6$ is nothing other than $x+6$), Badiou asserts that the characters, groupings and rules that hold for set theory are manipulations of the inherent inconsistency of being. 'The history of mathematics, for the concept of number as for any other concept, is precisely history—in principle interminable—of the rapport between the inconsistency of being as such and what of it we can make consist by our thought' (*NN*, p. 262).

The challenge for a mathematical ontology would be to determine what this inconsistency is apart from the manipulations with which it is made to consist. For Georg Cantor, the founder of set theory, the ontological validity of the infinite was equivalent to a formalized *thought* of the infinite. Mathematics was thus a form of freedom insofar as its content, the infinite, was purely immanent to thought; there was no need for mathematics to conform to an independently existing content.[7] Badiou follows this lead insofar as inconsistent multiplicity does not exist externally to mathematical thought. There is no other determination of this inconsistency apart from the formal operations of set theory itself. But it is just as true for Badiou that being does not derive *from* thought. That is, being is not purely generated in and by thinking itself. There must be a point of departure where being is posited. And this initial point is not, as some may imagine, the number one, but rather zero. Mathematical thought is a formalization of a being that is axiomatically posited at the outset in the form of zero. A mathematical thought of being, apart from its instantiation in symbols and manipulations, is nothing independently of these symbols and manipulations. And this nothing that is deemed to exist outside mathematical formalization is rudimentary for ontology as a whole. Zero exists.

What we are left with, then, is not the belief that being is made up of numbers, but rather that numbers are designated forms of being that can, like Spinozist substance, be traced back to a minimal axiomatic framework. Badiou's thesis is that ontology is a *discourse* of being; it pronounces what is *expressible* of being through no other qualification than being itself. As such, ontology needs no confirmation in the physical world to be valid (*EE*, p. 14-15).

The question of how exactly numbers are forms of being will be our first

---

5. An excellent introduction to the various fields of modern mathematics is Stewart Shapiro, *Thinking About Mathematics: The Philosophy of Mathematics*, Oxford, Oxford University Press, 2000.

6. Shapiro, *Thinking About Mathematics: The Philosophy of Mathematics*, p. 140. Shapiro: 'The various philosophies that go by the name of "formalism" pursue a claim that the *essence* of mathematics is the manipulation of characters. A list of the characters and allowed rules all but exhausts what there is to say about a given branch of mathematics. According to the formalist, then, mathematics is not, or need not be, about anything, or anything beyond the typographical characters and rules for manipulating them'.

7. The most succinct presentation of Cantor's belief in an actual infinite is given in chapter six of Joseph Warren Dauben, *Georg Cantor*, Princeton, Princeton University Press, 1979, pp. 120-48. See especially, p. 132.

concern here.[8] We will then follow through the consequences of Badiou's analysis to the impasses in ontology that open the thought of number onto another register: that of truth. I already stated that Cantor's postulation of the continuum hypothesis (CH) for his theory of the ordinals separated ontological questions of truth (at least insofar as these involved the existence or non-existence of cardinal numbers smaller than aleph zero) from epistemological questions of provability.[9] These impasses furthermore extended from the difficulty inherent to constructing models of axiomatic set theory (hereafter known as ZF) in which the continuum hypothesis could be proved or disproved, and this is not without enormous implications for a philosophical definition of truth. For this implies first that no system can designate its own criteria for verification, thus leaving open the possibility for truth beyond the tenets of empirical provability. By extension, the failure of a constructible model of ZF to designate the possibility or impossibility of CH strikes a blow at the convictions of logical constructivism which, for my purposes at least, will carry any debate about the usefulness of set theory beyond the fruitless arguments concerning the existence of numbers as conceptual fictions or logical facts.

At its root, Badiou's equation of set theory with ontology hinges upon a decision (that is, an axiomatic foundation) at the same time that it subscribes to two criteria for its justification. The first criterion is that being-qua-being (*l'être-en-tant-qu'être*) is pure multiplicity, irreducible to any principle of unity at either an atomic or global level. 'Mathematics', writes Badiou, 'is the kind of thought, and consequently the kind of discourse, that apprehends the configurations of multiplicity independently of any characteristic other than multiplicity'.[10] This privileging of multiplicity entails that if unity, or the one, exists, it does so through the operations of a *count-as-one*, which is exerted upon a multiplicity that pre-exists the count, albeit retroactively. Second, given that ontology is what is expressly sayable about being-qua-being, the *content* (being) is given directly through the *formal* operations of mathematics. Mathematical thought does not operate upon a being that is peripheral to mathematical operations: it is only by way of the operations which axiomatically posit and order multiplicity that infinity is posited as the proper domain of both Cantorian set theory and philosophical ontology. Set theory actively engages thought with its proper ontological domain, insofar as the formal operations that constitute set theory (axioms, well-ordering, generic proof) constitute a discourse of being that takes no other qualification than multiplicity as its criteria.

In some sense, then, Badiou's reader must accept a tautological correlation between being, thought and multiplicity. Thought is multiple insofar as there

---

8. The reader may notice my shift here to the less awkward 'numbers' as opposed to 'Number'. This will only be a temporary convenience, given that Badiou resolutely distinguishes Number from numbers.

9. See chapter 1, footnote 27.

10. [Editor's Note: unable to locate the exact source of this quote but similar statements can be found throughout Badiou, cf. Appendix 2 of *EE*, p. 483-6; *BE*, p. 443-7].

is a multiplicity of thoughts that already exist, at the same time that it is necessary, for philosophy, to assume that it is possible for there to be more thoughts. While some (notably, Heideggerians) might find it problematic to assume this at the outset, it is equally problematic to have an ontology that does not have a specified field as its point of reference. Otherwise, how could the validity of any ontology be assessed? Clearly, there cannot be some meta-ontological criteria of what being-qua-being is if ontology alone tells us what being-qua-being is. Thus, taken in this sense, ontology cannot follow a logic of correspondence between its statements and an external state of affairs. Much like the Lacanian refutation of a metalanguage, for Badiou, *there is no meta-ontology* apart from the meta-ontological thesis that mathematics is ontology. But if ontology is determined in and through its own operations, it is just as difficult to scrutinize it as a field and assess what being is without some criteria for delimiting its field of inquiry. At bottom, then, the decision Badiou has made for a set theoretical ontology depends less upon the choice for an ontology than it does upon a more primary decision that being is multiplicity and that set-theory offers the most sophisticated means there is for speaking of that multiplicity.

I have already mentioned the failure of meta-ontology. The implication of this is that being is not an external object, or reserve, upon which thought operates. Like it is for Parmenides,[11] or even Hegel, the multiplicity of being is directly conveyed in and through thought: mathematics presents multiplicity, but this organization and presentation offer nothing other than presentation and organization itself. 'Strictly speaking, mathematics *presents nothing*, without constituting, for all that, an empty game' (*EE*, p. 13). And this lack-of-any object is what a proper ontology requires.[12]

Nevertheless, if philosophers have been foiled in their attempts to obtain a proper grasp of being-qua-being, it is just as true that few mathematicians would have considered that what they were doing was ontology. There is thus a rather powerful jump that one must make from mathematics to Badiou's philosophy, and to adequately assess the reasons for making it a certain familiarity with the mathematical terrain is necessary. There are three 'modern' mathematical positions with which Badiou aligns his philosophy. The first is that zero exists. The second is that the one exists as the result of an operation (which Badiou will call the 'destitution of the one'). And the third is that infinity exists. These three assertions tell us something about being and its manifestations, and do so beyond being a purely empty game of mathematical operations. Yet these are conclusions that are derived from mathematical operations that are indeed just that: purely empty formalist procedures of arranging multiplicities into sets. To think through these positions will require a brief overview of the founding thinkers of these positions: Frege and Russell, but most importantly Cantor and his followers (Zermelo, Fraenkel, and Von Neumann).

---

11. Badiou has cited Parmenides' maxim that 'the same, it is at once thinking and being' on countless occasions.

12. 'If I am right, the truth is that there are no mathematical objects'. *NN*, p. 13.

I. Frege/Russell: Zero Exists

Twentieth-century mathematics was divided between three dominant strains of thought: formalism, logicism, and intuitionism. Badiou unquestionably aligns his philosophy with the first tendency: mathematics is concerned with the formal groupings and orderings of multiplicities rather than with any logical relations between a set and its elements. Mathematics, at its foundations, is not concerned with *meaning* in the way that logic is, and Cantorian set theory is not a descriptive logic. A set is not a collection of elements that possess a certain property (for example, set of all black objects, set of all oranges, etc). A set is defined by the composition of its elements independently of any property they possess.

Gottlob Frege is undoubtedly the forerunner of twentieth-century mathematical logic, and his theory of sets defined a set through its property: a set is defined by a property that subsumes any, or no, objects that possess it. What comes first, then, is the logical property: the existence of any objects possessing that property is a purely ontological addendum. But Frege questioned whether it was possible to derive a definition of number without having to make an ontological leap. Could number be generated from pure logic alone? His attempt to answer this question lay in defining number as a *trait of a concept;* a number is assigned to a concept that subsumes a given number of objects (*NN*, p.27). For example, the concept 'seasons of the year' subsumes four 'objects' (winter, spring, summer, autumn) to which the number 'four' is assigned. Likewise, the concept 'square circle' subsumes no possible objects of experience: thus, the number 'zero' is assigned to it. Numbers don't really have their own concept in this scheme; they simply count empirical objects. The jump we make from a concept that subsumes an object to a concept that subsumes numbers is through *redoubling* the original concept through equivalence. For example, the number 'four' is subsumed by the concept 'equal to the concept "seasons of the year."'

However, for Frege, the redoubling of empirical concepts was not enough to generate a purely logical definition of number, since nothing logical dictates that there should be four seasons in the year instead of five or three. For the purposes of deriving a purely logical definition of number, then, Frege turned to Leibniz's principle of identity: two things are identical if they can be substituted for each other without a loss of truth. A thing is the same as itself, since it can certainly be substituted for itself without a loss of truth. For Frege, this is a sufficiently logical criterion to derive a definition of number, since a number would certainly, like everything else, be subject to being equal to itself.[13] Unfortunately for Frege, 'everything' was not a number. But if the logic is reversed, and we come up with the property 'not equal to itself', we have the first logical concept that subsumes a number. *No object* falls under the concept 'not equal to itself', and to that lack of object, we can assign a number, zero. This can be taken a step further. If we take the concept 'identical to zero', it is true that an object falls under it, the number

---

13. On this point alone Badiou finds fault in Frege, since for Badiou, the statement 'every object is equal to itself' is not purely logical at all—it is ontological. *NN*, p. 30.

zero, to which a new number can be assigned one. And in the following manner, the procession of *all* numbers can be generated though pure logic. Existence, for Frege, proceeds from thought.

It is well-known that Bertrand Russell wrote a letter to Frege in 1903, outlining a famous paradox that spelled a flaw in Frege's system.[14] The paradox in effect demonstrates that it is impossible to generate the existence of number from a purely logical (or purely linguistic) criterion. For if we take the concept 'being a set that is not a member of itself' (which is surely as logical a concept as 'not identical to itself') and then subsume all the sets that possess that property, a problem occurs. What happens to the set of all these sets? Does it belong to itself? If it does, then by definition, it violates its own property of not belonging to itself. But if it does not belong to itself, then it must, by the very same property, belong to itself. We are left with an impasse.

In 1908, Ernst Zermelo proposed a way around this paradox with the postulation of the axiom of separation. It essentially proposed that a set is separate from the class of objects it collects together. By implication, a set cannot belong to itself because it is not given alongside the class of objects it subsumes. So we can speak of a set of all the sets that don't belong to themselves if we separate that sum-total set from the class of sets that it collects. The far-reaching implication of this axiom is that no *set* can belong to itself. At the same time that a set is separate from a class, the axiom of separation also entails that being is separate from language (*EE*, p. 58). A descriptive, linguistic property can only act upon a pre-given domain, or class, of objects that is given at the outset. If existence must be presupposed, it cannot be derived from language.

While the axiom of separation offers a way around Russell's famous paradox, it does little to salvage the logicism of Frege. For it does not allow a person to deduce the existence of an object from pure thought. As Badiou notes, 'If the universe were absolutely void, it would remain logically admissible that, if a thing existed (which would not be the case), it would be restricted to being equal to itself. The statement "all x is equal to itself" would be valid, but there would be no x' (*NN*, p. 34). In effect, there is a huge ontological leap from the statement 'all x is equal to itself' to the assertion that such an x exists.

If, for Badiou, existence cannot be derived from a concept, or from logic, then where does it come from? Ultimately, for Badiou, existence extends from a primary assertion of existence, from which a thought, or concept, of number can proceed. What is required, then, to ground existence is an *axiom*. For Badiou, as for axiomatic set theory, there is one axiom that alone posits existence, that makes an inaugural claim to existence: the empty-set axiom. In effect, a set exists that contains no elements. Set theory is established through the positing of the empty set to which zero, as a number, can be assigned.

---

14. This letter is reproduced in Jean van Heijenoort (ed.), *From Frege to Gödel: A Source Book in Mathematical Logic, 1879-1931*, Cambridge, Harvard University Press, 1967, pp. 124-5. A more familiar variant on Russell's paradox is: 'Tom the barber cuts the hair of all the men who don't cut their own'. Does Tom cut his own hair?

I mentioned earlier that existence is internal to the operations of mathematical thought, but the internality of those operations does not, as in Frege, proceed from thought to concept to existence. On the contrary, it is the positing of existence at the outset that the point from which thought proceeds is established.

Despite their obvious differences, Badiou, like Frege, departs from the inaugural existence of zero, as opposed to the one.[15] The one will be given through an operation exerted upon zero, and is thus the result of an operation of thought. It is not a purely ontological category. 'One' is the effect of counting, or grouping, the void that is the inconsistent multiple. For Badiou, the destitution of the one and the existence of zero constitute two of the challenges of modern number: how is zero to be thought apart from an atomic principle of unity? The challenge is not Badiou's alone: it is only in the past five hundred years that zero has been accepted as a legitimate number, alongside the infinity of the universe. To the modernity of zero and the destitution of the one, another existence is given as well: infinity. As one recent commentator has put it: 'Zero and infinity are two sides of the same coin—equal and opposite, yin and yang, equally powerful adversaries at either end of the realm of number'.[16] From zero, set theory has proved itself capable of weaving out the most complex infinities.[17] But formalist set theory is not the same as Frege's logic, and it is not to Frege, or even modern physics, that Badiou looks for thinking the infinite, but to the founding thinker of the infinite, Georg Cantor.

II. Cantor: Infinity and Inconsistency

Despite the fact that mathematics for Badiou constitutes a stable discourse of being-qua-being, it is nevertheless subject to various breaks, interventions and ruptures that constitute events. One such event was Cantor's discovery of the transfinite (a second-order infinity) at the end of the nineteenth century. While the infinite had been the source of much speculation and debate in philosophy—from Plato's *Parmenides* to Hegel's *Science of Logic*[18]—it was with Cantor that its existence was rigorously demonstrated in mathematical terms.

In the field of nineteenth-century mathematics, the dominant convention that Cantor's discoveries stood in resolute opposition to was finitism, a field of

---

15. 'Frege's attempt is in certain regards unique. It is not a question of creating new intra-mathematical concepts (like Dedekind or Cantor), but—using only the resources of a rigorous analysis—of elucidating what, among the possible objects of thought, singularizes those which fall under the concept of number. In this sense, my own effort follows along the same line'. *NN*, p. 35.

16. Seife, *Zero: The Biography of a Dangerous Idea*, pp. 131-2. See also Robert Kaplan, *The Nothing That Is: A Natural History of Zero*, Oxford, Oxford University Press, 1999.

17. For von Neuman, all numbers could be generated on the basis of the empty set. Zero, as an ordinal number, is the empty set ø; one is the set of the empty set {ø}; two is the empty set and its singleton, {ø,{ø}}; three is {ø,{ø,{ø}}}, and so on. See John von Neumann, 'On the Introduction of Transfinite Numbers', in Jean van Heijenoort (ed.), *From Frege to Gödel: A Source Book in Mathematical Logic, 1879-1931*, Cambridge, Harvard University Press, 1967, pp. 346-54, p. 347.

18. See meditations two and fifteen of *EE* for Badiou's take on those two texts.

mathematics that maintained that the natural numbers (or positive integers) were the foundation for all mathematics.[19] The name finitism extended this position, for, if the natural numbers were the foundation for mathematics, then infinity proved, at best, to be an unrealized potential for temporally bound human intuition. If infinity could only be founded upon a natural (hence temporal) progression of the positive integers (1, 2, 3, 4, ...), it could never be given beyond a finite series of natural numbers in that progression.

Cantor's innovation was to prove that the natural numbers, in fact, cannot provide a foundation for the entirety of mathematics because they are not all that is. The set of real numbers, to take the most prominent example, is of a greater magnitude than the natural numbers, which are themselves infinite. By extension, infinities of greater sizes could be said to exist: *there is more than one infinity.* The formal proofs through which Cantor arrived at his conclusions are quite simple,[20] even if the validity of the infinite is today still debated in the field of intuitionist mathematics.[21]

Cantor's diagonal proof is generally the simplest demonstration that there are infinities of different sizes. It explicitly states that the set of real numbers is of a greater magnitude than the set of positive integers. To establish this point, a means of comparing the sizes of their magnitude was necessary, even if either magnitude is impossible to give at any one time. For Cantor, the simplest means of comparison was given through a one-to-one correspondence which established that two sets had equal magnitudes if every element in one set could be paired off with only one other element of the other set. For example, all even natural numbers could be paired off in one-to-one fashion with the natural numbers in general, despite the fact that the even natural numbers are only 'part' of the natural numbers. The demonstration for this is remarkably simple:

```
1  2  3  4  5  ...
|  |  |  |  |
2  4  6  8  10 ...
```

The process could continue infinitely. Now a similar procedure could be used to compare the natural numbers with the real numbers. We would make a list coupling the natural numbers off with the real numbers. For example, the natural numbers could extend vertically down a left-hand column, while the real numbers could be listed down the right:

1. 51476589 ...
2. 63598324 ...

---

19. In addition to Dauben who gives the best overview of Cantor's struggle with the finitist Kroekner, see Lavine, *Understanding the Infinite*, p. 43.

20. The diagonal proof, as it appears here, can be found in almost any introductory source to set theory. I am closely borrowing the method employed by Seife, *Zero: The Biography of a Dangerous Idea*, pp. 145-54.

21. Although intuitionism is divided into various sectors, most accept the view that infinity can only be given potentially through a temporal process of counting. For a discussion of intuitionism, see Lavine, *Understanding the Infinite*, pp. 168-75.

3.17639543 ...
4.54721982 ...
5.87635210 ...

Cantor found a way to construct a real number that could never be matched with any positive integer in the left-hand column. Look at the first digit of the first real number on the list, 5. We can easily create a different number by changing that 5 to a 6. We know that this new number will not be matched with the number one, since the real number matched with the first positive integer must start with a 5. But how do we know that it won't be matched with the second positive integer? What we can do is change the second digit in the second real number to a new number as well: that is, we will change the 3 to a 4. Likewise, we will change the third digit in the third number to another number. In so doing, we will always construct a real number different from the positive integer it is paired with. We can then take that formula to construct a new number diagonally:

1.(5)1476589 ... make 5 a 6
2.6(3)598324 ... make 3 a 4
3.17(6)39543 ... make 6 a 7
4.547(2)1982 ... make 2 a 3
5.8763(5)210 ... make 5 a 6

In so doing, we yield a new number (.64736 ...) that will *never* be matched with any positive integer on the list, for in every positive integer n that appears on the left-hand column, our new number will always have a different integer in the nth place. As far as set theory goes, the demonstration is very simple, and it sets the standard for how mathematics is taught to schoolchildren. The counter-intuitive implication of the demonstration, however, is not only that there is infinity, but that there are infinities of different sizes.

If there are infinities beyond the magnitude of the natural numbers, the question arises as to whether these infinities followed a given order. Can they form sets in the same way the natural numbers did? In order to answer these questions, a principle of ordering was needed to both organize multiplicities and to compare the sizes of differing multiplicities. The principle for Cantor was that of *well-ordering*: a multiplicity was well-ordered (and therefore formed a set) if all its elements could be successively arranged such that each element was either greater than, equal to, or less than any other. In fact, well-ordering proved to be foundational for Cantor's definition of a set: a set was a set if its elements could be well-ordered.[22]

The ordinal numbers, which were defined *purely* by the place they were assigned in a series of numbers in a given multiple, constituted the backbone of

---

22. As Lavine states: 'Cantor regarded the process of bringing a set into the form of a well-ordered set, thereby specifying a definite succession of the elements of the set, as giving a way of counting the members of a set', Lavine, *Understanding the Infinite*, p. 53. A set was defined by its ability to be well-ordered: 'The transfinite sets are those that can be counted, or, equivalently given Cantor's analysis of counting, those that can be ordered by an ordinal or well-ordered', Lavine, *Understanding the Infinite*, p. 54.

Cantorian set theory. We could, as one mathematician has put it, think of the ordinals as marking a place in a queue: they constitute the mark of well-ordering. They do not, at least in the transfinite, mark a numerical quantity. Rather, they establish an *order*. They are defined by the position they occupy in a sequence and this was how they served as the fundament of Cantor's project.

But there is a problem that presents itself with this. If the ordinal numbers simply mark the succession of elements in a given series, what is there to distinguish them from the natural numbers that were the basis of the finitism which Cantor adamantly opposed? The natural numbers (1, 2, 3 ...) can certainly serve as the basis for a well-ordering. In fact, the natural numbers *are* ordinal numbers. But not all ordinal numbers are natural. Cantor's move beyond this, which was his initial novelty, was that he didn't limit himself to the finite (*NN*, p. 72). A limit can be assigned to the set of natural numbers: traditionally, this limit is written either as ω or ℵ0. ω, in fact, represents a special type of ordinal number, a cardinal. A cardinal number is the smallest possible ordinal number of its kind. Every natural number is a finite cardinal number, and the natural numbers as a whole have a cardinality, or measure, as well: ω, the first infinite cardinal and the smallest ordinal number that directly follows the natural numbers. The natural numbers, while infinite in number, are limited insofar as a 'second-order' infinity exceeds their magnitude. The need for such a limit followed from Cantor's famous diagonal proof, mentioned above, which determined the existence of infinities beyond that of the natural numbers. Since ω itself is the mark of a well-ordered set, it too must be an ordinal. Thus, beyond ω, we have the second-order infinite series, which simply follows the principle of generation for the natural numbers: ω, ω+1, ω+2 ... ; And beyond that, there is ω + ω, ω + ω+1, ω + ω+2, and so forth. This second order infinity, however, is limited by another cardinal limit, ℵ1, greater to all the numbers of the second-order number class, which then introduces a third-order infinity. Another limit inaugurates a fourth-order infinity, and so on.

There is a second respect in which the ordinals differ from the natural numbers. The ordinals are the result of an operation of well-ordering among various multiplicities, or sets. An ordinal represents a well-ordered set; in fact, for John Von Neumann, they are sets. We can put it another way. One-to-one correspondence states that two sets are isomorphic if each element can be paired off with one and only one element of the other. Now, taking all the sets that are isomorphic to each other, can these sets represent a particular type of well ordering particular to them? *This*, writes Badiou, is what is represented by an ordinal: 'an ordinal is the marking of a possible figure (or form, or morphism) of well-ordering, isomorphic to all the sets that structure this form. An ordinal is the number of the figure of a well-ordering' (*NN*, p. 73).

Cantor had a reason to make the ordinal numbers the skeleton of his mathematics: he wanted the infinite to have an order to it beyond the figure of the natural numbers. And if the very principle by which they were understood was in fact well-ordering itself, the form in which he understood the infinite was what determined its content *as* following a given order. Badiou is thus quite right to contend that Cantor's ordinal numbers 'authorize themselves on the basis of what they pretend to clarify' (*NN*, p. 76). In the process, however, Cantor faced certain impasses in determining infinity through ordered succession.

One is the famous continuum hypothesis: if ω is the first infinite ordinal number, Cantor believed that the next cardinal number (that is, the next ordinal number that was the smallest of its kind, closed under successor) directly following ω was an ordinal number that would be representative for the set of real numbers. The natural numbers have a cardinality marked by ℵ0. Cantor firmly believed that the next cardinal number, ℵ1 would measure the cardinality of the set of real numbers. If the continuum hypothesis was correct, no cardinal number appeared between the natural numbers and the real numbers. In other words, if the ordinal numbers were the mark of order themselves, then the cardinality of these sets that they could be collected into was not simply a random magnitude, but rather that of the natural and real numbers. We could put it another way. If we take a geometrical line, and then break it down into an infinite number of points, the continuum hypothesis would hold that these points could be placed in one-to-one correspondence with the set of real numbers: the magnitude of these points was measured by ℵ1. In other words, the continuum, as represented by a line, could not be measured by an arbitrary magnitude. The continuum hypothesis remained unanswered in Cantor's lifetime, and was determined to be unprovable by Gödel from within set theory as an axiomatic system. In 1964, the mathematician Paul Cohen created a generic model in which the continuum hypothesis could be disproved. I mention this because Cohen's generic set-theory would prove highly influential for Badiou, particularly in the second half of *Being and Event*. It is, however, a fairly difficult and lengthy task to go into it in any kind of detail at present, and furthermore takes us a step beyond the simpler project of Badiou's ontology. We will refer to it in subsequent chapters.

The second problem that Cantor faced was that the ordinal numbers as an entirety could not form a set without a paradox arising. The paradox is quite similar to Russell's paradox: the set of 'all' the ordinals must be an ordinal number, given that ordinal numbers are measures of the length of a well-ordered collection. If this is the case, the set of all ordinals will thus belong to itself (since it is an ordinal among the others) and not belong to itself at the same time (since an ordinal number cannot be counted in the series of well-ordered elements it totalizes).[23] For Cantor, this is not a problem: the ordinal numbers taken as a whole are simply an *inconsistent* multiplicity that exceeds well ordering. They were not a set. For Cantor, then, they could serve as a figure for the absolute.[24]

For Badiou, resolute atheist that he is, the philosophical implication of this

---

23. Although Cantor's is different from Russell's paradox (insofar as it extends from a very different premise), both paradoxes end up with an idea of the impossibility of a closed universe.

24. For Cantor, then, these paradoxes were simply proof of the existence of an Absolute that could never be approximated by human thought. 'The absolutely infinite sequence of numbers therefore seem to me in a certain sense a suitable figure of the absolute'. See Lavine, *Understanding the Infinite*, p. 55.

is that the idea of a whole is an impossibility for thought. One can recognize and define an ordinal, but one cannot form an extended set with an extension of all the ordinals that exist. Ontologically, totality is not. Like unity, totality functions as a result of the operations of what Badiou will call the count. This will be pertinent for Badiou's definition of a situation: a situation is a multiple counted as one. As for the ordinals, they function, for Badiou, as a way of ordering multiplicity.[25] They are the backbone of how we understand the natural world. Their existence can be generated on the basis of the empty set, since one is simply the set of the empty set, two is simply that set plus the empty set and so forth. Much like the regulative practices of what Badiou will call a situation, the ordinals are the result of an operatory principle, or law, that is exerted upon an inconsistent multiplicity.

II. Badiou: Mathematics is Ontology, the Void is the Name of Being

As previously stated, this rudimentary backbone of mathematics at the turn of the nineteenth century feeds Badiou's ontology with its constitutive premises: zero, infinity, and the destitution of the one. While the first two are taken as purely axiomatic suppositions at the outset by Badiou, they in fact form two axioms of Zermelo-Frankel's addendum to Cantorian set theory (hereafter known as ZF): the empty set axiom and the axiom of infinity. The empty set axiom, which, as its name would suggest, supposes the existence of a set containing no elements, is in fact the only axiom in ZF that posits existence. As we saw from the impasses that Frege stumbled upon in Russell's famous paradox, the existence of zero can in no way be directly induced from pure logic. An axiom is required at the outset. '"Zero exists" is inevitably a *primary* assertion, the very one that fixes an existence from which all others will proceed' (*NN*, p. 35).

Infinity requires an axiom as well. If the ordinal numbers themselves do not form a set, if they cannot be given in their totality, we cannot look to them as a whole for proof of the infinite. Infinity can be demonstrated to exist, but not given as a domain of experience. Although it is somewhat more complex to deduce than the empty-set axiom, Cantor prior to ZF already axiomatized infinity: *a limit ordinal exists* that is closed under successor. For any ordinal a that is less than ω, $a+1$ will also always be less than ω. Which means, in other words, that an ordinal exists that will never be reached through a process of finite succession. The axiom was simplified in ZF, but the essential premise still holds. In fact, the version of the axiom that Badiou retains is closer to Cantor's original axiom: for Badiou, simply, 'a limit ordinal exists' (*EE*, p. 176).

While all of the axioms in ZF find their way into *Being and Event*, the axiomatic positing of the empty-set and an ordinal limit are the most ontologically rudimentary. While the assertion that 'the empty-set exists' and 'a limit ordinal

---

25. 'A natural multiple structures, through number, the multiple of which it makes one, and its one-name coincides with this number-multiple. It is thus true that "nature" and "number" are substitutable'. *EE*, p. 159.

exists' are both existential *assertions*, the only existential *axiom* in ZF is the empty set axiom. All numbers, indeed all sets, can be generated on its basis. As Badiou writes 'There are only the void and Ideas. The axiom "a limit ordinal exists" is an Idea hidden under the assertion of existence' (*EE*, p. 176). This is to say that, for Badiou, the finite is existentially first, since it is on the basis of the empty set and its reiteration under the count as one that numbers, and hence mathematical formalization, is possible.[26] There is no infinity given at the outset. Conceptually, however, it is the infinite that comes first, the finite ordinals are only regions of being that comprise only a very small portion of numbers that, for Badiou, actually exist (*EE*, p. 179).

At the outset of *Being and Event*, Badiou integrates these two axioms, along with the count-as-one, into a theory of what being-qua-being is. Badiou's ontology poses that mathematics presents what is presentable of being-qua-being and does so by establishing a *situation* where such a presentation can occur. At a basic level, a situation—whether ontological or not—is simply a 'presented multiplicity'. As one situation among others, mathematics presents being-qua-being through formalization, that is, through the characters and groupings that organize multiplicity into well-ordered collections. The crux of this point hinges upon the status of the term *presentation*. It is not that things themselves are presented, or that multiplicity as inherently inconsistent matter or 'stuff' is directly given to thought through mathematics. Indeed, it would be difficult to suggest how something is consistent or inconsistent in and of itself since well-ordering, the mark of consistency, is simply the application of a rule. Even if inconsistent multiplicity is the fundamental content of set theory, it is also true that inconsistent infinity is never presented as such: presentation is only possible through the operations of the count-as-one. 'Nothing is presentable other than through the effect of structure, thus in the form of the one and its composition in consistent multiplicities' (*EE*, p. 65). In non-ontological situations, presentation operates in this manner: a microbiologist may recognize cells as singular entities (and thus count them as one), a phenomenologist may collect those cells together to form human beings—or any kind of objects—that count as one, while a politician may assemble various people into regions, districts, or cities that count as one. Unity is a purely operatory result of presentation, of the count-as-one, which is a rudimentary operation for establishing ontology as a situation. But presented being is not exhaustive for what being-qua-being is, any more than the instantiation of thought can exhaust thought's proper capacity.

Any multiplicity that falls under the count is, by definition, consistent. But not everything can fall under the count; multiplicity cannot be exhausted by the operations of the count since, from Russell's paradox onwards, any attempt to count multiplicity as a whole leads thought into impasses. Thus, in the split

---

26. As mentioned in a fn. 17 of ch. 3, von Neumann's definition of the ordinals departs from the very same principle: you have zero, ø, then one, {ø}, then two {ø,{ø}}, then three, {ø{ø,{ø}}}, and so on infinitely. '*The single term from which ontology weaves its compositions without concept is inevitably the void*'. *EE*, p. 70.

between direct presentation (of a consistent multiple) and indirect inference (of an inconsistent multiple that escapes the count), Badiou's theory of the multiple is forced to divide itself in two: 'there is a multiplicity of inertia—that of presentation—and a multiplicity of composition, which is that of number and the effect of structure' (*EE*, p. 33).

In other words, the presentation of inconsistent multiplicity is possible only on the basis of consistent presentation that follows from the count as one. Inconsistency is the retroactive determination of what remains unstructured, or unexhausted, in the ordering of multiplicity through the logic of the count. Two conclusions follow from this: first, a multiplicity is determined to be consistent *not* at an ontological level, but rather through a *law*, an effect of structure. Second, an inconsistent multiplicity, as a retroactive determination of consistency, is subtracted from presentation, since presentation is only possible on the basis of structure that uses the count-as-one as its primary operation. For these two conditions to coexist leaves Badiou and his reader with a dilemma: the following two conclusions must both be true at once:

1. The multiple from which ontology makes up the situation is composed only of multiplicities. There is no one. Or, every multiple is a multiple of multiples.
2. The count-for-one is the only system of conditions through which the multiple can be recognized as multiple (*EE*, p. 37).

The ambiguity of the term presentation, then, is that it refers to two very different things at the same time. Inconsistent multiplicity is what is presented, but subtracted from the law of the count, at the same time that presentation is possible only through the law of the count. The way out of this impasse, for Badiou, is to propose that ontological presentation is a *presentation of presentation*. That is, the doubling of a multiple into its consistent and inconsistent counterparts is what allows for the distinction between *presentation* and the *presentation of presentation*. The count-as-one is a presentation under a law, but what is inferred from its presentation, inconsistent multiplicity, is what is presented *in* that presentation.

One could, of course, easily ask why Badiou chooses to call this presented inconsistency infinite or multiple at all, if it is entirely lacking in any determinant content other than presentation. It is easy enough to acknowledge that what is not counted as one is not one, but why deem it to exist at all? Why would inconsistent multiplicity be being-qua-being as subtracted from the count? Would it rather not be nothing? The answer to this problematic is twofold for Badiou. One answer is to draw upon the axioms of set theory to find a primary ontological assertion. The second is to nominate the void as the primary name of being. The two answers, in fact, are coextensive, since the existence of the void is the primary assertion of ontology—its initial point of departure—at the same time that it is the end-point of ontology as well, insofar at the void names the inconsistency of what is not counted. That is, the void is also the name for the inconsistent multiplicity that is subtracted from the laws of presentation, at the same time that this inconsistency is formalized, grouped and woven out of that initial posting of being qua void. What presentation presupposes in a splitting of the multiple into its two counterparts (inconsistent and consistent) is a dialectic of the one and the multiple. What lies diagonal to this dialectic is the void itself, since, in and of itself, it is nothing other than a neutral univocity of being from which the dialectic of the one and the multiple proceeds. It depends upon the route that extends from one's original point of departure. From the perspective of experience or language, the void is simply an empty name for indeterminate being. But taken at a purely ontological level, that indetermination can be made determinant in and through an axiomatic system that takes the existence of nothing as its point of departure.

But back to ontology, it is only through an axiomatic that takes the void as its initial point of departure that thought avoids the pitfalls that occur when it attempts to think being apart from its particular appearance or manifestation in language or experience. Certainly, a strict materialist could assume that the void is nothing more than a residual name for some indeterminate being that escapes presentation. But if materialism is understood in the sense of a thought that is adequate to its content, then an axiomatic system departs from nothing other than thought. And that is why Badiou's ontology could be said to offer the most rational depiction of being as multiplicity since Spinoza. The great ideas through which being-qua-being are given to thought are very few in number: there are only nine axioms in classical ZF set theory. And only one posits existence. Nothing in the axioms themselves, the variables or symbols, directly designates multiplicity externally to what they posit. If we take an axiomatic as the foundation of this rational project, then we find unification between a thought of being and the world localized in a singular point.

In other words, the void names the limit of any ontological project that seeks to think being-qua-being as a totalizable field. That is, it does not subsist as void independently of a materialist project that attempts to make being entirely adequate to the operations of a thought of being as multiplicity. Whether or not this limit has anything in common with the Kantian supersensible limit that occurred in his famous antinomies (precisely at the point in which totality failed to be given as an adequate object for thought) is an open field of inquiry that invites comparisons between Badiou's ontology and a rich philosophical heritage that precedes the advent of set theory. Of course, the tenets of a vulgar materialism would ultimately call the positing of the void into question, since the acknowledgment of the existence of a void would suggest that *not all* being is a phenomenal object of experience: something falls outside the count, left to the resources of a transcendent speculation, for which the void would then be the empty name for what is not adequate to the resources of thought—that is, indeterminate being. From a classically philosophical perspective, we can see here the remnants of Hegel's critique of the Kantian thing-in-itself:

> since the things of which they are to be assigned are at the same time supposed to be *things-in-themselves*, which means, in effect, *to be without determination*, the question is thoughtlessly made impossible to answer,

or else only an absurd answer is given [...]. What is *in* these things-in-themselves, therefore, we know quite well; they are as such nothing but truthless, empty abstractions.[27]

Hegel, of course, would not be prone to making all being a totalizable field of discrete, countable entities, but his criticism of Kant is telling for the problematic of Badiou's ontology. If we assume that a materialist account of being is one in which being is adequate to thought, and if the operations of that thought follow the procedure of an act of presentation by which the multiplicity of being-qua-being is given to thought, does the positing of the void as the unexhausted resources of presentation simply reintroduce the transcendent into his system, albeit one that remains empty and indeterminate (that is, *void*)? Perhaps, but such an objection would only hold if we maintain that the opposite perspective is more cogent: that is, that all being can in fact be given as a possible object of experience, that everything can be counted as one. And this runs in direct contrast to a philosophy oriented around the new. Certainly, if one insists that philosophy is ontology, then the void, as the limit to what can be thought of being-qua-being as a whole, remains a name for the internal limits of a non-totalizable system—it is nothing more than an empty name for the internal impasse that thought encounters when it attempts to think infinity as an adequate object for thought.

A little unexpectedly, perhaps, I maintain that such a criticism is indeed valid, but only insofar as one remains at a level where the project of philosophy is nothing more than an exposition on being. The goal, for a philosophy of novelty, is to determine the void beyond its empty designation as a mere name, and for this, something other than ontology is required. The movement beyond a 'pure' ontology will consist of making that indetermination of being determinant in and through the production of a truth, as we will see in later chapters. It is at this point that a shift must be made from ontology as a foundation for Badiou's system to a theory of the event and truth as the possible arenas in which a determination of the limits of any given system occurs. That is, the move beyond ontology will consist of various efforts to redetermine knowledge precisely at those sites where it encounters its own failures: that is, around the void of any given situation. And these redeterminations will not be the exclusive project of philosophy, but rather will occur in *specific* situations, in which knowledge and truth operate: politics, science, art and love.

IV. Towards the Situation

To shift from a pure exegesis of Badiou's system to a more critical terrain, I would like to pose two questions. The first should be obvious enough in its generality: why should set theory offer a model for ontology over and above any other? While it can produce axioms and formulations that are internally

---

27. G. W. F. Hegel, *Science of Logic*, trans. A.V. Miller, London, Allen and Unwin, 1969, p. 121. Emphasis added.

consistent, it is an entirely other thing to say that it can speak for being as such, particularly if we assume that being is a property shared by many different things. The second question is somewhat more complex: while set theory can perfectly well determine multiplicity at a local level (say, that of the natural numbers), it is structurally impossible to determine multiplicity as a totality, and thus impossible to determine it *as* a multiplicity from any other perspective than one that is internally limited.

The two questions may in fact be two sides of the same coin as long as we accept, with Badiou, that being and multiplicity are synonymous. If Badiou wants to separate ontology from any sort of description of the physical world (however atomic or global), then surely some criteria for correlating the two is required. What we would need in order to 'prove' that the two categories correspond is a *meta-ontological* argument that could hold ontology (as thought) up to being *as being*. Of course, Badiou clearly distinguishes the operations of counting and well-ordering from what is being counted and ordered, but simply to split multiplicity (or being) into two divisions—inconsistent and consistent—does little to help matters if both determinations are entirely immanent to the operations of set theory.

V. Meta-structure: The State and its Excesses

My first approach to answering the above questions, then, will be decisively simplistic in its Quinean leanings: Badiou's adoption of set theory depends—at least in part—upon its *usefulness* for his project. If we consider matters from the perspective of science, for example, we can see that Euclidean geometry has a usefulness for classical physics, but not for relativity theory, which employed Riemannian geometry to determine gravity as the warping of space and time. The physical world, however, is still taken as the proper domain of physics in either respect, and no one would question the validity of any scientific project that used a mathematical model to its appropriate ends. We could transfer this example to philosophy in order to argue that while set theory provides a certain usefulness for describing multiplicity in a mathematical framework, it would not, unlike differential calculus, have much to say about the movement of a body. For a 'dynamic' ontology like Deleuze's, we can see how differential calculus, or Riemann's geometry, would provide a decisive mathematical interest for his ontology: the former measures a rate of change to any moving body (and not the movement of a body at any fixed point), the latter defines a topological manifold intrinsically.

But for Badiou, the above two examples are not exclusively ontological: they are more applicable for describing flux and change that exist in the physical world. Now, it is not unproblematic to say that, for Badiou, a body's movement is not, properly speaking an ontological phenomenon. But why would set theory—which is, despite its adequation to infinity, a fairly inert mathematical system—be ontological? If we are to answer this question through the route of usefulness, we should be able to say what Badiou would consider to be useful.

One way to arrive at an answer to this question is by looking at the second problem that was raised above: how can set theory be said to determine multiplicity if its operations are internal to it as a given model? The operations of set theory are internally limited since their proper domain, infinity, can never be given as a complete object of knowledge. The 'proof' of infinity results from an impasse that is internal to thought, and not from any act of designating infinity as a proper object for field of experience. In other words, set theory cannot properly *represent* infinity as its proper domain because inconsistent infinity cannot be directly presented in the first place. The count, as presentation, only presents individual multiplicities *one at a time* to constitute a situation; what escapes the count is the count itself as a structural operation. Or rather, the count is structure, but it does not structure itself. While a person can certainly see how the one, as an effect of structure, exists as an operation exerted upon multiplicity, it is still an open question as to whether that operation itself has resources in a higher principle of unity. Badiou's answer to this problem is to double *presentation* with a second operation of *representation*. Presentation is what posits a multiplicity under the count as one, representation is what counts that count. And if presentation is an activity that is immanent to the situation, representation is the domain of the situation's meta-structure, what Badiou will call the state of the situation.

There are two ways of thinking the relation between presentation and representation; one is through analogy, the other through set theory. For the sake of clarity, I will initially illustrate the point through an analogy. Take a political situation. We could think of a political body composed of its citizens. Each individual citizen is counted in the situation as a singular entity: they are given a number, they register to vote, they fill out income tax forms, etc. Very generally, this relation of belonging can fall under the banner of 'being a citizen of x', of possessing a certain property. But this initial presentation of an initial set is doubled by the operations of the state by which those presented citizens are represented. They are divided into various groups (or *subsets*) of the situation which can then be represented according to various categories: who they voted for in the last election, what income bracket they fall into, whether they are married, etc. These demographic comportments comprise subsets of the situation that, at least in the ideal vision of things, would more or less assure the regulative jurisdiction of the state over the situation.

The above example, however, is not explicitly an ontological understanding of the relation between belonging and inclusion. To think the relation between belonging and inclusion on an ontological level requires a turn to set theory in order to think the relation between a set, its elements and its subsets. If we refuse to define a set through a logical property, we are left to conclude that a set is composed of the elements that belong to it. Take, for example, a simple set with three elements, $\{1, 2, 3\}$. How many subsets does it have? We can start with the set itself, and then take its elements as atomic components: thus, we have $\{1, 2, 3\}$ and $\{1\}$, $\{2\}$ and $\{3\}$. Then there are the various combinations that can be made by using the elements: {1, 2}, {1, 3} and {2, 3}. That gives us seven subsets. But there is one more: the empty set, ø, is a subset as well since, being a set, it collects all of the remaining elements of {1, 2, 3} that have not been collected into subsets already—which is precisely *no element*. There are thus eight subsets for three elements. Incidentally, the number eight is two to the power of three: 2^3; for every set, the cardinality of its power set will be two to the power of the first set's cardinality. A set with four elements will have 16 subsets, a set with five elements will have 32 subsets, and so on.

Two conclusions derive from this. One is that a set, *any* set (including the empty set), will always have more subsets than elements. There will always be an excess of subsets over sets, inclusion over belonging, or representation over presentation. The second conclusion is that the empty set, the void, although not presented in non-ontological (or 'ordinary') situations, is nonetheless *included* as a subset of every situation. It is universally included. There is thus the void as inconsistent multiple that is subtracted from the count, and there is the void as subset of any situation. This is not to say that there are two voids, but rather two ways in which the void appears through the operations of presentation and representation. This is what will effectively allow us to draw a link between ordinary situations and their latent being-qua-being, which set theory alone authorizes. In any situation, whether ontological or not, the void is included. What is that status of the void with regard to a situation, that is, to a presented multiplicity? If it is included at an ontological level, does it come to be represented by the state as a proper subset of the situation?

To answer this question, we have to examine the function of the state. In effect, the state is there to assure the consistency of the situation. Even if it supposes an excess of representation over presentation, the aims of the state are ultimately to assure an equilibrium between presentation and representation, a minimal amount of excess. The state is not what disrupts the consistency of presentation, but rather what assures it through doubling the count of presentation with the official nature of representation. But given the fact that there is always a greater number of subsets than sets, it is not possible for there to be an ideal equilibrium between belonging and inclusion. From the position of the state, there are three possible relations of belonging and inclusion that can be held for any given term.

There are first *normal* terms, which both belong to and are included in a situation. Every representation, in such an instance, presupposes a belonging. In the previous chapter, we saw how such an approach could be imputed to Spinoza. If finite modes are determined to be caused by substance to the extent that they produce a given effect, then their representation (their producing a given effect) is what presupposes their belonging to substance; that is, their presentation. As Badiou writes of Spinoza: 'Everything that belongs is included, everything that is included belongs' (*EE*, p. 131).

There are *excessive* terms, which are represented but not presented. For example, certain demographic or economic categories can be constructed from and by the state that collects certain multiples of a situation together. Global capitalism, for example, can establish connections between various terms that are themselves geographically disparate, and thus create groupings and exchanges that can only take place at the level of statist representation (that is, at the level of capital). Or various demographic categories that figure in demographic polls or the social sciences can collect and relate individuals who have never met each other before (*NN*, p. 12). We can see how these various subsets only make sense at the level of the state, and not at a level of presentation.

There are, finally, *singular* terms, or '*abnormal*' multiples, which are presented in the situation, but are not represented. To explain them, I'll turn again to the example of contemporary politics. In looking at the political situation in contemporary France, and the alarming popularity of Le Pen's *Front Nationale*, we can look at the status of the *sans-papiers*, clandestine workers without permits. They are presented in the situation 'France' (insofar as they live there), but they are not represented by the state as French citizens. They are not counted by the state. Singular terms will be significant for Badiou, and not just ontologically. It is the singular terms that will compose the site from which an event will be declared.

In making the turn to the figure of the state and representation, I have of course shifted the discussion away from an understanding of purely ontological situations. But to repose the question of representation at an ontological level (and certainly, there is the power set axiom which posits the existence of subsets),[28] it is pertinent to ask if ontology has a state. Is there a state for set theory? The question ultimately assumes the completion of set theory as a situation. Within ZF, the power-set axiom is one axiom among others, and there is thus always the possibility of there being an excess of inclusion over belonging for *any* well formed set, whether finite or infinite. But however excessive the state is to presentation, it is also what normalizes the situation by rendering it complete, that is by achieving a maximum possible equilibrium between what is presented and what is represented. The state thus acts as an encyclopaedic determination of the situation and its various terms. For example, in a political situation, what the state represents are not presented individuals as such, but rather classes of individuals who can be categorized by way of regulative principles. Representation, in such an instance, takes precedence over presentation. This holds for 'ordinary', non-ontological, situations, as the political analogies have shown. But at an ontological level, it is difficult to say if anything is represented in set theory.

Furthermore, if we were to speak of a state for ontology, we are constrained to think two multiplicities: one that is presented and one that is represented. But if set theory presents nothing apart from presentation itself, we would then have to conclude that set theory is a representation of the presentation of presentation. It is thus impossible to separate representation from presentation if there is no possible separation between a presented term and presentation itself. In

---

28. The power-set axiom is also known as the axiom of subsets. For any set, the set of its subsets—the power set—will also be given. The power set will always contain more elements than the initial set.

non-ontological situations, by contrast, you can have the presentation of terms (of people, of atoms, of literary works), which can thus be classified and represented under various categories, classes or groups. In ontology, on the other hand, there is no separation between presentation and what is presented, and hence no way in which inclusion cannot imply belonging. Everything that is included in the proliferation of multiples also belongs. From this, Badiou concludes that for ontology, *there is no state* (*EE*, p. 105). Set theory, and consequently being itself, is a fundamentally incomplete situation. It lacks a state that can count it as one.

The importance of ontology is not that it acts as a model for describing other types of situations, but rather that it tells us about being-qua-being. The relation between ontology and a particular situation will thus involve the possibility of thinking the ontological being of an ordinary situation through its possible, and latent, grounding in what set theory can say about its being. Two things become necessary to do this, and I will address them in further detail in the ensuing chapters. The first objective will be to think a situation apart from its determination by the state. The second objective concerns the strategies that will be necessary to do this, that is, to find a particular site of the situation in which this can be achieved. To realize the first objective, it will be necessary to think through the possible relation between a particular situation and its inherent being, as the latter is given to thought through mathematics. As for the second objective, there will be particular multiples that escape the count of the state, and they will thus be determined to exist at a level other than that of representation. But if such multiples exist, in what terms could they be said to do so? Thinking through these particular difficulties will entail that the void, as a category for Badiou, is not exclusively ontological, but is rather tied to the action that will come to create determinate being in the situation through the production of truths.

I previously drew a distinction between continuous and discrete multiplicities in order to illustrate a contrast between Badiou and Deleuze that I would later undo. Initially, I presumed that Deleuze was a thinker of the continuity of change, while Badiou was a resolute thinker of the rarity of the new, of the discrete point. This is a distinction I still maintain, but with regard to their competing definitions of multiplicity, it is difficult to find an ontological constant that would support a division between the two. For, on one hand, Deleuze certainly grants singularities as much importance as he does the metaphysics of the whole. The existence of singularities challenges Deleuze's reader to locate a singular point for which the whole of a multiplicity can assume form. Likewise, for Badiou, the emergence of an event (which will always to some extent be peripheral to consistent ontological presentation) extends from an isolated point from which the inconsistent multiplicity of any situation will have been revealed to escape the count (that is, insofar as we have isolated the void of any situation). The problem for each thinker is not simply one of thinking multiplicity *qua* multiplicity, but rather of finding a discrete site from which a given multiple can be structurally determined or redetermined.

Philosophically, the distinction between discrete and continuous multiplicities is quite classic, as the earlier example from Zeno's paradox shows. While Kant tried to give sensible form to this distinction (such that space was continuous and time was discrete), Hegel's *Science of Logic* retraced the procedure through which the continuous, 'good' infinity could proceed from the repetition of discrete, successive marks. Badiou accepts this distinction at the same time that he refounds it. Certainly, the natural numbers could be considered discrete, and thus finite, even if they are infinite in number. The same could be said of the ordinals, which operate as an organizing principle for situations in general, most notably natural situations. But when considering the real numbers, it is evident that they are everywhere dense, hence continuous. Between any two isolated points on a number line, there are infinite neighbourhoods of real numbers that must be thought apart from any notions of discrete quantity that can be enumerated by successive marks (*NN*, p. 176). The goal will be to create, within the parameters of a discretely ordered situation, a site from which the inconsistent multiplicity of the real can surge forth with transformative effect in the situation.

In effect, then, Badiou posits two kinds of multiplicity: the ordinal numbers as discrete and the real numbers as continuous. But if this is true, it is just as evident that the two kinds of multiplicity obey different principles, since the ordinal numbers are what serve as an organizing principle of situations, while the real numbers—as inconsistent multiplicity—can be said to escape the count, precisely because they cannot be put into any kind of correspondence with the natural numbers. And if, at an ideal level of being-qua-being, the real numbers can be said to be everywhere dense, it is just as true that from the perspective of a situation, they are subtracted from the count, and are thus named void. The reason, however, that they are just that—nothing more than void—is the same reason that thought must be capable of thinking inconsistent being as a mere void. It must be able to determine the indeterminacy of the void through the production of truths.

Of course, there is a curious correlation between infinity and the void that can be traced further back historically than Badiou. The reason the void introduced infinity into mathematics, and the reason it was perceived as such a dangerous concept, is that it did not measure anything that could be accounted for from the perspective of experience. We could even go so far as to assume that the existence of zero amounted to a denial of change. Either change has always existed (for which there would be no empty period of time prior to the advent of change) or it never did exist (and hence, the universe is itself void and unchanging). In such a dilemma, you either have change, or you have a void: the two concepts are incompatible. As my point of departure was the overturning of this assumption, there will thus have to be a fairly strong counter-argument to the above paradox. How does the positing of nothing enable thought, or anything at all? The following three points can serve as a preamble to further discussion.

In the first place, it must be possible to separate the question of the new from that of mere change. Doing this will not necessarily deny the existence of change. There will always be difference and variation in history, developments and evolutions in the natural sciences, and movements and periods in the arts. While Badiou will not deny their existence, he will nonetheless separate the question of this kind of change from what is philosophically new. What Badiou seeks, and what mathematics provides, is a minimal foundation for the occurrence of thought. In a sense, we have three minimal assertions of the power of thought that are derived from the void. The axiom of the void is the minimal condition under which thought can assert existence. The event is the minimal encounter of thought with its own limits—thought is forced to confront something that does not follow from a previous instantiation. And truth, for Badiou, constitutes a firm break with any logic of external correspondence or internal verification, and does so by building upon, and amending, the axiomatic system of set theory. But the criteria for truth, as immanent to thought, does not in any way fill thought with any positive content. Badiou's immanence (the fact that he thinks thought through nothing other than thought itself) is a direct refutation of a Deleuzian immanence of power and positivity.

Second, the void should not be thought of as something that measures a given state of affairs, but rather as the local site of a situation from which an event can be extracted. Certainly, if you posit a universe devoid of change, you can give zero as the number that measures, or represents the rate of change in that world. The problem is that such a conclusion is incompatible with Badiou's entire system. The measurement of change is a function of representation. The void escapes representation, as does the change that proceeds from it. From the position of the state, the void and the event are invisible, and what makes an event an event *for thought* is that thought encounters something for which there is no given representation. If one chooses not to ignore this encounter, there is always the possibility for knowledge of the unknowable to increase. The challenge, however, is to see in what manner this growth in knowledge can be more than mere speculation. How is it possible for thought to gain truth about the indeterminate?

To answer this latter question, it must be possible to think the possibility for innovation in and through the concept of truth. A truth is what occurs in a situation, such that the situation will have been fundamentally transformed. One could object that if innovation has occurred in politics, art and science independently of set-theory and philosophy, there really isn't any need for philosophy in order for something new to occur. While Badiou will certainly agree with this, given that he is a resolute thinker of action and commitment above thought, he is nevertheless forced to ask what role philosophy might play in these kinds of changes. One possibility, as we will see, involves determining the extent to which something can be said to have occurred, and this is compatible with a theory of truth. While thinkers such as Kuhn, Foucault and Deleuze have thought the question of the new apart from any concept of truth, it is to Badiou's credit that the question of the new has been thought alongside a renovation of the concept of truth. Truth is the proper activity of thought, above and beyond its ability to think being. The challenge in the upcoming chapters of this book will be to understand what truth and its foundations precisely are.

Of the above three points, the first is obviously the simplest. It simply states that from a philosophical perspective, the new is rare. There are thus some rather heavy restrictions upon what Badiou deems to be philosophically significant, and this takes us to the problems that occur in the second and third point. A further explication of Badiou's ontology can perhaps clarify the second point, but in order to understand its possible repercussions for the new, we will now have to establish the possible connections between ontology and the question of the new.

4

Beyond Being: Badiou's Doctrine of Truth

As we have seen, Badiou's philosophy is divided into what at first sight seem to be the two mutually exclusive categories of being and the event. This division appears to constitute a foundation for his system as a whole. On the one hand, there is the banal multiplicity of being-qua-being, which is axiomatically posited at the outset, available to thought through mathematical formalization. On the other hand, there is the rarity of the event, of what is *not* being-qua-being, which comes with no guarantee. Events can never be predicted. One could say that Badiou's statement, 'mathematics is ontology', is put forth in order to separate philosophy from ontology: there is no need to make the question of being-qua-being the exclusive project of philosophy if Cantorian set theory can easily make the inherent multiplicity of being immanent to thought through the process of demonstration. In other words, in an apparent swipe at Heidegger's project, set theory ostensibly saves the philosopher the trouble of doing ontology. Badiou has confirmed this position by stating in an interview that: 'the thesis that mathematics is ontology has the double-negative virtue of disconnecting philosophy from the question of being and freeing it from the theme of finitude.'[1]

A mathematical demonstration of being disconnects philosophy from ontology in order to clear room for the activity that is proper to it: its concern with the event, the subject and truth. In contrast to being, an event is never demonstrable—its ontological status is always undecidable with regard to those situations in which it appears. The militant work of a subject is necessary to bring that undecidablity to the point of fruition in which it becomes decided—in which a truth comes to appear in the situation. Unlike the inherent inhuman and asubjective nature of ontology, an event always depends upon subjective action and the appearance of a truth as its retroactive determination. From such a perspective, then, the division of Badiou's work into the separate categories of being and the event is absolute: ontology simply tells us about *what is*, while the event is what

---

1. See Alain Badiou and L. Sedofsky, 'Being by Numbers', *Artforum*, vol. 33, no. 2, 1994, pp. 84-90, p. 86.

retroactively *comes to be* installed in a situation through a truth that will decide the undecidable.

I maintain, however, that the above opposition is erroneously posed, and that it is impossible to think the category of truth apart from the foundations that a mathematical ontology provides. Following the initial assertion that mathematics is ontology is a second assertion that all truths are post-eventual. The challenge, for the present, will be to examine the extent to which the appearance of a truth is enabled through the mathematization of being. While it may not be the case that all being is mathematical, that there are also post-eventual truths, it is only through the initial thesis that we can say what constitutes a truth as truth. To think through the relation between ontology and truth, the reader is required to do two things. The first is to re-question, or reinvigorate, truth as a philosophical category. The second will be to ask what sort of foundations will be necessary for there to be such a conception of truth. For, however open Badiou's theory of truth may be to non-mathematical interpretations (such as found in Žižek, Critchley, Bruno Bosteels), it is in fact only through a thorough exposition of Paul Cohen's generic set-theory that we can adequately grasp what Badiou is doing with the classical category of truth. And this will be a rigorously mathematical procedure.

But a word or two of warning at this point. The final chapters (or 'meditations') of *Being and Event* are quite difficult and far more mathematically technical than the 350 pages that precede them. A re-examination of the philosophical implications of what is, at bottom, a mathematical argument would require a book-length study in itself. Since my own analysis, however, concerns a broader exegesis of the theme of novelty, the present chapter will attempt to render Badiou's theory in an accessible manner while at the same time offering possible points of reference as to where such a theory could apply (e.g. those non-scientific conditions in philosophy, politics, love, and perhaps art in which a theory of truth holds).

In an attempt to mitigate the inherent difficulty of the material, this chapter will shuttle between a technical exegesis of Badiou's theory of truth and the more familiar terrain of philosophy and political theory. Insofar as this will involve more complex material than has been addressed so far, the following overview should be helpful. My argument departs from a consideration of conventional philosophical definitions of truth so as to examine the manner in which Badiou's own theory deviates from these positions. After a necessarily reduced and general overview of Badiou's own definition of truth, I will engage this theory with a continuation of the political discussion from the previous chapter. The questions raised by such an engagement will dovetail with a more technically refined specification of Badiou's own position. This will occur through a technical exegesis of Cohen's procedure, and a wider questioning of the cohesiveness of Badiou's philosophy as a systematic whole. I conclude by opening the discussion to a wider dialogue with thinkers whose positions on truth and novelty diverge from Badiou's.

I. Contesting Truth

Like being, truth is a classical category, and much in the same way that Badiou, following Heidegger, resurrects the classical question of being, the author of *Being and Event* is also a rare contemporary champion of truth. If philosophy, for Badiou, is no longer quite what it used to be (*MP*, p. 27), this is due in no small part to the permutations that the category of truth has been put through over the course of twentieth-century philosophy. Truth may not be obsolete, but it has become so subject to the scrutiny of language-based criticism that what remains of it in contemporary thought has been radically transformed so as to be almost unrecognizable. Perhaps the most significant manifestation of this transformation is the conclusion that propositional or correspondence-based theories of truth are no longer viable.[2] In his own way, Badiou has transformed the meaning of truth, but this transformation is also a radical reinvigoration. When one confronts the more polemical side of Badiou's writings, it is evident that there are three general tendencies towards which Badiou's criticism of his contemporaries is directed: the positivist, the hermeneutic and the pragmatic. In these three cases, truth is either subsumed to the limitations of what language can say or do,[3] or it is subject to an interpretative strategy of revealing presence and absence or, finally, it is viewed in terms of its usefulness for understanding and regulating a diversity of worldly affairs.

If Badiou proposes a break with the above three tendencies, he must surely offer an alternative model in which truth holds. To arrive at a succinct definition of what truth is for Badiou, it may be useful to say what Badiou is explicitly *not* doing with the category of truth. In the first place, he is not offering a propositional or correspondence-based model of truth where truth would be determined by the adequation of a statement to a state of affairs that assesses its truth value. There are several different variations on correspondence-based, or propositional, theories of truth. Such a state of affairs could be classically transcendent, as in the case of classically Platonic divisions (higher and lower, reality and appearance, being and becoming, Gods and giants, knowledge and opinion) that make truth possible. Truth, in such instances, is essentially determined through a process of correspondence between statements or propositions, on the one hand, and eternal, unchanging forms on the other. The sensible world of flux or change, while not unreal, was ontologically lower than the realm of forms.[4] Modern sci-

---

2. 'Modern philosophy is a critique of truth as adequation'. Alain Badiou, 'The Ethic of Truths: Construction and Potency', trans. Thelma Sowley, *Pli: Warwick Journal of Philosophy*, no. 12, 2001, pp. 245-55, p. 249.

3. For instance, Michael Dummett maintains that the only scientific philosophy is a philosophy of language that will provide the foundation for all other branches of philosophy. 'If the philosopher attempts to strip thought of its linguistic clothing and penetrate its pure naked essence, he will merely succeed in confusing the thought itself with the subjective inner accompaniments of thinking'. See Michael Dummett, 'Can Analytical Philosophy be Systematic?' in Kenneth Baynes, James Bohman and Thomas McCarthy (eds.), *After Philosophy: End or Transformation?*, Cambridge, MIT Press, 1987, pp. 189-215, p. 195.

4. See Plato, *The Republic*, trans. Desmond Lee, New York, Penguin Books, 1974, p. 265.

ence effectively transformed this by establishing an altogether different criterion for that correspondence. It is a distinction of modern philosophy that the spatio-temporal world is composed of and regulated by the mathematical laws that, for Plato, exclusively held for an ideal world. In a modern framework, in contrast, truth is essentially determined *within* space and time. If Platonic correspondence transpired between spatio-temporal phenomena and trans-worldly idealities, in a modern conception, truth constitutes true statements about a spatio-temporal world. The latter, scientific tendency entails that no truth could be stated outside the physical universe.

In a more contemporary vein, one could say that positivism offers a third model of propositional truth that is distinctly different from either Platonism or modern science. In positivism, the objectivity of an external state of affairs is entirely questionable, precisely because it is impossible to determine what a state of affairs would be independently of language.[5] The truth value of statements, then, depends upon their ability to state what is clearly expressible within language; its value is contingent upon the impossibility of there being an external state of affairs that corresponds to what is stated in the proposition. And yet, as a philosophy founded upon post-Fregian logicism, positivism purports to offer an entirely accurate model of truth. While statements such as 'the glass is full' or 'snow is white' may correspond to external objects or perceptions, one cannot claim that 'fullness' or 'whiteness' are properties of the objects independent of the statement that confers such properties upon them. The problem, of course, is that the existence of an external state of affairs is not something that can be determined from within the confines of language. And if philosophy has for its goal the securing of truths, the positivist project is founded upon a systematic means of securing the conditions under which something can be true *in* language. None of this, in and of itself, is news, and it should be enough to follow Russell's demonstration of the shortcomings of Frege's *Foundations of Arithmetic* to conclude that being, for Badiou, is separate from language. By extension, Badiou's theory of truth will be contingent on a demonstration of the existence of something external to language: 'The function of proof is not to prove. Rather, its function is to analogically assure the mathematical foundations of existence, and therefore to assure the rational compatibility of the undetermined with the proposed regime of determination.'[6]

If truth, for Badiou, is grounded in ontology—as I claim—then it is neces-

---

5. Richard Rorty has addressed this very difficulty of establishing such a criterion in the following manner: 'One can use language to criticize and enlarge itself, as one can exercise one's body to develop and strengthen and enlarge it, but one cannot see language-as-a-whole in relation to something else to which it applies, or for which it is a means to an end. The arts and the sciences, and philosophy as their self-reflection and integration, constitute such a process of enlargement and strengthening. But Philosophy, the attempt to say "how language relates to the world" by saying what *makes* certain sentences true, [...] is, on this view, impossible'. Richard Rorty, *Consequences of Pragmatism: Essays, 1972-1980*, Minneapolis, University of Minnesota Press, 1982, p. xix.

6. Alain Badiou, 'Metaphysics and the Critique of Metaphysics', trans. Alberto Toscano, *Pli: Warwick Journal of Philosophy*, no. 10, 2000, pp. 174-90, p. 184.

sary to consider his own position against that of Martin Heidegger, the primary *ontological* critic of modern propositional models of truth. If positivism offered a model in which veracity fell on the side of the limits of language, there is another contemporary take on truth for which questions of veracity fall entirely on the side of being. Badiou credits Heidegger with inaugurating the modern separation between truth and knowledge by subtracting truth (*aletheia*) from knowledge (*technē*) (*EE*, p. 9). Heidegger wrested truth from the proposition to locate it on the side of a being that revealed itself through self-concealment. If we take purportedly true statements, it is clear that what is presupposed to exist in any proposition is a state of affairs to which the statement corresponds. And in order to assume that this state of affairs exists, there must be an awareness of existence in general. What is assumed in every truth, then, is an ontological awareness of existence that underlies the proposition. The question for Heidegger was how this underlying ontology can be revealed to humans. In an exemplary essay, 'On the Essence of Truth', Heidegger maintained that what is correct in any proposition is its 'openness of comportment', its openness to being.[7] What is essential in this openness is not a particular being, but being as a whole. The distinction between particular being and being-qua-being in turn grounds the distinction between the scientific search for determinate results and the philosophical posing of the question of being; science yields determinate results about particular beings, while philosophy questions being in general. The problem of thinking being, then, extends from the fact that through the everyday occupations of man in the world, the whole is unattainable, covered over by the attention man devotes to particular things. But it is just as true that through that covering, the whole manifests itself. The whole of being is disclosed or uncovered to man *through* the covering that occurs in the practices of everyday Dasein: 'The disclosure of being as such is simultaneously and intrinsically the concealing of being as a whole.'[8]

The appeal of Heidegger's theory is that it is actually quite simple. If we sat down and thought long and hard enough about the being of things, it would reveal itself to us in some momentary manifestation of presence as absence (that is, absence of any material instantiation of being). What *aletheia* uncovers, then, is the *being* that constitutes a state of affairs for which there will be true propositions. What is necessary, in that uncovering, is a revealing of the being that is wrested from the particularity of any state of affairs. *Aletheia* thus furnishes a modern model of truth that is difficult for Badiou to ignore. Correlatively, we could say that a connection between Badiou and Heidegger is apparent: for each thinker, truth is not tied to particular statements, but to the grounding of particular beings to their latent being-qua-being. In Heidegger's terms: 'the essence of truth is not the empty "generality" of an "abstract" universality but rather that

---

7. Martin Heidegger, 'On the Essence of Truth', in David Farrell Krell (ed.), *Basic Writings: From Being and Time (1927) to The Task of Thinking (1964)*, Revised & Expanded ed., San Francisco, Harper & Row, 1993. Plato, it should be noted, observed that knowledge is related to what is, while ignorance is related to what is not. Plato, *The Republic*, p. 271.

8. Heidegger, 'On the Essence of Truth', p. 134.

which, self-concealing, is unique in the unremitting history of the disclosure of the "meaning" of what we call Being'.[9]

The challenge of thinking Badiou's own position consists in recognizing the manner in which Badiou's theory of truth differs from Heidegger's. We need a very convincing argument if we are going to assume, in the first place, that truth is ontological at the same time as being entirely distinct from truth as *aletheia*. The following quote from Badiou may help clarify matters (provided we understand that 'generic procedure' is tantamount to a truth procedure): 'As a de jure question, the existence of faithful generic procedures is a scientific question, a question of ontology: it is not the sort of question that can be dealt with by a simple knowledge, and the indiscernible occurs at the place of the being of the situation, qua being' (*EE*, p. 376).

Comparing these two statements by Badiou and Heidegger, one distinction should be obvious: Badiou mentions science while Heidegger does not. Badiou furthermore contrasts a science of ontology (that is, mathematics) with what can be discerned within simple or general knowledge, while Heidegger takes issue with truthless or empty abstractions of universality, to which he opposes the historical disclosure of the meaning of being. In other words, for Badiou, mathematics possesses a privileged relation to the indiscernibility of knowledge, from which, as we shall see, there can then be rational determinations of that indiscernibility in the form of *truths*. A generic procedure takes something that is indiscernible from the perspective of knowledge and grants it being in the form of truths that inhere in the situation. Heidegger, by contrast, ties the essence of truth directly to the disclosure of being, for which questioning (or later, the poem) was the means of realization. In other words, Badiou is concerned with the *being of truth*, with the manner in which the something that is indiscernible can come to have a transformative effect—and concomitantly, an *existence*—upon and within those situations in which truths occur. The term 'indiscernible', as it is transformed into a truth, thus has an immanent ontological status in the situation. Simply subtracting the indiscernibility of truth from knowledge would leave Badiou with a model of truth that is essentially no different from theology.[10] Insofar as the situation will be forced to acknowledge the *existence* of those indiscernible multiples, the procedure of a truth is ontological, and thus demands a rational determination of what remains subtracted from the dominant logic of the situation.

At bottom, however, the indiscernible is not an existing subset of the situation; rather it is a subset of conditions that exceeds the conditions that hold for members of the situation. Briefly, an indiscernible subset is simply a set of all the conditions that dominate the members of the situation. That is, if all members of a mathematical situation are constrained to 'only have 1's as elements', that condition will be 'dominated' by the two incompatible conditions of either 'having

---

9. Heidegger, 'On the Essence of Truth', p. 137.

10. 'In truth, a habitant of S [the situation] can only have faith that the indiscernible exists, for the reason that if it exists, it is outside the world [...]. For a habitant of S, it seems that only God can be indiscernible'. *EE*, p. 410.

only 1's as elements' or 'having at least one 0'. To be dominated is to extend the amount of information about the members of a situation. A subset will be called indiscernible if it intersects with *all* the dominations that hold for particular members of a situation, that is, if it contains no conditions that necessarily privilege or exclude certain members that fall under certain conditions. The manner in which that indiscernible will force its way into knowledge or experience is always a particular question, one that is always local to a particular situation. But the means by which the indiscernible is determined to exist will always, on the contrary, be thoroughly stripped of any particularity or subsumption within language. This is why the notion of the generic is so crucial for Badiou: it takes something that is indiscernible from the perspective of language or general knowledge and makes it the site of the being of a truth.

II. Towards the Generic

If Badiou breaks with both conventional and contemporary permutations of the category of truth, it goes without saying that what he offers is something that bears only a passing resemblance what is commonly understood as truth. There are two rudimentary features of Badiou's definition of truth. The first is that a truth is something new.[11] The criteria according to which we deem it to be new may be different from the manner in which we claim it to be true, but for Badiou, truths are nothing if not novel and transformative. The second is that truth is constituted by an infinite procedure for those situations in which it appears. Truth cannot be isolated in a single proposition or historical moment—it is the process through which continual evaluations of the indiscernible gradually expand thought's ability to determine the indeterminate. Modern physics, for example, constitutes such an open set of evaluations that are put forth and modified over a period of time by future physicists.[12] The act of positing these two requirements is complimented by the dual means through which he arrives at such conclusions. First, Badiou is concerned with what truth has historically been capable of with regard to those situations in which it has had transformative effects—a situation is changed by a truth. And second, he radically separates truth from anything that is merely verifiable within the situation as such: truth does not coincide with any logic of the situation that can categorize or determine individual beings.

Given that up to this point I have worked very hard to separate the question of the new from that of mere change, the above statement may seem puzzling. If situations do change through the advent of a truth, they must do so in a very specific way that would be distinct from merely sporadic or general change.

---

11. Badiou, 'The Ethic of Truths: Construction and Potency', p. 249.

12. 'For example, there does not exist, after Galileo, a closed and unified subset of knowledge that we could call "physics". There exists an infinite and open set of laws and experiments; even if we suppose this set to be terminated, no unique formula of language could resume it. There is no law of physical laws. So "the physical" is a generic set. Both infinite and indistinct. That is what the being of a physical truth is'. Badiou, 'The Ethic of Truths: Construction and Potency', p. 252.

Truth is a process by which an original situation becomes extended to encompass, or account for, elements that were not previously recognized. Such a process operates in stages, by a series of evaluations, some of which will have more profound effects than others. For example, as we saw, contemporary set theory began with Cantor who first demonstrated the existence of infinities of different sizes. Set theory ran into paradoxes with Russell, was axiomatized by Zermelo, had demonstrations of its consistency by Gödel. In the 1960s, the mathematician Paul Cohen inaugurated a branch of non-Cantorian set theory which led to further developments. 'Set theory' thus does not constitute a closed or unified field of mathematics; rather it is an open set of evaluations (by Cantor, Russell, Zermelo, Von Neumann, Gödel, Cohen) that successively invite further inquiry and reformation. Geometry has much the same history as well: with paradoxes (Zeno), axiomatics (Euclid), transformations (Gauss, Riemann), and applications in the physical science (Einstein). Taking these two fields as emblematic allows us to see how truth consists of the process by which these evaluations successively transform knowledge in two directions. In one direction, the process of truth redistributes existing knowledge; at the same time, it gradually gives information about the indiscernible upon which such a procedure operates. It operates in the situation (within knowledge) and at the limits of the situation (towards the indiscernible) at the same time.

Beyond the event, then, from what position in the situation does a truth procedure depart? Initially, there is a constructible model (or, as Badiou calls it, a 'quasi complete situation') for any situation that consists of the various terms and conditions with which elements of the situation are determined to exist, and with which certain statements are determined to be true or false. From within the situation, there will always be certain statements that cannot be answered from within that model itself. The axiomatic system of set theory, for example, contains some statements and axioms that are internally verified from within its own premises while at the same time certain axioms and theorems (most notably, the axiom of choice and the continuum hypothesis) will require something outside that model to assure their validity. From within the internal resources of an axiomatic system, they are intrinsically undecidable. Furthermore, the material to which the statements refer is fundamentally unknowable from within the resources of the initial model, as I will shortly explain. The truth or falsity of either the axiom of choice or the continuum hypothesis assumes a numerical domain in excess of what most of the fundamental axioms of set theory (except the power set axiom) can construct as sets. They are fundamentally undecidable because the domain upon which they operate is indiscernible within a constructible model.

For the purposes of clarity, I will shift the discussion back to the example of politics as a point of reference. For Badiou, this is not an analogy, since politics may have furnished him with his deep conviction that a truth procedure always operates against the dominant logic of the situation in which it occurs.[13] When

---

13. By this, I mean that if Badiou's theory of truth falls subject to a mathematical over-determin-

we speak about non-ontological situations—for example, France as a country—questions of who is included or represented in the situation France will depend upon certain properties (French citizenship, and the various legal criteria that come with determining it) that hold only for certain members of the situation. Thus, as we saw, the existence of *sans-papiers*, by virtue of being-there without authorization by the state, poses an open question with respect to state authority: are they entitled to rights on the same level of French citizens? What sort of status does their residing in France grant them? And furthermore, with respect to the problem that directly concerns us, if we assume that they are entitled to rights, would such an assumption necessarily be *true*? These kinds of questions are foreign to any statist authority of the situation because the terms of the situation that are assured within a limited model cannot discern the existence of the terms in question. Within the legal framework of the French state, they exceed a membership relation. Their status is thus undecidable from the position of the situation: they belong, they are not included; they are presented, but not represented. That is, what is foreign to the logic of the state (non-French citizens) presents itself as ontologically undecidable at the level of the situation. The question is one of making decisions on the basis of something that is presented but not represented. For clandestine workers, what will be needed is a re-determination of their existence that escapes the dominant logic of the state, an extension to the legal framework that constitutes a model for the situation. In extending that framework, the situation will be transformed so as to acknowledge their existence and rights as members of the situation.

Before I explicate how such a process occurs, I should also answer the other, perhaps more pressing, question of why this should have anything to do with truth. For Badiou, it is necessary to have truth in order to do politics, because it is only with cases of truth that situations *necessarily* transform themselves to accommodate the existence of something that had not been acknowledged until that point. Let us entertain, for the moment, a counter-argument to Badiou's position. One could certainly find reasons to extend a limited number of rights to clandestine workers that do not necessarily involve the concept of truth: for example, the fact that they offer cheap labour could make them appealing to various industries, and thus attractive to certain factions of the state, etc. From this, you could have changes and transformations in the situation that can accommodate the existence of the *sans-papiers*, or other disenfranchised groups. Contemporary capitalism is rife with such examples of various groups putting forth identities and pleas for recognition, to which the free market can respond with varying degrees of accommodation. None of this has to do with what Badiou sees as either novelty or truth. For example, various disenfranchised groups (women, gay people, black people) can makes themselves visible, establish communities or collective identities, and make various prescriptions against the state for legitimacy (the

---

ation, it is nonetheless true that his philosophy developed out of certain problems that presented themselves in his early, political work.

legalization of same-sex marriage, affirmative action, etc.). The state's decision to accommodate their existence (by amending legislation, for example or, in the example of mass communication, creating various products that can cater to and acknowledge a select audience) will depend, more often than not, upon factors such as economic viability, opinion polls and the strength and solidarity of collective struggle (for example, the ability of various groups to specify themselves as a community for purposes of visibility and solidarity). And, indeed, change could be said to follow from such examples, and be perfectly compatible with liberal democratic pluralism.

But if the example of contemporary identity politics could be said to offer a model in which change can occur, it is surely inadequate to constitute a true politics for Badiou. And as such, it is not an arena for the new. One reason for this is that in a situation where truth occurs, a transformation of an existing situation must *necessarily* occur, whereas in the case of a liberal-pluralist acceptance or accommodation of various ethnic or cultural identities, the reasons for such changes are usually derived from various economic or demographic circumstances that are entirely contingent. Only truth can effectively *force* a transformation to occur in the situation.

Conventionally speaking, it seems hardly necessary to have a concept of truth in order to do politics, whereas in contrast, truth is widely considered indispensable in order to do science. And of course, it is easier to see why transformations necessarily occur in science since, historically, various crises have occurred that forced practicing scientists to abandon certain models or paradigms and develop others in turn. The existence of certain factors or terms that were external to closed paradigms necessitated these crises and transformations. Politics for Badiou, as well as the other truth procedures, operates in much the same way, given that at various points (where events may occur) the existence of certain indiscernible elements is declared, for which the dominant logic of the situation *must* be transformed in order to incorporate their existence. Certainly, one could argue that the position of clandestine workers (or the proletariat, or other disenfranchised groups) are not necessarily indiscernible as much as they are marked by the situation as excluded, or less equal. Any given social system will, by necessity, mark certain members as excluded, as numerous European politicians have demonstrated in their recent campaigns against immigration. Thus, one could indeed say that immigrant workers fall under the logic of statist representation, and there is thus no need to transform the situation to accommodate their existence. They are accommodated, or recognized, in the situation as an excluded aberration. Perhaps this is a residual effect of the efforts of politicians to render the situation a completed whole—one simply names the void as an excluded aberration.[14] But this interpretation begs the question as to what exactly is indiscernible, if the *sans-*

---

14. This is perhaps close to the constructivist interpretation of universality, as given in the quasi-Lacanian social theory of Judith Butler. 'It is imperative to understand how specific mechanisms of exclusion produce, as it were, the effect of formalism at the level of universality'. See Judith Butler, Ernesto Laclau and Slavoj Žižek, *Contingency, Hegemony, Universality*, London, Verso, 2000, p. 137.

papiers (to give only one example) are a symbolically designated category? The answer, and concomitantly, a criterion for the concept of truth, will consist of the manner in which they are recognized by the situation. Are they recognized by the situation according to a logic that is common to all the members of the situation, or are they recognized as a particular group for whom various rights can be refused according to another logic: that of not possessing a particular property (for example, French citizenship)? In the latter case, any decision will be made according to a particular set of laws and regulative norms that are particular to single situations. This has nothing to do with truth. In the former case, however, the situation itself will be redetermined according to a logic that falls outside the authority of the state, since the conditions that hold for the *sans-papiers* will have to hold for *all* the members of the situation through a criterion that is universally applicable. By extension, no particular authority of the state will hold for such a redetermination, and thus, one will be forced to look outside the state for a possible criterion according to which one can make a claim for rights.

We are perhaps in a better position to understand what Badiou means, then, when he says that 'A truth shall thus be a generic part of the situation, "generic" designating that it is any part whatsoever of it, that it says nothing particular about the situation, except precisely its multiple-being as such' (*MP*, p. 107). In the example of politics, a claim for rights is made on the basis of belonging, yet such claims tell us nothing specific about the group for whom the prescriptions are being made, since belonging could be said to hold for all members of the situation. Nor, for that matter, is it necessarily the case that the rights that once belonged to French citizens are simply extended to the *sans-papiers*. In order to have truth, there must be a sharp distinction between what specifies each member of a given situation and what is general to all members of a given situation. For it is only from general properties of a situation's members that one can speak of the indiscernible. The reason for this should be obvious: from the logic of the situation, things either exist through the possession of particular properties, or they don't exist at all. A claim for rights, then, forces the logic of the situation in two directions—one towards the situation itself (where being is presented), another towards the state (where certain beings are represented). From the perspective of the situation, indiscernible elements or terms of the situation are deemed to belong, or be presented; from the resources of the state, they are either represented as excluded (for which their existence will be problematic) or they don't exist at all. In either case, from the position of the state, it is a matter of the ontological excess of the void which the state cannot tolerate. No subset of the state can categorize, or represent them within the resources of the situation. What will be needed for a transformation, then, is a new subset of the situation that can incorporate various new terms to account for the existence of the indiscernible of any situation.

How does the question of a generic property common to all members of the situation come to install itself in a situation where truths occur? In what manner does the situation change? Before I embark upon a more technical explication of a generic procedure, I will draw upon an example that is commonly used to explain it. Imagine there is a room, M, in which you place a person. We can add the provision that this person will only be able to know objects within that room—his or her knowledge will be limited to what is within the room. How, then, would a person come to know about objects outside the room? The aim is to create an extended model of the room into which information about what could exist outside can be admitted. To create such a model, one compiles a list of statements about the possible elements that exist outside that room. We may not know if such statements will necessarily be true, but the one thing we do know is that if the objects in the room are denumerable (that is, if we have a logic that can categorically list each thing that exists in the room), then the list of statements about the elements outside the room will be denumerable as well. What is needed to tell us if these statements are true or false will be a corresponding set of conditions that can answer each statement: that is, to every statement made about an indiscernible x outside the room, there will be a condition in the corresponding set that will tell us if x exists or not. The condition will force the given statement to be either true or false. Each statement will comprise a stage in the procedure in which our original model M is gradually extended. And in so doing, a knowledge of the indiscernible will have been gained. The problem is of knowing how such a set of conditions can be constituted, given the limitations of the original model. Herein resides the necessity of the twin concepts of the generic and forcing.

III. The Force is With You

At this point, we will need to move to a slightly more technical level. As a starting point, consider the two most problematic postulates of set theory: the axiom of choice and the continuum hypothesis. The first suggested that *any* set could be well ordered by virtue of a choice function, the other suggested that no cardinal number appears between the natural and real numbers.[15] Now, these postulates posed difficulties for ZF as a constructible model for set theory. Was their truth value independent of the elementary relations of set construction (belonging, equivalence, well-ordering) that comprised a first-order logic of set theory?[16] While it is generally accepted that the continuum hypothesis was not provable from within ZF, it was a hypothesis that Cantor nonetheless firmly embraced. The reason Cantor originally proposed it extended from his belief that the transfinite had an order. The only way to construct a denumerable set (or cardinal number) larger than the natural numbers was through the power set axiom, which would then generate a set whose size was 2 to the cardinality of the natural numbers, ω. If the continuum hypothesis was true, it could *not* be the case that a cardinal number would appear randomly in the transfinite: its existence would be constrained to following a logic of constructibility given in ZF. If

---

15. For an overview of these two axioms, and their special status with regards to both Badiou's philosophy, and set theory itself, see chapters 22 and 26 of *EE*.

16. See Tiles, *The Philosophy of Set Theory: An Historical Introduction to Cantor's Paradise*, pp. 175-91.

this is the case, all denumerable sets were constructible through ZF, and no set could appear between ω and its power set, whose magnitude would be 2 ω. Or, if a denumerable set (or infinite ordinal) occurred between ω and 2ω, then its denumerability would be determined by something other than what is constructible from within ZF.

What should be noticed here is the linking of constructibility (that is, of what can be stated within the limitations of a given model, ZF) to existence (of what may not hold within that model). From within an axiomatic model, all sets must be constructible in order to exist. By extension, to prove the independence of either the axiom of choice or the continuum hypothesis, one must separate the question of existence from constructibility (since denumerable sets would exist independently of what could be constructed from the basic axioms of ZF, such as a cardinal number that was not 2ω). That is, if something could be determined to exist independent of any principle of constructibility given in the model ZF, not only could the axiom of choice be true independently of a constructible model (since such a set could surely be well-ordered), but the question of the truth of such a claim would fall on the side of *existence and not language*.[17] It would also then be possible to say that a denumerable set larger than ω exists which falls somewhere in between the natural numbers and real numbers, but which is also *not* constructible. To do this, Paul Cohen devised a way of creating extended models of set theory in which both the axiom of choice and the continuum hypothesis were false. What needs to be done, then, is to take a model of ZF (we could call it M, and it would include all sets that can be generated by the axioms, with the exception of the axiom of choice) and extend it to add a denumerable subset that is less than 2ω.

What you do is create a subset of M (call it α), and then add that subset α to M to create an extended model of M (called N). Now, in order to speak about α, there must also be a means of speaking about its members. These members cannot be directly counted or intuited (since they are unconstructible); instead, one must gain a minimal, non-specific, amount of information about its elements. The simplest way of speaking of such a denumerable subset would be to *list* each element that could belong to α. These terms that will be listed will be made from within M, so the goal is to see if, to each term, there corresponds an element that belongs to α. That is, for each member of the denumerable infinite subset α, there will be a list of successive statements about the elements that belong to α or not. The difficulty, obviously, is that we have nothing outside of M that can tell us whether or not such elements even exist in α: we are simply extending a model from within its own limitations. What exactly are these terms naming?

Furthermore, does the relation between terms produced in M and elements that exist in α not introduce a correspondence-based theory of truth back into Cohen's—and ultimately Badiou's system? Cohen's strategy was to make each

---

17. Needless to say, I use language in the same way as 'constructible', since any constructible formula is clearly something that can be stated within the language of any given model or situation, but which may be true or false outside that model as well.

term in M correspond not to an 'actually existing' element (which could not be determined from within M anyway), but to a condition that will establish whether or not any given term within M will satisfy a condition of belonging to α. Within M, we will make a list of statements about the members of α and we will then subject them to a list of conditions that will determine if they name an element that belongs to α. So what each term made within M corresponds to is not an element inasmuch as a *condition* that will determine if the term can name an element that can exist in α. Thus, there is the original model M and the terms *t* that are made within it, on the one hand, and, on the other, a generic set G, and the various conditions *p* that will give us some information that can decide if, to each term *t* in M, there will be a member of a set that could be said to exist.

The problem is that it is only from the perspective of an extended model N that we can have a full set of conditions that will determine the existence of members of α, and thus the truth or falsity of statements made within M that concern its members. But how can this be possible if we can only arrive at N through constructing α from within M? Resolving this conflict was, for Cohen, a way of developing a non-Cantorian set theory. If the set G is to have any kind of validity for creating an extended model of M, it must be capable of encoding enough information to finally arrive at our extended model N. Obviously, since the extended model N will be infinite, it is impossible to assemble a complete list of conditions that will be able to decide if, for every *t* in M, there will be a member that does or does not belong to α. Cohen was able to posit the existence of such a subset by making G generic—which means that there will be a *p* in G that will decide if every statement *t* corresponds to a member of α. Thus, from within M, when we ask of a hypothetical member of α (which we speak of through a term *t*) 'do you belong to α or not?' there will be a *p* in G that will tell us yes or no. Thus, each *p* will effectively 'force' an answer to our original question. The trick, in constructing G, is to make sure that it is consistent: that is, for any *p* or *q* in G, we will not have it the case that *p* forces one term *t* to be true, while *q* would force it to be false. Now, Cohen used the principle of induction to define a consistent forcing relation within G: *p* forces the falsity of any term in M if and only if for all *q* extending *p*, it is not the case that *q* forces that statement to be true. This is different from saying that *p* will force the falsity of a statement if it doesn't force its truth, for we may not have enough information. We want *p* to force the falsity of a statement if, no matter how much information an extended *q* gives us, the given statement is still not forced to be true. The more technical aspect of what these conditions are is a bit difficult, and has been explained elsewhere. It is enough to know, however, that if the statements within M are denumerable, then so too (by the principle of induction) is the set of conditions in G. From within M, a person can understand the principles of forcing, and thus questions about the indiscernible N can be decided from within M. This not only holds for non-Cantorian versions of set theory, but for any theory of truth in Badiou's philosophy.

Cohen was able to create different models of non-Cantorian set theory in which both the continuum hypothesis and the axiom of choice were determined to be independent of ZF, and he also constructed another model in which the continuum hypothesis was false. The validity of these given models, however, is a less important contribution to philosophy than his twin theories of the generic and forcing. The question of existence has been separated from that of constructibility. Something (an infinite, denumerable subset) has been determined to exist that does not coincide with a regulative term of the situation (i.e., it is not constructible from within the given model ZF). This is what a stage in a truth procedure is: a demonstration of the existence of something that falls outside the logic of a given situation. And the infinite subset that is established in the service of that existence is both infinite (its procedures do not end) at the same time that each investigation is a finite, or local, status of such an investigation.

What Badiou is attempting is a unique and ambitious project that effectively unites ontology and truth through a mathematical formalization that effectively grounds the latter in the former. More explicitly, truth is a process of 'filtering' the particular determinations of a situation through its latent being that set theory authorizes. Set theory authorizes this on two counts because it provides the foundation for thinking the ontological potential for an event (that is, through a theory of the void as site for a potential event), and because it allows for a thinking of what could possibly be common to all the members of a situation.

IV. Towards the Situation (Again)

Being and Event puts forward two theses around which the rest of Badiou's philosophy coalesces. The first is the familiar argument for mathematics as ontology. The second, perhaps just as familiar to his readers, is that all truth is post-eventual. In many respects, people have taken these two theses to operate independently of one another: insofar as the status of the event is not directly ontological (its status is neither being nor non-being), its presence is immune to the compartmental structure of set theory. That is, one could argue that the first thesis, mathematics is ontology, is a thesis of inertia, of a discourse of being that remains subtracted from any principle of change that could be said to occur in experience. It is there as a background against which the second thesis, all truths are post-eventual, appears as a true break or rupture. In such a line of thought, not only could the two theses be said to be independent of one another, they are diametrically opposed insofar as they operate according to very different principles.

In the following chapter I counter such a presupposition because it is clear that the second thesis can be put forward only on the basis of the assumption that mathematics is ontology. Certainly, one could argue that mathematics itself is subject to breaks, ruptures, and events (set theory, in fact, is such an event for Badiou), and thus the establishment of mathematics as ontology is itself established from a theory of events and truths that, one presumes, Badiou's philosophy made possible in the first place.

If truth is an open process for Badiou, those evaluations that gradually extend situations put time into play in the situation to the extent that their truth value anticipates the extension of the original model in order to be registered as true or false. But even this runs counter to the primary argument of this chapter, which is that it is only on the basis of a mathematical ontology that there can be a theory of truth that comes to be installed in particular situations. What makes truth true for Badiou is not simply that it 'produces holes in knowledge', but also that the conditions under which a truth will be true as such must be true for every member of the situation, whether the members are discernible or not. And the determinations of what holds for all the members of a situation cannot be derived from a particular knowledge of the situation, but rather through what can be said about the situation on an ontological level. What this in turn presupposes are several different domains that must possibly coincide in order for there to be a cohesive philosophy that connects ontology to a theory of truth. On the one hand, there is set theory as ontology, a pure formalization of multiplicity in and through the manipulation of mathematical symbols.[18] Second, there is the situation, which is simply a multiplicity presented as one, and redoubled and regulated by the practices of the state. Third, there is the indiscernible of the situation—a subset of conditions that escapes what may hold for the members of a situation.

For Badiou, not one of these domains are defined by philosophy. As for mathematics, philosophy simply supplies the meta-ontological thesis that it is ontology. A situation is simply an unproblematic multiplicity that comes to be determined as one. In that respect then, one could call the cells that form a human body situations, as indeed the organs or the bodies of those humans. But the determination of that unity, for Badiou, depends not so much upon any ontological status of the one as upon a mechanistic conception of ordering multiplicity: there is multiplicity that falls under the operations of a count. And the indiscernible, in and of itself, is simply the by-product of what holds for logical constructivist models: there is nothing to say that an indiscernible subset exists in the same way that members of the situation exist. It is only insofar as there are truths that are produced by a subject that the indiscernible can be said to hold in situations.

What we need to turn these rather inert domains into something that is significant for philosophy are possible relations that can allow the three to interact. For example, one needs to think the possible relation between a situation and its being-qua-being, which neither a mathematician nor a member of the situation necessarily do. Or we would need to establish the connection between the indiscernible subset of a situation, and the generic being of the situation that set theory alone authorizes. And the question of how exactly to achieve this will be the topic of the remainder of this book. Obviously, Badiou's philosophy is rigor-

---

18. See Shapiro, *Thinking About Mathematics: The Philosophy of Mathematics*. Shapiro: 'The various philosophies that go by the name of "formalism" pursue a claim that the essence of mathematics is the manipulation of characters. A list of the characters and all allowed rules all but exhausts what there is to say about a given branch of mathematics. According to the formalist, then, mathematics is not, or need not be, about anything, or anything beyond the typographical characters and rules for manipulating them', p. 140.

ously revisionist, or foundational. It extracts possible concepts from the world that provide purely formal foundations in which innovation can occur. Philosophy provides that framework. But when we inquire into the possible site in which those foundations can themselves enable practice, it is to the situation that one must look. Now, what seems all too clear is that for philosophy to be what it is for Badiou, a certain degree of exteriority that can overlook the possible relations between a situation, its being and the indiscernible is necessary. The problem with this is that from the perspective of the situation, it is difficult to say if those foundations will hold. It is difficult even to say if a situation, from the perspective of an inhabitant, can even be delimited. I can refer to myself as an inhabitant of a situation, but it is difficult for me to say exactly which situation, since a rather complex means of statist categorization (I am an American, a son, a homosexual, etc.) makes it difficult for me to delimit one situation (out of possibly several situations) which can then be a protocol for transformative action.

And, foundations aside, this remains one of the more formidable challenges facing Badiou's philosophy. What we have for the most part is a philosophy that provides foundations for experiences that could just as easily *not* occur: events are quite rare for Badiou, being is founded on the axiomatic assertion that nothing exists, and the state plays a more or less arbitrary mode in determining the being of the situation ('arbitrary' insofar as the state's logic of discernment takes no protocol from anything other than itself). More often than not, situations are regulated by what is transmissible within knowledge. But it is just as true that Badiou firmly maintains that he is 'an absolute immanentist [...] if there is truth, it isn't something transcendent, it's in the situation.'[19] So it would seem that there are two necessary points of departure for a truth procedure, one being the mathematical foundations that underpin the latent being of any situation (the event site, the indiscernible, generic sets etc.), and another being the situation itself (which may not be formalized in a directly mathematical sense at all). But the question of what constitutes a situation has been left relatively unproblematic up until now: situations are simply multiplicities that can come to be counted as one. One initial consequence that follows from this is that situations in which events do not occur are simply non-problematic for Badiou: they operate according to a regulative state of affairs and thus do not require the intervention of a militant subject, or philosopher for that matter.

But this seems to be the least of the problems left open by Badiou's neglect of a situation. We can assume that situations constitute sites in which truths come to be given, since truth is only ontological insofar as the being of a truth (and not a purely ontological being of being) is forced into the language of the situation. 'Truth is not of the order of something that supplants experience: it proceeds there, where it insists as a singular figure of immanence' (*CS*, p. 198). An ontologist can immediately recognize this. But it insists as something that is subtracted from any categorization that exists in the situation. A situation where truth oc-

---

19. Badiou and Sedofsky, 'Being by Numbers', p. 87.

curs, then, is determined as a site of truth to the extent that it remains determined by something that is fundamentally heteronomous to the order of knowledge or experience. And if this is the case, Badiou's theory of what constitutes a situation remains fundamentally under-theorized on two counts.

In the first place, it seems that a method of specifying what constitutes an individual situation as a situation is needed to unravel the necessary relations that make an event and, by extension a truth procedure, a process that is fully immanent to the situation. That is, if we are to believe Badiou when he claims he is an immanentist, surely there must be some criteria for determining how the occurrence of a truth operates. Truths do not ontologically present or subtract themselves from situations, any more than they contract themselves around the circulation of opinions; they first and foremost occur in those situations. And if this is so, a means for accounting for the *relation* between a situation and its generic subset (such that it occurs in a procedure of truth) needs elaboration in Badiou's own project following *Being and Event*.[20]

But second, if truths appear in a situation insofar as they constitute a hole in knowledge that is nonetheless determining for a situation, some criteria for determining the heteronomy (that is, the fact that it remains structurally determined by something that is neither of its order nor determinant apart from that order itself) of a situation is needed. Certainly, one can say that mathematics serves Badiou's purposes well, insofar as it can safely separate questions of being from those of language. As philosophical concepts, being and truth remain Badiou's strong points insofar as they are open to a rigorous mathematical demonstration. The problem, however, is that knowledge and the situation simply fall back upon the more unproblematic concepts of organization and classification. What they fail to serve, for Badiou's purposes, is any account of how they would necessarily be affected by the existence of generic subsets or indiscernibility. Subtracted from knowledge, these concepts would simply be negligible from the position of the state of a situation. While we can certainly see how mathematics can theorize an ontological incompletion, insofar as it takes infinity as its domain of inquiry, it is another thing to say how it could theorize the ontological incompletion of any particular situation as such, given that it operates, as does philosophy, with a good degree of removal from particular situations.

Foucault, one could say, was a pioneer of a descriptive methodology—that is, of a theory of continuity that served to unify a given 'discursive field'. While one could take this continuity as a general principle of the continuity of change, there were, for Foucault, other methods of ascribing secret or hidden origins to what would otherwise appear a unique break or rupture in historical continuity. These origins, while strictly foundational, nonetheless produce effects in novelty that denies their altogether radical character. An historical analysis of discourse

---

20. [Editor's Note: This has been addressed in works of Badiou's published since Gillespie's death in 2003. See for example Alain Badiou, *Theoretical Writings*, trans. Ray Brassier and Alberto Toscano, London, Continuum Books, 2004, Alain Badiou, *Logiques des mondes: L'être et l'événement 2*, Paris, Seuil, 2006.]

(Foucault's term) could seek to install beneath or prior to any historical advent an historically indeterminate origin from which it could be said to have been enabled (the apparent swipe here perhaps being the retroactive myth of the primal father that Freud installed in order to justify the advent of the family as a vector of repressive Victorian sexuality[21]). Of course the attack on origins as origins enabled Foucault to ask the more primary question of how these origins came to be invented at precise moments in history—that is, how they are constituted in and through the discursive fields in which they occur. To answer this question, an altogether different methodology was required. For Foucault, this was essentially a descriptive[22] methodology that took as its point of departure not any foundation but rather the groupings, or relations, that could be established to allow certain statements to emerge as radically new. Certainly, these statements may constitute events but they do so on the basis of various relations that arise from within a given discursive field. We can, for example, consider the following comment of Foucault's:

> Even though the 'event' has been for some while now a category little esteemed by historians, I wonder whether, understood in a certain sense, 'eventalization' may not be useful procedure of analysis. What do I mean by this term? First of all, a breach of self-evidence. It means making visible a *singularity* at places where there is a temptation to invoke a historical constant, an immediate anthropological trait, or an obviousness that imposes itself uniformly on all.[23]

The striking similarity between Badiou and Foucault on this count hinges upon the fact that they both link the category of the event to what is unpredictable or unforeseeable. Something occurs. In this respect, the two thinkers share the same interest in the emergence of the singular, from which the new derives. They are furthermore united in their questioning of what can emerge from such singular occurrences. But for Foucault, such an interest is centred upon new forms, or regimes, of rationality that coalesce around the appearance of an event. He retains the event, while dispensing with truth. Foucault, the great thinker of knowledge, continues his previous quote by stating that:

> It's true that practices don't exist without a certain regime of rationality. But, rather than measuring this regime against a value of reason, I would prefer to analyze it according to two axes: on the one hand, that of codification/prescription (how it forms an ensemble of rules, procedures,

---

21. Michel Foucault, *The Archaeology of Knowledge*, trans. A.M. Sheridan Smith, London, Routledge, 1989, p. 27.

22. 'Before approaching, with any degree of certainty, a science, or novels, or political speeches, or the *oeuvre* of an author, or even a single book, the material with which one is dealing is, in its raw, neutral state, a population of events in the space of discourse in general. One is led therefore to the project of a *pure description of discursive events* as the horizon for the search for the unities that form within it'. Foucault, *The Archaeology of Knowledge*, pp. 29-30.

23. Michel Foucault, 'Questions of Method: An Interview with Michel Foucault', in Kenneth Baynes, James Bohman and Thomas McCarthy (eds.), *After Philosophy: End or Transformation?*, Cambridge, MIT Press, 1987, pp. 100-17, p. 104.

means to an end, etc.) and on the other, that of true or false formulation (how it determines a domain of objects about which it is possible to articulate true or false propositions.[24]

What Foucault has effectively done, then, is anchor the primary concepts of Badiou's philosophy (the event and truth) in a network of *relations* that constitute them. In other words, it is as if Badiou and Foucault approached the same field with entirely different questions. Foucault has, in effect, effectively transposed what Badiou has taken great pains to theorize in his philosophy and transformed this into discursive relations that, for Badiou, would appear to be philosophically negligible. There is nothing inherent to Badiou's definition of a situation that allows him to think that it could enable anything resembling an event or truth. And this is because Badiou disconnects the event or truth from anything that can be recognized within the situation. Events and truths, in order to be truly transformative, must avoid any coincidence with what the situation dictates to be knowable. Now, if Badiou easily sees a downside to Foucault's argument, given that Foucault thought little about how such events or interruptions can come about independently of their appearance as effects that are taken as enabling causes, it is telling that despite his critique of Foucault's dismissal of origins (as the arena for an inquiry into various breaks and ruptures), this will be what remains radically under-theorized in Badiou's own thought: that is, the situation in which the relations that acknowledge events and redistribute knowledge occur. Certainly, these events or truths may have their philosophically defined origins outside the situations in which they occur, but it is nonetheless true that their presence is felt in the situation as such by subjects who are gripped and seized by them.[25]

Peter Hallward observes that 'set theory, founded on the axiom of extensionality, rigorously excludes all considerations of the relations between the elements of a set from a description of that set. The set {a, b, c} is exactly the same as {b, c, a}.'[26] In other words, Hallward argues that Badiou's philosophy lacks a coherent understanding of relations that organize situations. Against Hallward, I would argue that set theory has relations that are constitutive for a definition of a set (for example, the axiom of choice orders the members of a set, the union set axiom breaks a set down into its atomic components, etc.). It is nonetheless true that these relations remain purely formal and could hold for any particular member of a situation, and thus do not provide any reason, say, for creating one particular subset at the expense of others. But this privileging of certain elements over oth-

---

24. Foucault, 'Questions of Method: An Interview with Michel Foucault', p. 107.

25. When Badiou speaks of something that happens, the terms he employs possess an uncharacteristic display of sentiment. Consider this personal quote in reference to the events of May 1968 in Paris: 'for what was taking place, yes, we were the genuine actors, but actors absolutely seized by what was happening to them, as by something extraordinary, something properly incalculable'. See Alain Badiou, 'Politics and Philosophy', *Ethics: An Essay on the Understanding of Evil*, trans. Peter Hallward, London, Verso, 2001, p. 124.

26. Peter Hallward, 'Generic Sovereignty: The Philosophy of Alain Badiou', *Angelaki*, vol. 3, no. 3, 1998, pp. 87-111, p. 104. It is not true, however, that set theory is 'founded' upon the axiom of extensionality.

ers is precisely how a state operates over the situation, and one could say in turn that it has a decisive effect on what can or cannot occur in a situation.

If the state plays a role in setting the conditions of possibility for subjective action, this introduces the problem of limits into Badiou's system. While Badiou is certainly capable of theorizing the ontological incompletion of situations vis-à-vis set theory, it is an altogether different matter to assess the incompletion of the situation through the situation itself. How does a member of a situation know if any situation does or does not have a limit or end point that could potentially complete it? The impossibility, for example, of Kant's antinomies alludes to this very problem: how do we determine the existence of the universe if it is impossible to give the universe as a complete object of knowledge? The problem, of course, is not so much the stream of phenomena that potentially goes on without end, as the lack of a supersensible limit that could say whether or not the universe (to take only one rather large example of a situation) is infinite or finite.[27]

Undoubtedly, it is Lacan who has proved a decisive influence on Badiou with respect to thinking the point of impasse of any situation's completion. And it would not be controversial to argue that Lacan's methodology stands in direct opposition to that of Foucault. We have already clarified that Foucault rejected any notion of a foundation for the continuity of change so as to enable change purely through the relations that are established within a discursive field, such that any notion of transcendence to that field itself denied the altogether radical or novel appearance of the new. It is notable, then, that contemporary theorists have deliberately used Lacan to take issue with Foucault on precisely this count: a theorization of something outside a given discursive field is necessary if one is to avoid reducing that field to the relations that occupy it. Moreover, it is necessary if philosophy is to be something more than a descriptive account of those relations.

The great Lacanian concept that Badiou has expropriated for his own purposes is of course the Real. While the term has suffered some abuse and misuse with the advent of Lacanian cultural studies, its centrality to Badiou's own project cannot be overestimated. In many respects, the influence is easy enough to observe, given that a given situation is always determined and predetermined through an order that remains at one subtracted remove from any discursive principle that regulates existing knowledge in that situation. We can think the subtractive relation between the situation and its latent being in the same manner in which we think the anchoring of the Lacanian Symbolic to the Real. If one had to give a quick definition of the Real for Lacan, I would simply say that the Real is a direct result of the failure of language to properly speak its own being. From within language, *there is no metalanguage*, but the statement, 'there is no metalanguage', is itself a statement made *within language* about the failure of something to exist *outside language* that can properly ground speech in something outside its

---

27. Russell's paradox could do little to answer the question if its application to any particular situation is uncertain.

own articulation. The Real results from a very real separation of language from being, and the very failure of language to properly designate something outside itself (notably the existence of the speaking subject) is coincident with the Real (precisely, the unconscious subject, the subject of language).

While there are many ways in which Badiou and Lacan converge and diverge, here I want to draw attention to just one detail. In the Lacanian approach I have just outlined, it is clear that the statements made regarding the Real are made *entirely within* language: they grant no autonomy or existence to the Real apart from the language that fails to say everything. That is, Lacan's materialism effectively flattens existence into what can be expressed in language, at the same time that, through internal impasses of language itself, something falls outside its grasp. We have in Lacan, then, an internal model of the incompletion of the Symbolic itself. This is somewhat different from the position Badiou takes with respect to situations, which, from the perspective of philosophy, is located on the side of what mathematics can say about being-qua-being. Or rather, Badiou can think the incompletion of situations, but he does so through a mathematical ontology that, in and of itself, is operative at one remove from the situation and the language that determines it.

'Mathematics alone reaches a real', wrote Lacan.[28] It is perhaps in Badiou that Lacan found a great heir to his statement. Clearly, we can see how each thinker attempted to give determination to something that is not directly expressible in language or experience, and it is obviously at the site of the Real of any situation that the potential for transformation will be sought. Or rather, it is not enough simply to change what can be said in a situation, but rather to transform that situation at its foundations which always remain heteronymous to the various opinions, norms and regulative principles that circulate in any given world. The fact that there is a coincidence with Lacan on this count is one of the things that drew me to the work of Badiou in the first place, and one of the advantages I can find in his system over thinkers such as Deleuze, and particularly Foucault.

But the relationship between Badiou and Lacan is not one that can simply be established through a mapping of one thinker's concepts onto the other: psychoanalysis is not philosophy and Badiou, the philosopher, may not subscribe to the linguistic materialism that informs Lacan's psychoanalysis. In many respects, this may be all the more advantageous for Badiou, given that, for me, the distinction between being and language is philosophically crucial, and that Badiou's equation of mathematics and ontology is the cornerstone of that separation. It is nonetheless true that Badiou faces a formidable challenge in establishing an internal coherence to his system, given that much of what operates within it is not strictly philosophical at all (mathematics in dialogue with science, art and politics). There are situations, or worlds, that exist and are inhabited independently of any philosophical mind that thinks them. And there are militant subjects

---

28. Lacan, *On Feminine Sexuality: The Limits of Love and Knowledge - The Seminar of Jacques Lacan, Book XX, Encore*, p. 131.

who act on the basis of a radical commitment to their cause, and not on behalf of any principle of generic truth. Philosophy is what oversees these domains, and thinks through the possible compatibility between the various (artistic, scientific, amorous, or political) truths that can be produced within these various worlds. Philosophy, for Badiou, does not have a proper content apart from the possible relations it establishes between being, situations and various truths. It is itself a relation. And if this is the case, it is odd to see so little theorization, from within Badiou's system, of the possible relations that establish situations themselves, apart from a rather arid and mechanistic conception of Statist representation.

5

Giving Form to Its Own Existence: Anxiety and the Subject of Truth

Up to this point, we have been almost exclusively concerned with the connection between Badiou's ontology and his theory of truth. Even the most casual reader of Badiou will have noticed that apart from a brief exposition earlier, an engagement with Badiou's theory of the event has been absent from the discussion. The reason is not accidental. My concern has been to investigate how a theory of novelty can be compatible with truth, and how such truths can be thought in their rarity. Mathematics, I have argued, provides such a foundation for this theory of the new insofar as it fundamentally reorients the knowledge of a situation to a determination of its inconsistent being: this reorientation is, for Badiou, constitutive of truth itself insofar as it is a process. From what has been outlined thus far, the connection between a mathematical ontology and a generic theory of truths rests upon the provision that Paul Cohen's amendments to classical Cantorian set theory provide a means with which to answer certain questions that, from a perspective that is either finite or bound by experience, are fundamentally unanswerable. The step from ontology to truth, then, necessitates a subreption of the indiscernible, an imposition of an order to give consistency to what is fundamentally inconsistent.

But one must take an additional step in order for such a reorientation to occur, which is that something must occur to disrupt the ordinary state of affairs that determines the stability of individual situations. This occurrence, as should be obvious to most readers of Badiou, is an event. The ultimate difficulty with reconciling events with ontology is that events are sporadic and unpredictable while ontology is purely demonstrable—events cannot be said to emerge *from* the inert presentation of being-qua-being that is qualified by set theory. Rather, they disrupt that presentation. And this is not simply because events as such are rare: it is also because at the moment of their appearance, they are recognized only by certain subjects, while others regard them either as non-existent or as aberrations. The event, in other words, is a subjective category, while ontology is not.

While these subjects are not necessarily individual human subjects who possess faculties of cognition and recognition (there can be collective subjects), a certain phenomenology to account for what it is that occurs when subjects recognize (or don't recognize) events may be necessary if Badiou's theory of the event is to have any possible foundation other than a problematic circularity. That is, Badiou seems to posit both that subjects are what name and give form to the fleeting appearance of events, and that subjects *are* only insofar as there are events that call them into being. The fact that events are tautological can be traced back to some basic problems in Badiou's ontology: Badiou believes, in the first instance, that there is an inconsistency that cannot be exhausted by presentation. But this inconsistent being has no other material support than the presentation under the count as one. Strictly speaking, inconsistency is nothing apart from the presentation through which it consists. How does this nothing come to manifest itself apart from presentation? It is from this question that Badiou was led to theorize the event as a direct eruption, or non-presentation, of inconsistency, that has potentially transformative effects in a situation. The question I wish to address in this chapter concerns the cause of events: do they derive from inconsistency in itself, or are they the result of subjective action? If it is the latter, we need to ask exactly what it is that constitutes a subject for Badiou.

What I would like to do here is to establish a certain supplementary framework through which to discuss how it is that events occur and the manner in which they grip subjects. The reason for the absence of such a framework from the initial setup of *Being and Event* seems to be in part a residual effect of Badiou's decision for a mathematical ontology. As an ontology, set theory is founded on an inert structure of the presentation of multiples. It contains little that could account for how it manifests itself in particular existences, or particular situations. Even less does it concern an account of subjectivity.[1] We saw how, in a previous chapter, I deflected this difficulty back onto Badiou's inability to account for how it is that situations are formed. To this extent, I was largely echoing Peter Hallward's objections that Badiou lacks a theory of relations that are internal to a situation, and that he fails to account for what makes singular situations what they are. In what follows, I want to take an additional step by proposing that, at the level of the event, a supplementary framework is needed to account for what it is that comes to grip or seize subjects as they encounter events. It is here that I will attempt to account for the influence of Lacan on Badiou's work.

This move to Lacan is not a supplement to the stated goal of this book, although I will insist that the category of the event cannot be derived from ontology in itself. Rather, I feel that if one is to give an account of Badiou's event and subject, a supplementary framework is necessary, something that can account for what occurs at the moment a subject is gripped or seized by an event. The need for an additional framework may simply be that it is necessary to elucidate what

---

1. On the contrary, for Badiou, most of the logic for specifying situations, or possible worlds, comes from the operations of the state.

it is that mobilizes subjects, whether collective or individual, in the pursuit of either truth or change. Oddly enough, it was just such a problem that concerned Badiou's work in the 1970s, where a theory of the political subject was central to his thought. If the work of the late 1980s signalled an attempt to ground and restrain such problems within the more classically philosophical categories of being and truth, it did so at the price of asking how militant subjectivity is possible within an ontology that is indifferent to the distinction between something and nothing. More explicitly, while ontology could be said to take the void as being, it is an entirely different question when something comes to announce itself in the situation as an event and call a subject *into* existence. For while events are not directly presented in situations, they are nonetheless experienced, if not instituted by subjects.

One of Badiou's recent critics, Conor Cunningham, writes that Badiou's philosophy is an attempt 'to have the nothing as something; to be without being'.[2] In other words, his minimalist metaphysics can assert that being is nothing (or void) at the same time that this ontological statement may have no bearing upon presented entities in situations that are fully something. This is what a subtractive ontology entails. What follows from this (or, perhaps for Cunningham, any scientific attitude) is that distinctions between something and nothing (or, say, between life and death) become either irrelevant for a philosophical system, or simply nonexistent. At an ontological level (provided we are Cantorian ontologists) this assumption is perfectly valid. But when we consider how Badiou distinguishes his position from that of theology (for which the indiscernible would simply be an empty, indeterminate nothingness), we must acknowledge that truths are forced to exist in the situation: they do, indeed, become something. This conversion of nothing (the indiscernible) into something (qua production of truths) is a central moment in Badiou's project. Acknowledging this requires a rudimentary distinction between something and nothing.

Not surprisingly, it is on this very point that Slavoj Žižek distinguishes Badiou's position from that of Lacan: 'In Lacan, act is a purely *negative* category: to put it in Badiou's terms, it stands for the gesture of breaking out of the constraints of Being, for the reference to the Void at its core, *prior to filling this Void*'.[3] For Žižek, one presumes, there is no need to force the indiscernible into truth—one can simply remain in a pure void. In opposition to Žižek, I will argue that it is precisely in Lacan's work that we find a possible framework for a distinction between something and nothing, that acting is not a 'purely negative' category, but rather the very means by which nothing does become something. In Badiou's work prior to *Being and Event*, we see an employment of Lacan (via Hegel) that was deliberately set up to destabilize a structural system of placement: the structural determination of the Symbolic is always threatened by the indeterminate excess of the Real.

---

2. Conor Cunningham, *A Genealogy of Nihilism: Philosophies of Nothing and the Difference of Theology*, London, Routledge, 2002, p. 243.

3. Slavoj Žižek, *The Ticklish Subject: The Absent Centre of Political Ontology*, London, Verso, 1999, p. 160.

In this respect, subjective action was properly thought in terms of destruction. So far, this analysis remains concomitant with Žižek's comments above: for the early Badiou, action was a purely negative activity of destruction. Badiou's move from the dialectical model of *Theory of the Subject* to the mathematical rationality of *Being and Event*, although certainly a move away from defining subjective action as pure negation, does not mean that Badiou somehow shifted theoretical alliances for or against Lacan.[4] Rather, we need to ask what use Badiou makes of Lacan (and Jacques-Alain Miller) at the time of *Being and Event*. As I will argue, if Badiou extracts his theory of ontology and truth from Cantor and Paul Cohen, it is from Lacan he derives his theory of the event.

I. Rudimentary Ontology: An Overview

For those who are now willing to accept the two primary theses of *Being and Event*—that mathematics is ontology, and that there is an inconsistency that cannot be exhausted by presentation—a number of questions still immediately follow. To accept that mathematics is ontology may prove useful for one particular set of problems (such as for finding the most adequate means of understanding multiplicity, for example), but this only opens the door to a whole series of other problems. To give only the most general and obvious example, there is an uncertainty surrounding the particular relation between mathematical being (inconsistent multiplicity) and its manifestation in particular situations. Badiou maintains that the relations between a situation and its latent being are purely subtractive insofar as presentation is an operation that presents particular beings *as multiples* and not multiplicity as such. What we are left with, then, is not so much a relation that follows from the inherent limitations of either presentation or language (however limited they may in fact be), but rather an axiomatic presupposition that the nothingness that escapes presentation is an inaugural existence. Being, in other words, is not inferred from presentation, but is axiomatized.[5] And as we have seen from Deleuze's reading of Spinoza, axioms can just as readily generate positive manifestations (or expressions) of being. This creates problems if Badiou wishes to create an effective connection between axiomatized being and its manifestation in situations (through presentation or forcing).

---

4. The belief that Badiou's work could be read as being in some sort of competitive relation of repudiation or affirmation of Lacan is suggested not only by Badiou, but by Bruno Bosteels as well, who actually sees the developments of *Being and Event* to be a more radical affirmation of Badiou's Lacanian heritage.

5. The axiomatization of being, while itself being an axiomatization of nothing, nonetheless inaugurates certain properties (say, of multiplicity or equality) which can produce decisive effects in situations. This is nowhere more true than in politics as a truth procedure for Badiou. The Lacanian Joan Copjec extends from Badiou's need for an axiomatic in her recent writing: 'One must start from the notion of infinity because it is impossible to introduce it by the path of the finite. And one must begin with an axiom of equality rather than foolishly trying to bring it into being through some Other who would recognize and validate individual pleasures'. See Joan Copjec, *Imagine There's No Woman: Ethics and Sublimation*, Cambridge, MIT Press, 2002, p. 175. One could, in a Badiouian move, substitute Copjec's 'pleasures' with 'interests'.

What the difficulty of an axiomatization raises is a set of particularly puzzling questions concerning why Badiou confers existence onto nothing (a supposition that, for Cunningham, is the acme of nihilism).[6] Furthermore, it also overlooks any inquiry into the particular process that informs the manifestation of being-qua-being in possible or particular situations. Of course, when this is posed as a problem, what is overlooked is the fact that Badiou accords an extreme importance to the operations of both presentation (the count) and representation as the means by which particular situations and worlds are formed. The difficulty, however, is that for Badiou, presentation is not a direct presentation of being-qua-being; it is rather a constitution of a situation from which being-qua-being is subtracted. And with respect to the fact that presentation is simply the operation of the count as one, Badiou maintains that the one does not exist at all:

> it is purely the result of an operation. What this assumes is that only sets have an existential validity—operations don't. As a theory, this hardly seems consistent with John Van Neumann's belief that an axiomatic set theory can depart from the existence of functions alone—the existence of sets will follow from them.[7]

I am not looking make an argument for an ontological principle of unity in Badiou as much as I am asking why the operation of the count, the material support of number, has any less ontological validity than the existence of the void. The operations of thought, for example, are certainly capable of producing thoughts that together constitute a multiplicity, but this is very different from positing thought as something that is irreducibly infinite. In the process of the constitution of thought, singular thoughts come first. It becomes difficult, furthermore, to separate an ontological theory of multiplicity from any unifying principle of presentation if we interrogate the status of the term inconsistency. In a strict set-theoretical sense, nothing is inconsistent in and of itself: something is inconsistent only insofar as it cannot follow a principle of well-ordering which departs from a principle of presentation and ordering under the count as one. From this perspective, it is difficult to then grant multiplicity an ontological primacy over and against the one. And to return to a point that frames this entire chapter, the situation, the subject and the event are categories of experience that depend upon a theorization of the one as much as they do upon any notion of transfinite infinity. Badiou's displacement of a theory of the one runs the risk of contempt of those domains of experience on which his philosophy ultimately depends.

What is missing is thus an account, on the one hand, of the process through which possible situations or possible worlds are formed, as well as the various cat-

---

6. Cunningham has written that Badiou's philosophy is an attempt 'to have the nothing as something; to be without being'. See Cunningham, *A Genealogy of Nihilism: Philosophies of Nothing and the Difference of Theology*, p. 243.

7. '[I]t is formally simpler to base the notion of set on that of function than conversely'. John von Neumann, 'An Axiomatization of Set Theory', in Jean van Heijenoort (ed.), *From Frege to Gödel: A Source Book in Mathematical Logic, 1879-1931*, Cambridge, Harvard University Press, 1967, pp. 393-413, p. 396.

egories that are transitive to both ontology and the situation itself, on the other. This is not to say that mathematics does not provide an adequate foundation for ontology, and by extension, a philosophical system. It is rather that something is required in addition to that framework that can come to constitute situations, subjects and events. Badiou's mathematical formalism, which is perfectly capable of weaving complex multiplicities and rules out of nothing, is simply an empty game of manipulating symbols. The problem is not just that of giving the operation of presentation the same ontological validity as sets; rather, what is needed is an analysis of why being must depend upon presentation as its material support, and what sort of framework may be necessary for such a dependency. One can put this more simply: in talking about material objects (a chair, say), one would not say that it is a presentation of a chair—it is a chair. Presentation, that is, is not a direct presentation of the inconsistency of being, but rather the material instantiation of being. This holds even for a number, for which there is no ontic/ontological doubling between the being and its Being. In other words, being-qua-being is nothing apart from its material instantiation, and this nothing then becomes the rudimentary means through which being can be mathematically ordered by set theory. Even the number zero is not a direct presentation of nothing, but a mark of that nothing that enables it to become ordered as multiplicity. This is where Badiou's reader enters a quandary: if there is an excess of inconsistency which is, in itself, nothing, can it become manifest over and above presentation? This, I believe, is where Badiou was led to posit his theory of the event. The only direct presentation there could be is the event, which is simply the eruption of nothing into the situation. The pressing question, then, is how nothing comes to announce itself.

If we are to make any kind of move from ontology to particular situations, or from truth procedures to particular truths, various questions that concern the status of particular situations, or particular truths and the effects that ensue from them inevitably follow. In his small but important book *Ethics*, Badiou made the point that a generalized ethics (of human rights or life, for example) 'equates man with a simple mortal animal, it is the symptom of a disturbing conservatism, and—because of its abstract, statistical generality—it prevents us from thinking the singularity of situations'.[8] The statement is startling, not least because it foregrounds a weakness in Badiou's own thought: no one would argue that set theory, a pure multiplicity of nothing, allows one to think particular situations. In fact, Badiou's precise point is that set theory is purely rational—it is ontology irrespective of any applicability to experience. Nor would one expect the singularity of situations to be the starting point for human action, since the event from which subjective action emanates is, as I understand it, perfectly generalizable and transitive to any situation: the inclusion of the void, in fact, follows not from situations but from a set-theoretical axiomatic. And from this perspective, taking the singularity of situations as a starting point for subjective actions is immedi-

---

8. Badiou, *Ethics: An Essay on the Understanding of Evil*, p. 16.

ately questionable. As I see it, Badiou devises his own protocol for ethical action by replacing one set of general tropes (life, human rights, respect for others) with a mathematical framework that is resolutely indifferent to the singularity of situations altogether.

This is only one particular manifestation of a very general problem for Badiou. How can a philosophy with minimal foundations that are grounded, in effect, *upon nothing*, account for novelty in any effective sense? Badiou's philosophy may provide a cohesive system that is purely foundational for subjective action and the various truths that result from it, but any kind of criteria for speaking about particular situations or—perhaps more importantly—predicting, in the present, the foreseeable change that results from subjective commitment seems altogether absent from the system outlined in *Being and Event*. What makes Badiou's thought what it is results from the fact that it is independent of experience. Certainly, thinkers such as Kant and Hegel depart from purely formal, if not empty, foundations, but these are altogether different from what Badiou proposes, if these formal foundations can provide the possible conditions of experience (as in Kant) or determination as a procedural operation (as in Hegel). If there is to be a possible movement in Badiou's philosophy beyond the sterility of the system put forth in *Being and Event*, two supplementary trajectories are required.

On the one hand, there needs to be some sort of possible application of the categories of being and truth to the situations that can be thought in a manner other than subtraction. And second, there needs to be some possible phenomenology of subjectivity that could serve as a unifying principle to relate the particularity of situations to the various actions and evaluations (which ultimately are purely mathematical) that define subjective engagement. The first approach would lean towards Foucault's various attempts to define and engage with historically specific situations—with the particular problems that certain situations established for themselves as their transcendental, albeit historical, conditions of possibility. And, as for the latter question of subjectivity, it is Lacan who may provide the framework for speaking of a subject's relation to the inconsistent presentation of an event.

As regards the first problem (the specificity of situations), I will put Foucault aside and instead examine a question internal to Badiou's philosophy. I asked previously whether there is any way of thinking the relation between being and the situation apart from subtraction. It is not as if this question was left unanswered by Badiou, given the centrality of the category of the event. The event, insofar as it is not derived from any given term of the situation, is neither a category of presentation or representation. To put it schematically, it is an unpresentation. The status of this unpresentation rests upon a problematic circularity, since events are events insofar as they are named and put into play in situations, which seems to be the exact same operation that informs presentation. Presentation presents, and this is constitutive of situations, while the naming of events is what is constitutive of truth procedures, but in both cases what is presented or named is purely nothing: what presentation presents is neither more nor less inconsistent than the events that are named. Being, in this instance, is univocal. But this leaves us with a problem. The only manner in which we can distinguish the appearance of inconsistent multiplicity (qua presentation and representation) from the appearance of inconsistent multiplicity (qua event) is through a rather crude recourse to experience. That is, we can assume that presented multiples are more or less recognized by everyone (given a proper paradigmatic framework), whereas events are presented or seen only by those subjects who declare it and recognize it as such. The distinction, then, hinges upon the ability of a select number of human beings to recognize events.

I emphasize this as a problem not simply because it necessarily falls back upon a purely empirical account for distinguishing presentation from events. What I find more surprising is the fact that Badiou does not appear to think that the conditions under which events occur require any other foundation than naming and recognition as such. The problem with this is that it is tautological: subjects constitute events at the same time that subjects are miraculously constituted by the naming and recognition of events.[9]

Given that events and subjects are coextensive with one another (insofar as it is impossible to have events without subjects or subjects without events), it is difficult to find a third term to account for their coextensive relation. As has already been established, this is why Badiou grounds the possibilities for each in the possible disjunction between presented multiples and the representative practices of the state: those singular multiples that events name. 'The fundamental ontological characteristic of the event is to inscribe, to name, the situated void of that for which it is an event'.[10]

Here Badiou seems to refer the term 'void' to something that is situated. This is very different from the inherent inconsistency of a situation's latent being that is subtracted from presentation. To be subtracted is to not be situated at all. But the question is what the situated void is, if it is neither a presented multiple among others, subtracted being, nor the event itself (insofar as the event is what inscribes the situated void)? As previously stated, singular multiples are presented but not represented—they provide the site for events at an ontological level. But at the same time, there seems to be the event itself, which names not simply that void, but the *subjective conditions* under which that void will be taken up in a truth procedure. To establish the event both as the inconsistency of the situation and a part of the situation itself, Badiou is forced to divide the event in two: part of it is directed towards that situated void, and part is directed towards that aspect of the event that escapes the situation. If exclusive emphasis is placed on the former part of the event, then it simply becomes another version of the state: it is simply a non-statist way of counting indiscernible elements. In order to avoid doubling the event with the state, another part of the event is needed which exceeds the situation, and in so doing, calls upon nothing other than itself for its own validity.

---

9. '[...] only an *interpreting intervention* can declare that an event *is* present in the situation; as the arrival in being of non-being, the arrival amidst the visible of the invisible,' *EE*, p. 202.

10. Badiou, *Ethics: An Essay on the Understanding of Evil*, p. 69.

It is this part of the event that instigates subjective action. The event now supplements the situation and it is this, rather than presented or unpresented multiples, that is the true catalyst for subjective action or fidelity. Such principles, along with the definitions of the subject and the event, are supplementary to the rather closed connection between ontology and truth, as Badiou is well aware insofar as he believes that, beyond the static presentation of multiplicity set theory makes available, something must happen in order for there to be a transformation, in order for there to be truth. In ontology, I would argue, nothing happens; things simply are.

So far I have been focusing on the set theoretical foundations of Badiou's philosophy. In order to do this, I have overlooked the fact that events emerge in an unpredictable manner, and thus require a possible framework outside ontology to explain how they happen. This is not to say of course that events are not engaged with unknown multiplicities that have their grounding in a mathematical ontology: it is to say, rather, that events and their subjects are what force the plastic univocity of being to assume new or unforeseeable trajectories, new truths and modalities of existence. This, at bottom, is novelty in Badiou. But in order to effect a possible movement from ontology to truth, Badiou's system must add an additional step that is extrinsic to ontology. As I mentioned already, when Badiou speaks of something that happens, his terms reveal an uncharacteristic display of sentiment. In a personal quote in reference to the events of May of 1968 in Paris, for example, he stated that: 'for what was taking place, yes, we were the genuine actors, but actors absolutely seized by what was happening to them, as by something extraordinary, something properly incalculable' (*Ethics*, p. 124).

What is initially so striking about this quote (and others like it that one finds periodically in Badiou) is that it makes recourse to personal experiences that are otherwise entirely absent in Badiou's philosophy. In particular, here Badiou seems to be appealing to categories of affect that presuppose a subject of experience who is gripped or seized by something incalculable, who becomes a catalyst for all possible action. What seems to be potentially overlooked, then, within the overall sterile, formal framework of the ontology of *Being and Event* is any possible theory of affect that could account for that very act of gripping the subject. This absence is telling when it comes to addressing the manner in which subjects are gripped by events.

If this objection seems to imply a reproach that is entirely at odds with what makes Badiou's philosophy what it is (a minimalist metaphysics), consider the following two points. First, it seems necessary to fall back upon some category of affect if we are to account for the processes through which subjects and events mutually enable one anther.[11] That is, there may need to be something of a necessary engagement with the possible conditions that seize and grip subjects in the

---

11. As Hardt and Negri observe, this could be part of a wider politics of accounting for affect in politics. Michael Hardt and Antonio Negri, *Empire*, Cambridge, Harvard University Press, 2001.

constitution of events, and which may define a political mode of subjectivity. I would be arguing here for fidelity as a certain drive that propels a subject forward in the pursuit of truths.

The second consideration is even more ambitious. In Badiou's thought, there are four conditions under which truth can occur, art being one among others. It seems, however, that a classical philosophical engagement with art is impossible in Badiou's system—there is no possibility for aesthetics for Badiou. Given that the mathematization of ontology entirely strips being of any notion of affect, and given that it is precisely affect or sensation that aesthetics studies, the only possibility for a philosophical engagement with art in Badiou's philosophy is through *inaesthetics*—that is, the means through which philosophy can oversee the possible creation of truths in the arts. Art, in other words, is one instantiation of the void as truth. Now, this is only one instance of what occurs when Badiou subordinates a possible arena of human action and engagement to the foundations that philosophy sets for it through science. In other words, art is philosophically important only insofar as it is capable of producing truths that are subject to various conditions established by mathematics (and, by extension, science). I argued earlier, by looking at Deleuze, that it is possible to have a theory of novelty that is not necessarily subjected to a criterion of truth. One could say that, despite its concessions to science, Deleuze's philosophy is an aesthetic philosophy through and through. By making a move to Lacan, however, one finds a possible vocabulary for speaking of artistic production that is, on the one hand, compatible with Badiou's overall theory of the new, while nonetheless being independent of the criterion of truth.

To summarize the argument so far. I am claiming that Badiou needs a framework through which one can speak of how subjects are gripped by events. Lacan, I suggest, provides such a conception in his relation of the subject to its indiscernible being, its own real. The catalyst for action (what Badiou calls fidelity) will be found in Lacan's notion of the drive—the means through which subjects create new modalities of relating to, or experiencing, being. And the drive, my argument will go, can also provide a framework for artistic production that thinks action through an impersonalization of being at the same time that it is independent of the category of truth as such.

This move becomes necessary because it strikes me that the condition of art is the most problematic for Badiou's philosophy in terms of the category of truth. There certainly can be various movements in art that establish formal groupings that resemble Paul Cohen's process of constructing a generic set, but it would seem unnecessarily restrictive to subordinate these formal groupings to generic conditions set to it by this addendum to Cantorian set theory. In other words, one is left with a rather brute minimalism to account for what truth can be in artistic practice. For this reason, there can only be inaesthetics in Badiou's philosophy. What a psychoanalytic notion of the drive—and, by extension, sublimation—might entail is a broadening of the protocol that Badiou uses for subjective action (a response to the indiscernibility of being) that is not necessarily confined to truth. Whether or not such an aesthetics can be philosophical is an altogether different question: it may be that such an aesthetics is a properly psychoanalytic affair. All the same, it may be necessary to explore such an option so as to accomplish two things: one, to think the proper framework that determines subjective action and two, to think through the problematic category of art as a truth condition.

II. The Void: Subject or Being?

Lacan's influence upon Badiou is evident. One could compile a book length study on the subject, but perhaps it is more useful here to take the primary differences between the two as our point of departure. Badiou has been prominent in stating that he proposes a different 'localization' of the void than Lacan and that, unlike for Lacan, being for Badiou is separate from the Real. The implication of this is that philosophy and psychoanalysis presuppose different points of departure: one departs from being as a foundation, while the other starts with the position of a subject immersed in language. The question that immediately arises, then, is whether the void is localized in being, for which it is an ontological category, or is it the place from which the subject speaks?

If Lacan aligns himself with the latter position, Badiou unhesitatingly opts for the former. It should be clear that Badiou's void is 'inhuman and asubjective', whereas for Lacan, on the contrary, the void is the main core of subjectivity. The barred subject, $, is the void that is marked as a subject of lack, a subject alienated from its own being through the mediation of the signifier. The inscription of such a lack (void) in a linguistic chain of signifiers is what makes the subject's ability to relate to the world through the shifting of signifiers possible.[12] The subject that those signifiers represent, however, is nothing but the mark of an excluded existence inside an inert symbolic framework that is necessary for experience. The subject is that void that emerges dead on arrival in the symbolic register.

One could take issue with this distinction almost immediately. From a Lacanian perspective, it is not entirely certain that the subject is simply a void *tout court*. The subject as void exists only insofar as it is marked and designated by the signifier, and not as some sort of substantial absence that can be uncovered through a procedural stripping away of material signifiers. The void is always stained or tainted by the signifier that designates the subject as lack. The subject, in such a perspective, is as material as it is empty. Judith Butler, among others, has consistently argued that the Lacanian category of the Real depends upon some instantiation of a kernel that resists symbolization, and this is what makes it an ahistorical and oppressive category. She asks: 'On the one hand, we are to accept that "the Real" means nothing other than the constitutive limit of the subject; yet on the other hand, why is it that any effort to refer to the constitutive

---

12. The classically psychoanalytic statement 'I feel like a motherless child' is possible on the basis of substituting one signifier, 'I', for another, 'motherless child'.

limit of the subject in ways that do not use that nomenclature are considered a failure to understand its proper operation?'[13] Butler's argument extends to argue that conceiving the Real as the constitutive limit to the social (which is the place of the subject) amounts to determining the subject as outside the social. This is how Butler qualifies her Hegelianism: the Real is simply an empty void of determination. In other words, to use the terms from the Badiou of *Theory of the Subject*, to refer to the subject as void overlooks the fact that lack is more likely the result of a structural law of placement rather than an excess of lack over and above that system. Thus, lack is a thoroughly immanent category.

The crucial point that Butler misses in her argument, however, is that it is precisely the point that the Real does not designate something outside the social—it is *nothing* outside language. In other words, Butler's criticism overlooks the fact that speaking subjects designate their own Real in and through the materiality of language and the limits it presupposes, not through some determinate process of exclusion. The Lacanian subject is the place of that nothing outside language, just as Badiou's void is the name for the nothing that exceeds particular instantiations of either thought or being. For the Lacanian subject, then, there is nothing outside the history that the signifier induces and the place of this nothing is the void of the subject. The void of the subject is not something that exists outside the symbolic chain. Rather, the unique position of the subject extends from the fact that there is *nothing* outside the symbolic chain. This is what makes the Lacanian subject a structurally determinate category: the impasses that render the closure of the symbolic impossible would result in a failure to determine the symbolic as a structured system were it not for the fact that a speaking subject fills that empty place of indetermination. In other words, the failure of the Symbolic to inscribe itself as a closed totality is constitutive of the failure of the subject to be fully present to itself through the medium of speech.

This has, I believe, direct implications for Badiou's theory of the subject. For it asks: how is it that a subject can be propelled to act through something that is manifest only through negation? Whether that negation designates the place of the subject or the place of being is a moot point: the fact of the matter is that it is a question of a determinate nothing. To interrogate the relation between the two thinkers, it will be necessary to retrace certain steps in Badiou's thought. We could start with a primary text of Lacan's theory of the subject. In his seminal essay 'Suture', Lacan's disciple Jacques-Alain Miller produced a comparative reading of Lacanian psychoanalysis with Frege's logic, which functioned as an implicit critique of the logical assumption that one can have existence without a subject.[14] Given that Frege founded his thought of numbers upon the exclusion of any psychological subject of reflection, the subject was excluded from Frege's systematic account of the genesis of numbers through a purely logical necessity.

---

13. Judith Butler, 'Competing Universalities', in Judith Butler, Ernesto Laclau and Slavoj Žižek (eds.), *Contingency, Hegemony, Universality*, London, Verso, 2000, pp. 136-81, p. 152.

14. Jacques-Alain Miller, 'Suture (Elements of the Logic of the Signifier)', *Screen*, vol. 18, no. 4, 1977-8, pp. 24-34.

This was a simple assertion that the existence of numbers does not depend upon the existence of a subject who thinks them. According to Miller, however, the subject re-emerged in his system at that very point where Frege sought to derive an existence through logic alone. In Frege's system, zero was the primary logical number, insofar as it was the only number that could be attributed to a 'purely logical', non-empirical concept. The point for Miller is that the assignation of the number zero to the lack of an illogical object is the very relation that defines the subject's relation to the signifying chain. In other words, zero is the marking of the subject as a lacking subject who tries to compensate for its own lack of being through a substitution of one signifier for another (in the same way that the number 1 in Frege marks the number 0 as the number assigned to the concept 'not-equal-to-itself'). What makes Miller's essay more than a simple analogy between Lacan and Frege is that it also aims to be an explicit critique of science itself. Science, which is presumed to exist independently of a subject, must reintroduce a subject in order to sustain the progression of number. We are left to assume, then, that a psychoanalytic theory of the subject is the very sustenance of a logical (or scientific) system.

In an early essay, 'Marque et manque', Badiou took issue with this very assumption insofar as he remained sceptical that science requires a concept of either a subject or of suture.[15] Given the tenets of Gödel's theorem of incompletion, there was no need for a logical system to be closed in upon itself in order to function as a consistent system for producing knowledge. Science, that is, did not need closure in order to function: 'Stratified to infinity, regulating its passages, science is a pure space, without an outside or mark, or place of what is excluded' (*MM*, p. 161). This position entails that if there is no need to mark what is excluded from a scientific order—insofar as in science 'the not-substitutable-with itself is foreclosed with neither recourse or mark' (*MM*, p. 157)—then there is no subject of science. This is, of course, in striking contrast to the position he would develop in *Being and Event* where subjects only exist in and through truth procedures, of which science is one. But this does not mean that Badiou saw suture as a useless category; it founded a subject's relation to ideology. Departing from a classically Althusserian distinction between science and ideology, Badiou puts forth the theory that psychoanalysis has nothing to say about science, and that this is the negative determination of the desire that is operative in ideology. The negative determination of desire in psychoanalysis is a direct effect of the impossibility of giving a distinctly scientific account of the structural relations that make that desire possible. That is, the psychoanalytic definition of desire as lack is a desire for a scientific knowledge that can account for a subject's conditions of possibility at the same time that, at the level of that desire, such an account is strictly speaking impossible. The subject who passes from representation (ideology) into knowledge is a subject that would cease to exist at the moment of its gaining sci-

---

15. Alain Badiou, 'Marque et manque: à propos du zero', *Cahiers pour l'analyse*, vol. 10, 1969, pp. 150-73. Hereafter cited in the text as *MM*.

entific knowledge. What we are left with, then, is the notion of a subject that plays a constitutive role in the 'production' of science as truth, even if that role is itself nothing more than a transitory stage towards the gaining of that knowledge.

The shift from this position (where the subject is an ideological, non-scientific category) to the work of the 1970s (where the subject was a dialectical, political subject) to the current position (where there can be both political and scientific subjects) presupposes a potentially broad set of factors that could have influenced the development of Badiou's work. On the one hand, in 1967 he maintained that, if there is no subject of science, it is because science is the proper subject of philosophy. But by the work of the 1970s, science had taken a backseat to politics—both as a subject of philosophy and as a condition for subjectivity altogether. In other words, there are only political subjects.

The shift to a set theoretical ontology in *Being and Event* signalled two changes in Badiou's thinking. There was first the possible coexistence of both political and scientific (as well as artistic and amorous) subjects, at the same time that the void became an exclusively ontological category. It is this second move that firmly distinguishes Badiou from Lacan, such that, by the time of *Being and Event*:

> The choice here is between a structural recurrence, which thinks the subject-effect of the empty-set, so exposed in the unified network of experience, and a hypothesis of the rarity of the subject, which defers its occurrence to the event, to the intervention, and to the generic paths of fidelity, referring back and founding the void on the suturing of being for which mathematics exclusively commands knowledge. (*EE*, p. 451)

The rarity of the subject is what is put in the service of a mathematical determination of the void as non-subject, at the same time that subjective action is rendered possible through both the intervention of an event, as well as the void of local situations that becomes determinate in and through the forcing of truths. The subject, from such a perspective, is defined through its action. In the Lacanian register, in contrast, Badiou posits the void as the 'subject-effect of the empty set', which is nothing other than the purely empty-place of inequality that allows for the movement from one signifier to the next, and for which the subject is the unified condition of possibility. Ostensibly, this severs the subject from any possibility of transformation or change, given that the void that is the subject works exclusively in the interests of a structural system of determination. Aside from language, there is nothing.

The above distinction is made possible on the basis of a single question: what does the void do differently in philosophy than in psychoanalysis? In departing from the above distinction, Badiou concludes that being is distinct from the Lacanian Real insofar as the Real is only possible on the basis of a subject, while for philosophy, the void *is* independently of a subject. That is, the void is the primary name for an inhuman and asubjective being that precedes any possible advent of subjectivity. Such a position should hardly surprise anyone: it is entirely consistent with the outlined trajectory of *Being and Event*, and it is concomitant with any philosophy that takes ontology as foundational. It would be absurd to make ontology a subjective category given that many non-human, or non-subjective entities have an ontological validity.

If so, why does Badiou bother to have a subject in his philosophy at all? Why did he move from declaring science to be the subject of philosophy to writing a book on the philosophy of the subject? The reason, I believe, depends on the conditions under which something new can occur. For the new to emerge, something needs to disrupt the structural. In order to account for the supplementary means with which subjects and events appear in Badiou, it becomes necessary to appeal to categories that were central to Lacan. To determine the manner in which they inform Badiou's own position, perhaps more intimately than he realizes, one will have to undo the above distinction that Badiou has drawn between Lacan and himself.

Consider the assumption that the Lacanian subject is a pure void, a barred subject—in short, $. Is it really the case that the subject is nothing other than a void that receives its determination through a linguistic structure that exceeds it, on the one hand, while being nothing but an empty system of structural determination, on the other? This position falls prey to an interpretation of the subject as nothing but its symbolic designation, given that the lack of the subject is, strictly speaking, nothing at all. This would be no different from a rather crude interpretation of psychoanalysis as a variant of constructivist logic—the subject is insofar as it is constructed in language. Such a perspective fundamentally misinterprets the radical nature of Lacan's definition of subjectivity insofar as it reduces the question of the subject as the foundation for the constitution of meaning (insofar as it is from this position of the subject that meaning is constituted) into a definition of the subject as a determinate effect of meaning (that is, the subject as it is posited in language). Is the emphasis here put upon the materiality of language which, in some variant of behaviourist psychology, comes to determine an identity? Or is it rather that the exclusion of being that is essential for language as a closed system exerts an influence upon the meaning that the speaking subject produces? In other words, the lack that sutures the subject to the signifying chain, if it is to be something more than an indeterminate nothing that escapes the grip of language, must play a constitutive role in Lacanian psychoanalysis.

The implications of this distinction do not hold exclusively for sorting out the internal coherence of Lacanian psychoanalysis; they are also what found Badiou's entire critique of constructivist mathematical logic—that is, the belief that existence can only be given through the discernibility of language. To counter constructivism is, of course, to maintain that there is an existence that is not exclusively subsumed within the tenets of what can be demonstrated within language. The Lacanian Real is one such manifestation of an anti-constructivist tendency, given that it is what remains of being in the aftermath of the failure of meta-language. The Real, as a subjective function, is the result of the following paradox. On the one hand, there is no metalanguage—everything is explicitly posited in language; on the other hand, language cannot totalize itself as a closed system for which it can then definitively state that there is nothing outside it.[16]

Thus, while one can maintain that the subject is purely a void, that it receives its only material support through the signifier, this is quite different from arguing that the subject is nothing other than a lack conjoined to a signifier. There is an additional something that fills out this gap between the failure of a meta-language and the impossibility of determining language as a closed system (for which the nothing outside language would be truly nothing). This something is Lacan's famous *objet petit* (a). The object (a) is not subsumed within language, and thus does not exist as one signifier among others. At the same time, however, what makes object (a) what it is results directly from the fact that language fails to subsume the totality of being: the object (a) is the emergence, in the symbolic, of that which remains outside its grasp, a positive determination of the negative indeterminate. Like Badiou's event, the object (a) is the appearance of something that is anterior to presentation; at the same time, it is subtracted from what is subtracted. It is neither being-qua-being, nor a consistent presentation, but rather a category of the subject.

Lacan's famous formula for the fantasy is the conjoining of a barred subject to its virtual object: ($S \lozenge a$). To the lack in the subject instituted by the signifier corresponds a determination of that lack in the form of a phantasm of presence (say, in a psychoanalytic context, the desire of the analyst). What lies behind that phantasm is precisely nothing, but it is a nothing that gains determinate form in the various desires, repetitions, or sublimations of the psychoanalytic subject that desires presence beyond language. At the risk of making a mere analogy, is this not the very same logic informing Badiou's theory of the event—precisely the fleeting appearance of that which is indiscernible from the position of experience, and which is given determinate form through the activity of a subject? The very problematic status of the event in Badiou hinges upon a paradox: on the one hand, there is an excess of being over presentation; on the other hand, this excess is purely nothing. How can nothing present itself? Precisely insofar as there are events that are given form by those subjects who recognize them. We can only understand the possible correspondence between Badiou's event and Lacan's object (a) if we understand that the former is not a phenomenal event any more than the object (a) is a phenomenal object. Instead, both are what one could call 'supplements' to presentation itself that makes the move from a purely subtractive theory of presentation to a direct determination of the indeterminate possible. That is, the event is what facilitates a movement from a negative ontology (in which the question of inconsistency remains a negative determination

---

16. As Joan Copjec has put it: 'Whenever the split between being and appearance is denied, you can bet that one particular inscription is being overlooked: that which marks the very failure of metalanguage. Language speaks voluminously in positive statements, but it also copiously speaks of its own lack of self-sufficiency, its inability to speak the whole unvarnished truth directly and without recourse to further, exegetical speech. Some elision or negation of its powers writes itself in language *as* the lack of meta-language. This negation is no less an inscription for its not being formulated in a statement, and the being it poses presents no less a claim for our consideration'. Copjec, *Read My Desire: Lacan Against the Historicists*, p. 9.

of something that is subtracted from presentation) to a positive determination of that subtracted inconsistency qua production of truths. Likewise, in order to move from a purely negative determination of desire (which always hinges upon the immanent failure of some impossible object), the psychoanalytic subject must shift its activity to the drive, where it gives form and determination to the empty ground of its causality in and through the formation of an object (a). A distinctly Lacanian question is, how does the subject give form to its own existence?

One possibility was put forth in Lacan's theory of sublimation. In a rudimentary sense, sublimation is the creation of determinate things in and out of a constitutive lack that is inherent to experience. It emerges out of the constitutive relation of the subject's relation to its own real. In what follows, then, I want to examine the potential relations that inhere between Lacan's theory of sublimation and Badiou's theory of truth, while looking to Lacan's theory of the drive (which is closely linked to sublimation) for a possible account for the subjective conditions that enable such activity. Doing so will allow me to initially reconsider the supplementary framework that is necessary to account for Badiou's theory of the event, the subject, and fidelity. It will also put us in a position to question the ultimate aims of Badiou's entire project—the knotting of novelty to truth.

Now, in order to adequately assess the possible connections between Lacan's object (a) and Badiou's event, we have to ask after the ontological status of each. The reason I say 'ontological' is because the event, in and of itself, is not exclusively an ontological category: 'with the event, we have the first *exterior* concept to the field of mathematical ontology' (*EE*, p. 205). The event supplements presentation and, by extension, ontology. For example, when considering the French revolution, there are states of affairs that are presented in the situation (to name only a few: the bourgeoisie, Jacobins, the guillotine, the massacres, the storming of the Bastille) which, in and of themselves, are a multiplicity of elements that lack a unifying principle without the name 'French Revolution' that creates of these elements an event from which a political procedure can be derived. The event 'French Revolution' is not one multiple among others (insofar as it is not, in itself, presented among the other multiplicities). It is what unifies these disparate multiplicities under the banner of its occurrence. Or, to put it another way, the event takes these elements and adds something more that exceeds direct presentation. But this something more, insofar as it is not presented, cannot be accounted for as something. Insofar as it escapes presentation, it is ontologically undecidable.

Now, in a parallel trajectory, what exactly is Lacan's object (a) if it is neither an object nor a strictly linguistic designation? How can something be said to exist if it is not articulated in language? Consider one of the most basic examples of an object (a), the breast. It would be a mistake to assume that the object simply is the breast on account of its breast-like properties. That is, the breast is not *in itself* an object of satisfaction. An infant could presumably be just as satisfied with the warm milk it provides, the pleasure it produces when digested in the body, and the satisfaction that is associated with the act of suckling. The breast, as the object (a), however, is what is imputed to give the coupling of bodies and organs the satisfaction that are proper to them: it represents something more than just one subsidiary object among others. It is the object that acts as a support for the satisfaction proper to these objects. The object (a), then, is not the object of satisfaction but that something more that satisfaction aims at. As Alenka Zupančič puts it:

> After a need is satisfied, and the subject gets the demanded object, desire continues on its own; it is not 'extinguished' by the satisfaction of a need. The moment the subject attains the object she demands, the *objet petit a* appears, as a marker of that which the subject 'has not got,' or *does not have*—and this itself constitutes the '*echte*' object of desire.[17]

What Lacan's object (a) represents is a surplus satisfaction that language fails to produce. That is, if a psychoanalytic subject enters language, she does so at a price: there is a necessary acceptance that an unmediated relation to one's being falls out of the equation. What is left in its place is the installation of a lack.[18] This is not to say, however, that this lack is simply left to persist on its own accord: something re-emerges to the subject that comes to fill that lack, as it presents itself in the form of an object that embodies the surplus-value of a being anterior to language. Likewise for Badiou, if inconsistent being-qua-being must, by structural necessity, be subtracted from consistent presentation under the law of the count, that subtracted being can nevertheless come to supplement the consistent presentation of a situation in and through the fleeting appearance of an event. Both Badiou's event and Lacan's object (a) are what resist the structural necessity of subtraction of exclusion: they subtract themselves from their initial subtraction as inconsistent being at the same time that their supplementation of a given field provides a unity for disparate phenomena.

One immediate objection presents itself with the above analogy. For the purposes of the present discussion, it is questionable whether the object (a) is in any way a catalyst for action. One could argue that the cause of a subject's desire is a determination of the subject as pure passivity whose desire exists in a negative relation to its posited object. In contrast, Badiou's event calls a subject into being in such a way that its residual effects will hinge upon the action and decisions taken by the subject that retroactively give form to it. The event is determined in and though subjective activity. To make an analogy between Badiou and Lacan is problematic if we lack a means of ascribing an active agency to the Lacanian subject. What possible forms can the object (a) assume that directly result from the activity of the Lacanian subject?

We can start with the rudimentary assumption of Lacan's that the subject's

---

17. Alenka Zupančič, *Ethics of the Real: Kant, Lacan*, London, Verso, 2000, p. 18.

18. In Lacan's Seminar VII, which led to his eventual conceptualization of object (a), this constitutive lack, or unnamed being, was called *das Ding*. '*Das Ding* is which I will call the beyond-of-the-signified. It is as a function of this beyond-of-the-signified and of an emotional relationship to it that the subject keeps its distance and is constituted in a kind of relationship characterized by primary affect, prior to any repression'. Jacques Lacan, *The Ethics of Psychoanalysis, 1959-1960*, Jacques-Alain Miller (ed.), trans. Dennis Porter, New York, Norton, 1992, p. 54.

relation to the signifier is a structural relation to emptiness, or lack. The question that emerges from this is one of the possible relations the subject can form with that lack. One obvious example of such a relation would be the avoidance, or repression, of that lack that is constitutive of neurosis. Neurotic subjectivity may in fact have some coincidence with situations in which the void is foreclosed from presentation—in either case, normativity or stability depends upon a foreclosure of the void. But there are other possible relations of the subject to its own lack that presuppose the direct activity of the subject in determining that relation, and thus determining the lack. One such possibility was given in Freud's account of sublimation that was subsequently modified by Lacan. Sublimation is conventionally taken to be the desexualization of libido in and through the production of scientific and artistic objects and knowledge. In contrast, the drive is usually taken to be the realization of primal, destructive impulses. The former would be the cultural purification of the latter. Lacan's radical move is to have united the two terms—drive and sublimation—in the very notion of an object (a): in each case, it is the activity of the subject that gives form to the object as satisfaction. This means that the object is the residual effect of subjective action and not the object that determines a subject's desire.[19] Thus, the sexual activity of bodies could be one possible (perhaps convenient) way of producing modalities of affect (that is, of aiming at a being beyond language), while the production of objects or knowledge in science, religion and art could exemplify other possibilities of giving determinate form to the negative determinations of the real. Science would entail a quest for the complete symbolization or determination of the Real—anything that remains unsymbolizable within it would simply imply a limitation in our own knowledge. Religion attempts to fill out this lack through the imposition of a radically transcendent other—while art, it is argued—is the realization of this lack in and through its representation as something. That is, it renders the impossibility of the Real possible in and through the medium of representation (a result of the paradox that the Real cannot be represented). Art, it would appear, has a unique relation to the Real insofar as it neither fully excludes it from experience (as in the case of religion) or fully incorporates it within knowledge (as in science). And this may have implications for Badiou's theory of art as a truth procedure, given that, for Badiou, truth is determined through mathematics.

Badiou, no less than Lacan, defines art as an instantiation of the void: the artists he designates as exemplary producers of truth can all be noted for their minimalist tendencies: Beckett, Mallarmé, Pessoa, Schoenberg. 'Art is [...] mobilized, not because it has worth in and of itself, or with an imitative and cathartic aim, but to raise the void of Truth up to the point at which dialectical sequential link-

---

19. Alenka Zupančič has opposed the drive to sublimation as such: 'if the drive is a "headless" procedure, sublimation is not. Sublimation is a kind of "navigator" of the drives, and this is why it plays such an important role in society'. Sublimation can thus lead to productions of determinate modes of that nothing, whereas the drive is simply the expenditure of that nothing—a drive towards nothing. See Alenka Zupančič, 'The Splendor of Creation: Kant, Lacan, Nietzsche', *Umbr(a): A Journal of the Unconscious*, no. 1, 1999, pp. 35-42, p. 40.

ing is suspended' (*MP*, p. 125). This notion of a purification of being is, of course, not altogether dissimilar to the commonplace notion of sublimation in Freud, who saw the sublimation of an instinct or drive as the purification of crude, and potentially destructive, instincts, into higher aims that could be met with social approval.[20] It is a telling sign of Freud's conservative, and under-theorized, take on the matter of sublimation that his aesthetics tended, more often than not, to focus on the classical or conventional: Michelangelo, Leonardo, Shakespeare. In 1930, at the time of *Civilization and its Discontents*, where he put forward his theory of the cultural value of arts, the work of Picasso, Lizzitsky, Duchamp, and others, was left unmentioned. Freud's theory of sublimation not only ran the risk of subscribing to a conservative sexual morality (an accusation commonly levelled against psychoanalysis regardless); it fell prey, to put it mildly, to a conventional aesthetics that denied art its potential for innovation.

Freud's notion of sublimation, then, was articulated as a function of the superego, insofar as it sought a way for the satisfaction of instincts in means that were subject to cultural approval. Lacan's response, although quite contrary to Freud's, did not lead to a rejection of the notion of sublimation. Sublimation for Lacan did result in the purification of affect, but these emotions were precisely those that were instigated by the cultural demands of the superego—fear and pity. Lacan's theory aims to subvert the very cultural authority that Freud's theory of sublimation put to work. To unravel the possible conflict between the two great psychoanalysts, we will have to consider the initial mockery that Lacan made of Freud's own views. In 1964, Lacan proposed the following Freudian interpretation of sublimation and its correlate in the drive:

> In other words—for the moment, I am not fucking, I am talking to you. Well! I can have exactly the same satisfaction as if I were fucking. That's what it means. Indeed, it raises the question of whether in fact I am not fucking at this moment. Between these two terms—drive and satisfaction—there is set up an extreme antinomy that reminds us that the use of the function of the drive has for me no other purpose than to put in question what is meant by satisfaction.[21]

The end of the above quote proposes the following contrast: if the drive is opposed to satisfaction, it is contradictory to speak of the satisfaction of a drive. Taken further, it is clear that satisfaction itself is a contradictory notion, insofar as there are individuals who are clearly capable of producing a certain stability in their lives in and through the manifestation of their symptoms (say, compulsive hand-washing)—this stability, while forever frustrated and dissatisfied, is what

---

20. 'A satisfaction of this kind, such as an artist's joy in creating, in giving his phantasies body, or a scientist's in solving problems or discovering truths, has a special quality which we shall certainly one day be able to characterize in metapsychological terms'. Sigmund Freud, 'Civilization and its Discontents', in Albert Dickson (ed.), *Civilization, Society and Religion*, trans. James Strachey, vol. XII Penguin Freud Library, London, Penguin, 1991, pp. 243-340, p. 267.

21. Jacques Lacan, *The Four Fundamental Concepts of Psychoanalysis*, Jacques-Alain Miller (ed.), trans. Alan Sheridan, New York, Norton, 1981, pp. 165-66.

satisfaction aims at. To borrow the famous term of Slavoj Žižek, the command to 'enjoy your symptom' does not result in a possible attainment of an aim, but in a prolongation of frustrated desire that typifies neurosis. But it is just as clear that individuals who manifest neurotic symptoms are nonetheless discontented despite their attainment of satisfaction: just as, we could assume, the act of speaking does not result in the same sort of jouissance that can be enjoyed in sexual intercourse. This is what Lacan means when he opposes drive to satisfaction. The question then is what exactly the drive or sublimation aims at if not satisfaction. How exactly does the drive play out a trajectory of impossibility?

This question brings us to the centrality of the Lacanian Real. From most of the cultural literature that has come out in the past fifteen years on the topic, it should be evident that the Real is the impossible. The impossibility, that is, of having an ontology from within the parameters of psychoanalysis. Or, yet again: the impossibility of the Real results from the paradoxical conclusion that there is no meta-language at the same time that language cannot foreclose the possibility of an existence that escapes language. For the speaking subject, there is no meta-discursive position from which one can state with certainty that there is nothing outside language. The Real is thus the minimal ontological framework that results from the fact that, within language, being is excluded at the same time that no definitive limits for that exclusion can be demarcated. We have already established that the subject occupies the limit point from which language proceeds, but there is also the question of the excess of being that is not exhausted by the presentative capacity of language. The minimal ontological form this being takes is that of the object (a), or, in Badiou's case, the event. The question that intimately links Lacan's object (a) to Badiou's event properly concerns the activity of the subject: how does the subject give form to being beyond simply leaving it as an empty, indeterminate excess?

For Badiou, it is evident that that the indiscernible is granted form through the forcing of truths. And it is unquestionably just as true that the conditions under which forcing can occur depend upon a generic, and thus universalizable, framework put into place. Truth is universal, for all.[22] The contrast with Lacan should be obvious: if the drive is itself an attainment of Lacanian jouissance, should not jouissance be universalizable, had by all?[23] Moreover, the drive itself, as an answer of sorts to the problems that irrational forms of enjoyment may represent to the subject, remains an ultimately individual notion: there can be no collective solution to the problem of jouissance precisely because, from the perspective of psychoanalysis, only individuals can be treated on the couch. There

---

22. This is not simply a formal mathematical counterpart to Badiou's ontology: a sufficient account of universalizability was given in Badiou's account of Saint Paul. See Alain Badiou, *Saint Paul: The Foundation of Universalism*, trans. Ray Brassier, Stanford, Stanford University Press, 2003.

23. This is a bit of a lengthy argument in itself. The basic premise behind it is that no matter how much one enjoys, there will always be others who enjoy more. This would appear to be the driving impetus behind Lacan's writing of 'Kant avec Sade', as well as Slavoj Zizek's recent writings on enjoyment as a political factor. See Jacques Lacan, 'Kant avec Sade', trans. James Swenson, *October*, vol. 51, 1989, pp. 55-104, p. 104.

cannot be a collective jouissance of the community.[24] As such, psychoanalysis would be an ultimately individual notion that carried very little truth. By extension, its usefulness for speaking about Badiou's notion of subjective fidelity would appear quite limited.

My response to the above objection is twofold. First, while there is certainly a connection between what happens at the level of a subject being gripped by an event and the universal truth that may follow from such an account, the universalizability of a truth cannot in any way serve as a criteria for what happens at the level of a subject being gripped by an event. A subject declares its fidelity to the event as a pure matter of faith. This is because, in a position Badiou may since have retracted, the truthfulness of an event cannot be decided at the time of its occurrence. And from this perspective, it is just as true that subjects gripped by events can form reactionary—and hence untrue—tendencies in response to events (say, collective unities who oppose political revolution, people who regarded Schoenberg's music as noise, etc.). Nothing at the level of universalizability can define the trajectory of the subject in response to something that has the power to form collective subjects out of individuals. A theory of what creates those subjective formations is what I am looking for in psychoanalysis.

Second, Badiou has, on at least two occasions, made concessions to the Lacanian cure as a potential truth procedure, insofar as the subject on the couch can, over the course of analysis, give form to the unconscious (or indiscernible) mechanisms that compel it to act.[25] At an immediate level, the answer is clearly that certain individuals make decisions to change their 'situations' (their individual lives) in order to form new relations to the being (the *jouissance*) they have to bear in everyday life. The hard work of analysis, then, could be regarded as a truth procedure among others that allows subjects (individual human subjects, say) to form new, hopefully more rational, means of existing. The manner in which we move from psychoanalysis, a specialist field that concerns individuals on couches, to arguing for its significance for philosophy will require something else: this is what I am looking for through the theory of sublimation. Sublimation can allow for the creation of something new in art, in a manner that will be applicable, if not useful, for Badiou's own writings on the topic.

The remainder of this chapter will thus attempt to go through these two points so as to assess what they may have to offer Badiou's theory of the event, the subject and fidelity. It is ultimately a question of affect as a principle of the subject, over and above the structural relations that make subjectivization possible. It may seem odd to appeal to Lacan for these purposes, given that he has

---

24. Ultimately, this is what Lacan meant with his maxim 'do not cede your desire!' That is, do not let an other dictate to you what your desire should be.

25. In *Theory of the Subject*, Badiou wrote that: 'We won't pay any attention to those who argue that a couch is not as serious as a concentration camp. To them we say without hesitation that this remains to be seen. The axiom of the *nouveaux philosophes*—"a camp is a camp"—is just as false as what the Chicago therapists wanted to promote through the excommunication of Lacan: "a couch is a couch". The fact is that the psychoanalytic cure has no other real aim than that of the readjustment of the subject to its own repetition'. See Alain Badiou, *Théorie du sujet*, Paris, Seuil, 1982.

often been accused of stripping psychoanalysis of *any* notion of affect. From such a perspective, it offers a cold and sterile framework for speaking about human behaviour. Philosophically, however, the psychoanalytic notion of the drive remains tainted by an irrationality that, more often than not, assumes morbid or abject vicissitudes (for example, Žižek's comparison of an encounter with the 'monstrous real' with Badiou's truth procedures). This psychoanalytic approach, for Žižek, constitutes an irrationality that underlies every philosophical approach to fill out the void of the indiscernible through the forcing of truths: in a Truth-Event, the void of the death drive, of radical negativity, a gap that momentarily suspends the Order of Being, continues to resonate'.[26]

In many ways, Žižek is entirely correct. In the first place, truth is indeed an empty category: behind any particular or local instantiation of it, there is nothing other than the void, just as ontology and thinking are nothing apart from their particular presentations or instantiations. But there is a surreptitious jump that Žižek makes from the emptiness of truth as a category to the fact that the truth procedures become nothing more than a way of regulating primordial psychic drives (whereby love is nothing other than the ability of human beings to rationalize an unbridled jouissance, politics becomes a means of modulating the non-universalizability of enjoyment as a political factor, art is a means of sublimating the abject horror of the Real into beautiful objects, etc.). Žižek's move is to ground *all* subjective action in impulses and interests that are applicable only to a psychoanalytic subject. In other words, at the bottom of Badiou's truth procedures lie libidinal impulses. What he has done, then, is oppose Lacan to Badiou without acknowledging that this distinction is possible on the basis of what distinguishes psychoanalysis from philosophy. And secondly, is it not the very point that sublimation, in supposing the desexualization of libido, makes categories such as 'unbridled' jouissance secondary to the ultimate aims of its activity? The applicability of the drive for Badiou's philosophy will hold only insofar as the drive ceases to be a purely individual notion and admits of a capacity for universalizability. In other words, I am in no way arguing for a correlation between Badiou and Lacan on the ground that subjective action presupposes a libidinal interest (in the same way that sublimation presupposes a drive), but rather that the elementary relation of a subject to its enjoyment (that is, a speaking subject to its unsaid being) is constitutive of the relation between Badiou's subject and the event. What is required, then, is not a sexualized content, but rather a minimal condition of affect that defines that relation.

III. Affect defined

Lacan's major writing on the topic of affect occurs in his tenth seminar, on anxiety. Anxiety, he says, is the only thing we can be sure of. I take this to mean that the other emotions that regulate human experience are always capable of

---

26. Žižek, *The Ticklish Subject: The Absent Centre of Political Ontology*, pp. 162-3.

deceiving. I have already mentioned fear and pity: clearly, with respect to contemporary events, there is no doubt that we live in a world where feared enemies and pitied victims proliferate. And their invocation in politics can often serve contradictory aims. For example, in relation to contemporary events, the same Muslim population we fear in the name of potential terrorist attacks is the same we pity in the name of the humanitarian interventions of 'just wars'.[27] Fear and pity, in either case, arouses the need for a resolution, just as readily as their transgression can find form in other, more threatening, extremes. Anxiety is something different, because it is instituted on an entirely different basis. What we fear or pity is conventionally what is other to us: in contrast, what arouses our anxiety is altogether intimate to us. It's hardly surprising that ethical indignation is often aroused with respect to people at a distance from ourselves (in Bosnia, Palestine, Iraq), rather than with regard to people we encounter in our everyday lives (UK and American citizens who live in poverty or are incarcerated).

What gives structure to anxiety is not a lack (a constitutive wound at the heart of experience), but rather, in Lacan's terms, a *lack of lack*. 'Anxiety is not the signal of a lack, but of something that you must manage to conceive of at this redoubled level of being the absence of this support of lack' (5.12.62). Subjective lack, which makes the emergence of the speaking subject in language possible, is also that which guarantees that the object (a), qua cause of desire, will always remain at a distance from that subject. It is always excluded, and thus open to various irrational vicissitudes. As an object of desire, the object (a) remains an impossible object which the subject relates to by virtue of some kind of constitutive failure. But in the absence of that lack, the object no longer remains at a distance; it emerges full-circle to the subject as the constitutive core of its grounding in being. And this being that is revealed to the subject as its own ground is precisely that empty place, that nothing that is the subject's own being. The confrontation of the subject with this being is the proper catalyst for action. The arousal of anxiety is thus unlike other psychological notions of affect that are constitutive of a subject's relation to the stability of their symbolic order. While fear and pity, among other affects, could be said to determine the manner in which subjects hold irrational relations to their jouissance and its various vicissitudes, it is anxiety, the encounter with the empty ground of being, that prompts an individual to go into analysis with the hope of forming other, preferably more rational, relations to their jouissance. Anxiety is the cause of subjective change precisely because it lacks a support in representation.

I will present this in the simplest form to provide a way into Badiou. In 'normal' situations, there may be certain elements that are subtracted. As we saw in the case of immigrant workers, some may be represented as excluded in the contemporary political situation of France, and this subtractive representation may arouse various feelings of disgust, pity or resentment. The arousal of these

---

27. See the admirable editorial by Jacqueline Rose, 'We are all afraid, but of what exactly?' *The Guardian*, 20 March 2003.

feelings depends upon their status as subtracted, as lacking what French citizens have (work permits, legal status, recognition by the state, etc). The movement that would facilitate the shift to an event would be to consider them not as subtracted elements of the situation 'France', but rather as human beings that, like French citizens, occupy the same place. If an event, or a political sequence, is to be established in their name, what is required is a recognition of the common being that is shared with French citizens, from which various prescriptions against the French state can be made on behalf of their ontological validity.

It is one thing to say that the example of the *sans-papiers* can provide one such example of a situation's recognition of its own subtracted being. It is another thing, however, to say that such a recognition arouses anxiety, or that such anxiety is the sole catalyst for subjective action, or fidelity. And, of course, anxiety is not an exclusively Lacanian notion, given that his work on the topic has been preceded by Kierkegaard, Heidegger and Freud, among others. If anything could be said to unite these latter three interpretations, it is the belief that anxiety is a subject's own confrontation with possibility: the possibility of moral obligation through the acknowledgment of guilt (Kierkegaard), or the possibility of one's own freedom to exist in the world (Heidegger). The indeterminateness of anxiety, then, is not anxiety about something in particular, but about being in general. And this revelation of being in general, the fact that it is not something that can be represented as excluded, and hence managed, is constitutive of a subject's relation to indeterminate being.

Taking this as our point of departure, we must then ask what it is that anxiety may provoke in psychoanalytic theory and what its counterpart may be in Badiou's truth procedure? The answer to the first part of the problem is simple enough: in contrast to emotions like fear and pity, anxiety is distinct from ordinary passionate attachments that define a subject's relation to the world. In other words, a person is compelled to go into analysis less on the basis of a compulsive need or desire for something (however much that can serve as a prop for their wish for analysis) as because of an underlying anxiety that makes ordinary life unbearable. The subject is seized by something it doesn't have a name for, and this is what could be said to prompt the series of investigations that ensue in the course of analysis. So far, this is quite concomitant with how Badiou sees a truth procedure. 'To speak brutally, I do not think that analysis is an interpretation, because it is regulated not by sense, but by truth. This is certainly not an uncovering of truth, of which we know that it is vain to think it could be uncovered, because it is generic' (*CS*, p. 208). Analysis does not uncover a pre-eisting truth, but is rather a means through which a subject gives form and shape to the indiscernible being that grounds its anxiety.

This final point is the pretext for the conclusion of this discussion. If analysis is ultimately something that individuals, as opposed to collective subjects, undergo, why should it then be seen as universal or generic? Isn't the whole point of Lacan's enterprise that jouissance cannot be universalized, had by all? Lacan's famous utilitarian analogy of jouissance as a white sheet illustrates this logic perfectly: if you cut enough holes in the sheet for everyone to stick their head through, you end up destroying the sheet in turn. The universalization of jouissance is its own abnegation. And if we conceive the ultimate goal of analysis to be new, more rational, relations subjects form with their jouissance, we are left with something that is fundamentally incompatible with Badiou's truth procedure. The crux of this problematic takes us to the difference between being and the real. I mentioned before that the Real is a category of the subject. What is implied by this is that the being of a truth that comes to be instituted in the situation traverses the individuality of the subject who chose to recognize it over others who did not. Badiou's subjects are unique subjects to the extent that they recognize events that others don't; however, if truth is for all, the particularity of the subject is abnegated. The move from psychoanalysis to philosophy, and from the Real to being requires that truth must pass over from being a subjective principle of fidelity to become a truth that exists for all qua forcing. The Real, as I see it, names that part of a truth that the subject operates in the service of, at the same time that the subject's actions traverse the individuality of the real.

I previously distinguished satisfaction from jouissance on the grounds that the former attains a certain stability that is rooted within language, whereas the latter is an explicit excess of being over language. Jouissance, at bottom, is Lacan's name for being. And the object (a), that bit of jouissance that supports subjective activity, is the correlate for Badiou's event. What the object (a) and the event both provide is a minimal framework through which a subject confronts being. Given that neither the event nor the object (a) have proper supports in representation, there is never a guarantee that disaster might not ensue from the subjective relations they establish. Perhaps their indeterminacy is what allows them to, quite often, assume irrational forms, as witnessed in the example of false truth procedures in Badiou, or in the obscure attachments that subjects form with obscure forms of enjoyment, in Lacan. The conditions of possibility of change and novelty in both Badiou or Lacan are just as readily the possible conditions for evil.

When Badiou remarks that analysis is not interpretation, he means that there is a point in the analytic situation that cannot be reduced to the dimension of language, which guides the subject forth in his or her pursuit of a truth. In the absence of a metalanguage, jouissance is that excess of the subject to itself, that part of the subject that is more than simply the sum total of its activity. When coupled with the object (a), then, the subject is driven in pursuit of something that is not reducible to its experience. And conversely, to see the Real as a category of the subject is to put the subject in tandem with something that exceeds its structural configuration in a linguistic network: it is that part of the subject that exceeds its own activity. What distinguishes Badiou's subject from Lacan's, then, is the process through which that subjective excess passes over from being a purely subjective principle (qua the Real of jouissance) into something that holds for a collective human situation in its totality (qua generic being of a truth). Forcing is what makes that shift possible. But it would be difficult to see how forcing would be possible were it not for the activity of a militant subject who is put in the service of something that exceeds all positive or representative value in the situation. Lacan, I have argued, provides the framework for Badiou's subjectivity.

The final question, then, concerns what we are to make of sublimation in Lacan. Is it a notion that is concomitant with art as a truth procedure in Badiou? The question returns us to Badiou's comment that truth in analysis cannot be uncovered because it is generic. Is there a generic, higher faculty of jouissance? Sublimation, I have suggested, offers one such possibility in and through the production of aesthetic objects that instantiate the empty ground of being that is annulled in and through the advent of language. And artistic sublimation may do this in a manner that is altogether different from the realizations that occur in religion or science.

When Badiou remarked that jouissance cannot be reduced to interpretation, he meant that it was that limit point of the situation which refuses closure. It becomes quite easy, then, to see that jouissance cannot be universalized: it cannot be given as a totality that can then be cut up and dived equally among all inhabitants of the situation. Like Russell's paradox, this is a direct effect of the inherent incompletion of being itself. What needs to be asked is whether it is possible for art to instantiate that incompletion. The artists that Badiou champions seem to share a tendency to strip away detail to uncover, or localize, the purity of the void. When Lacan describes sublimation as the 'elevation of an object into the dignity of a Thing',[28] I take him to mean that a Thing remains irreducible to the exchange or distribution of goods that typify stability in a social situation. This Thing, this object (a), that embodies our jouissance maintains its generic or universal value insofar as it is not reduced to the dominant logic of the situation, whether that be the baseness of fear or pity, or the customary circulation of goods in a capitalist society.

What sorts out the disparity of terms (jouissance, drive, sublimation, object (a), anxiety) with regard to the terms of Badiou's philosophy? For readers less familiar with Lacan, the following shortcut can provide an axiomatic framework with which to digest the preceding remarks:

1. The subject's declaration of an event defines a rudimentary means of relating to being. If the event is object (a), the affect that defines the subject's relation to that object (or event) is anxiety.
2. Being is distinct from the Real insofar as the Real is a category of a speaking subject's relation to its own (impossible) being. The Real presupposes a subject, while only the appearance of an event presupposes a subject. Events cannot be deduced from an asubjective, impersonal ontology.
3. If the drive can typify a subject's fidelity to an event (insofar as the psychoanalytic theory of the drive is a subject's instantiation of its object (a), sublimation is a means of instantiating the forms of indiscernible being that can be met with recognition from other subjects. It provides a productive form in which a drive can achieve satisfaction irrespective

---

28. Lacan, *The Ethics of Psychoanalysis, 1959-1960*, p. 112.

of its object. Thus, the value we impute to the artistic object depends less upon its usefulness or ability to satisfy human wants or interests, but rather upon the fact that it gives form to a being that eludes the speech of the speaking subject.

6

From Reflection to Transformation: What is Philosophy?

The previous chapters have provided an overview of the rudimentary categories that are internal to Badiou's philosophy: being, truth, the event and the subject. This final chapter will attempt to ask the broader question of what philosophy is. In the most general of senses, there are three possible ways to answer this question: one would be to define philosophy as it is 'in itself' with respect to basic questions; another could look at Badiou's philosophy alongside other thinkers; or one could interrogate the definition of philosophy with respect to other practices, such as art, science and politics. If the former two approaches have more or less dominated the discussion up to this point, it is the latter that will be our focus in what follows.

The preceding chapter attempted to separate the foundations that make events and subjects possible from the strictly ontological foundations that inform Badiou's doctrine of being, the situation, and truth. There is a supposition, in short, of two separate, but mutually sustaining, foundations that make truths—and by extension, novelty—possible. One (the ontological) is static and atemporal, while the other (the event) puts time into the situation by means of an intervention. If there is one concept of Badiou's that effectively unites the two, it is forcing, for it is in the act of forcing that the activity of a subject becomes united with its ontological ground in and through the production of truths. The determination of the ontologically indiscernible in and through the forcing of truths is that moment when an event becomes 'ontologized'—something that escapes the hold of the language of the situation (and is thus not deemed to exist) produces its residual effects in and through the instantiation of a truth (for which, then, truths could be said to exist).

If forcing is what effectively unites the event with a truth (through the retroactive determination of the former by the latter), it is nonetheless interesting to note that philosophy makes this connection at the same time that there are no philosophical events or truths as such. Events and truths occur in the four restricted domains of art, science, politics and love, and do so independently of any philosopher who labels them either true or evental. In this respect, philosophy does not seem to be necessary for novelty. At best, philosophy simply oversees the possible connections or conditions that made novelty possible—and, as an afterthought. From this perspective, one question is quite obvious in its simplicity: why bother doing philosophy at all if, in and of itself, it is incapable of producing something new?

This question can be truncated further: what exactly is philosophy in itself if it works in the service of four conditions that remain external to it? However rudimentary the question seems, it will be the guiding focus for this chapter. What precisely remains of philosophy if it is put in the service of peripheral conditions that produce concrete truths that philosophy is incapable of making in itself? Does philosophy provide a foundation of sorts (say, an ontology, or criterion) necessary for discerning truth as advent or novelty? If so, we could assume that philosophy is stable and unchanging, unlike science or politics, which are subject to innovation.

Or, on the contrary, we could assume that philosophy will be re-evaluated to the extent that there is novelty or innovation in other fields. That is, philosophers may be forced to think differently in response to the innovations of certain non-philosophical thinkers, such as Marx, Freud and Darwin, to name the most obvious. There is one clear example to support such an argument: Cantorian set theory was an historical innovation of the past century that came to have a decisive effect on the way Alain Badiou did philosophy. It remains to be seen how effectively Badiou's thought will translate into any kind of innovation in French philosophy as a whole, but it is possible that Cantorian set theory—considered a scientific advent by Badiou—could have implications for the manner in which philosophers do ontology.

Two different considerations need to be made with respect to the above points. The first is that Badiou's philosophy is quite radical in a very classical sense: it looks to certain basic concepts of philosophy (being, truth, the subject) so as to potentially reinvigorate it as a discipline. The fact that Badiou's philosophy is a foundational philosophy does seem to place a restriction on the manner in which it can change in response to innovation in other fields. That is, if philosophy provides a theory of ontology and truth that makes innovation and change possible, it seems difficult to see how a non-philosophical advent could have any effect on that foundation.

As a point of comparison, it should be noted that Badiou's reinvigoration of being and truth is not very different from Heidegger's efforts to return to a pre-Socratic questioning of being, or Edmund Husserl's efforts to arrive, philosophically, at a pre-Galilean origin of science. In other words, what Badiou is doing is not particularly novel with regard to twentieth-century, post-phenomenological philosophical claims that there are classical foundations to philosophy that precede scientific discovery. While Badiou may not hold the same set of prejudices against science as Heidegger, both presume that philosophy oversees the possible foundations that make science possible (even if, in Badiou's case, he certainly wouldn't suggest that philosophy makes scientific thought possible). This belief is widely held in much of continental philosophy. Bergson's project, in its response to Darwin, sought to install a metaphysics that made the theory of evolution possible; only philosophy could provide such a metaphysics. Husserl's phenomenology was preoccupied with the transcendental foundations of science, which eventually led to his preoccupations with consciousness. These two responses, whatever concessions they make to scientific innovation, ultimately maintained the superiority of philosophy over and above science, insofar as the conditions of possibility for doing the natural and physical sciences were properly thought only on the basis of philosophy.

Is there a necessary connection between relating philosophy to science in a foundational manner and assuming that, on this basis, philosophy is superior to science? A philosopher, for example, could claim that while biologists study life, only philosophers can provide a concept of what life is, or that neuro-psychologists study consciousness, but only philosophers can provide a proper concept of consciousness. These claims, presumably, would be made on the basis of the fact that philosophy is transitive to the delimited fields that are typically proper to the sciences, and is thus in a better position to answer certain questions. However different the possible relation between philosophy and science may be in different strands of continental philosophy, for many thinkers there seems to be an implicit assumption that philosophy is capable of doing something that science cannot. More generally, it seems that because philosophy is a discipline that lacks clearly defined borders, it can subsume other disciplines—including science—either by providing a possible foundation for science, or by producing concepts that science is incapable of producing itself. Even Deleuze, who has a fairly positive attitude towards the sciences, maintains that science is incapable of producing concepts: rather, it produces measurable functions that refer to the virtual ground they actualize, while missing the virtual entirely.

Of course, it is Heidegger who has been the most unequivocal in his condemnation of science. To give only one remark from many similar statements made late in his career, Heidegger wrote that, 'The development of philosophy into the independent sciences that, however, interdependently communicate among themselves ever more markedly, is the legitimate completion of philosophy. Philosophy is ending in the present age'.[1] Innovation in science signals the end of philosophy as such. One philosophical response to such a dilemma consists in a return to the origins of philosophy, whether in embracing its Greek origins—a tendency that can be witnessed in thinkers as diverse (or as close) as Heidegger, the Husserl of *The Crisis of European Sciences*, and Deleuze and Guattari in *What is Philosophy?* This approach is not altogether different from what Badiou himself attempts in *Being and Event*: a neo-Platonist (by way of Cantor) reinvigoration of

---

1. Martin Heidegger, *Basic Writings: From Being and Time (1927) to The Task of Thinking (1964)*, David Farrell Krell (ed.), Revised & Expanded ed., San Francisco, HarperSanFrancisco, 1993, p. 434.

classical philosophical categories. The one significant distinction between Badiou and other revisionist philosophers, however, is that Badiou in no way opposes philosophy to the proper capacity of science and, as we will see in this chapter, this is what makes his thought incompatible with a tradition of continental philosophy which has done little to hide its outright hostility to science.

More simply, for Badiou, it is not the case that philosophy makes science possible. Scientists (not to mention political activists or artists) can go about their work with little concern for any philosophical foundation for their activity. Philosophy is not a foundation in that respect. Rather, it looks at the domain of human activity (which, in its proper capacity, is the ability to think) and interrogates the degree to which thought is capable of producing truth in the disciplines that are proper to it. What distinguishes the disciplines of art, science, politics and love from other disciplines (such as culture, opinion, sexuality, mass communication) is that the former are capable of producing truths while the latter are not. This is a properly philosophical thesis: the belief that truth could hold for art or politics in the same way that it could for science.

Now, if such an argument is made on the basis of a *philosophical* definition of the category of truth, then it must surely also be acknowledged that philosophy is not a discipline in the same way that science is. Science is a specific domain in which it is possible to gain knowledge of a given field, precisely because it can be adequately defined and circumscribed. From this assumption comes Badiou's thesis that there are no philosophical truths: philosophy does not produce knowledge in and of itself, but rather assesses thought in and through the various truths and knowledges that are actualized in science. Philosophy can be forced to think differently, over time, about various things insofar as there is possible advent or novelty in art, science or politics. But it is hard to say if philosophy itself is capable of producing new thoughts spontaneously through nothing other than itself.

In addition to Badiou's respect for the integrity of science as a delimited field of enquiry, there is also his commitment to politics that cannot be reduced to a 'political philosophy'. He is a political activist who works directly with disenfranchised groups in modern France; his work as a philosopher is external to his activity as a political activist. And this commitment is, much like science, concerned with particular situations where events, actors, and thought engage. In other words, only science, politics and art have particular engagements with those arenas where novelty occurs; philosophy plays something of a subsidiary role, and this is what may make it so difficult for many people working in continental philosophy to readily grasp what he is doing. At the same time that Badiou offers a foundational philosophy, his project also challenges philosophy's authority to say anything interesting on political, scientific or artistic matters that undermines the capabilities of local actors (scientists, activists, artists) who engage in their local situations.

Allow me to give only one example of possible discrepancies in the reception of Badiou's work. *Being and Event* has been available in Italian, Portuguese and Spanish translations since 1995. These translations, moreover, seem to have been produced for and by an audience with an interest in uniting Badiou's political theories with his broader philosophical project. The interest in his work in these countries extend from a tradition of thinking that is rooted in Althusser and Foucault (and, to a lesser extent, Lacan) as practitioners of social and political change, with only a tangential relation to post-phenomenological questions of ontology. In contrast, the first few works of Badiou's to be translated in English have been those which secure him as a thinker within a great continental tradition that engages his philosophy with rival thinkers such as Heidegger and Deleuze. Even the *Ethics* book, despite its polemical and accessible tone, has been received as a response to the post-phenomenological 'return to ethics' that dominated much round-table discussions of continental philosophy in the past two decades.

There are a few obvious reasons for this. The most evident, as I have noted several times already, is that Badiou is a French philosopher, and is thus subject to being read in line with contemporaries such as Derrida, Lyotard, Deleuze and Nancy—thinkers who, with the possible exception of Deleuze, are generally understood as hostile to any possible relation between philosophy and mathematics (or science or logic). That is, quite simply, a French philosopher who states that 'mathematics is ontology' will be seen as foreign to what most English-speaking thinkers expect from a French philosopher. Second, the gulf between radical politics and philosophical thinking may be more pervasive in English-speaking countries, to the extent that the distinction between philosophical thought and political action is so pronounced that any possible reconciliation between the two could only result in subsuming the latter under the former—that is, political action is possible only insofar as thought exerts a sobering influence upon it.

The reason for going through a rather broad array of trends in contemporary thought in order to situate Badiou is that it seems difficult to answer the question, 'what is philosophy for Badiou?' without examining the traditions he both engages with and opposes. On the one hand, Badiou is a radical philosopher who, like Heidegger, seeks to revisit classical philosophical categories. On the other hand, he radically undermines philosophy's authority to speak about everything in any sort of meta-situational kind of sense. This poses a problem for what philosophy can say or do. For if philosophy cannot claim to speak about science or politics in any manner that is superior to what actual scientists or political activists do, then it becomes difficult to say what philosophy actually does. This isn't simply a complaint that philosophy is not some sort of pre-condition for doing science; it is rather the fact that, for Badiou, philosophy doesn't do anything at all.

In order to unravel these difficulties, we should probably look at the simplest definition of philosophy for Badiou. As Oliver Feltham and Justin Clemens have noted, for Badiou the task of philosophy is to 'reflect and learn from those transformations happening in contemporary historical situations'.[2] Although no longer

---

2. Justin Clemens and Oliver Feltham, 'An Introduction to Alain Badiou's Philosophy' in Alain Badiou, *Infinite Thought: Truth and the Return to Philosophy*, ed. and trans. Justin Clemens and Oliver Feltham, London, Continuum, 2003, p. 33. Henceforth cited as *IT*.

contemporary, one such transformation has been the reconfiguration of the category of the subject instituted by Marx and Freud. As duly noted in the first pages of *Being and Event*, the classical category of the subject has been regulated to non-philosophical practices of politics and clinical practice. In other words, a subject is defined by its action, and this (along with the innovations of Darwin) proposes a break with the classical category of the subject that spanned the lineage from Descartes to Husserl.

Lacan, as is well known, declared psychoanalysis to be anti-philosophy, by which I take him to mean that psychoanalysis, not unlike chemistry, physics and biology, is a delimited field of inquiry, dealing with speaking subjects in a clinical environment. While this fact might mean little for philosophy, it is important to note that Badiou follows Lacan by stating in an interview that 'in the end, I think that philosophy should always think as closely as possible to anti-philosophy' (*Ethics*, p. 122). For Badiou, this would mean that philosophy cannot help but engage with those non-philosophical domains that are capable of producing knowledge, if not advent or novelty. In so doing, there may be a possible change in the manner in which we do philosophy, and thus think in general. Philosophy, that is, develops in response to other fields, and not out of itself.

The one thinker who could be said to precede Badiou on thinking this very difficulty would be Louis Althusser, who, significantly, was not a philosopher in any strict kind of sense. Althusser, as is well known, saw Marxism as a science—that is, it was a delimited field of inquiry with a consistent theoretical framework that could yield adequate results. The very shift that Althusser saw in Marx's thought from Hegelian speculative thinking to historical materialism as a science radically questioned the authority of philosophy to engage in the political. At best, it occupied something of a transitory position. This insistence on the non-philosophical character of Marxism is what separates Althusser from the typical reception of all French thinkers within a post-phenomenological framework. A quote from *For Marx* illustrates the stakes succinctly:

> If the birth of a new philosophy is simultaneous with the foundation of a new science, and this science is the science of history, a crucial theoretical problem arises: by what necessity of principle should the foundation of the scientific theory of history *ipso facto* imply a theoretical revolution in philosophy? This same circumstance also entails a considerable practical consequence: as the new philosophy was only implicit in the new science it might be tempted *to confuse itself with it*. *The German Ideology* sanctions this confusion as it reduces philosophy, as we have noted, to a faint shadow of science, if not to the empty generality of positivism. This practical consequence is one of the keys to the remarkable history of Marxist philosophy, from its origins to the present day.[3]

The question, then, concerns what philosophy is capable of, if it is subject to changes that occur in the domain of science (a science, it should be noted, put in the service of the political). Does it remain an inferior version of science, a reac-

---

3. Louis Althusser, *For Marx*, trans. Ben Brewster, London, Verso, 1996, pp. 33-4.

tion to it, or does it perhaps open itself to new possibilities? Badiou, obviously enough, chooses the latter route, but in one deliberate manner that has not been noted in the discussion until now. It is not the innovation of Cantorian set theory (a scientific novelty) and its subsequent axiomatization by Zermelo and Fraenkel that provides philosophy with a foundation that remains transitive to other possible arenas of the new (although, to a great extent, this is very much true for Badiou's system). It is rather that this particular innovation reinvigorates a classical philosophical category—ontology—in such a way that philosophy can oversee a degree of compossibility between advents in science, art and politics that is made possible on the basis of an ontology that is common to them. The tenets that maintain this compossibility are precarious, to be sure, for it is certainly not the case (to give only one example) that the advent of quantum physics can furnish a complex model for political organization. Badiou seems to be asking a more ambitious, yet rudimentary question. Given that science has been capable of attaining truth, does it furnish a model of truth with applicability to domains of experience that are frequently open to dispute: that is, is it possible to have truth in politics and art?

To answer such a question, we would have to ask what such a model of truth would be (or, more generally, what is truth in science?) and then ask if it is possible that such models are operative in politics and art. Badiou has done this, I have argued, on the basis of two frameworks that are irreducible to each other. The first, ontological, foundation is perhaps the more systematic of the two to grasp: it presupposes that all situations have an ontological grounding in inconsistent multiplicity that admits of potentially new sites for the development of knowledge. All situations, that is, are ontologically incomplete, and the procedural manner of gaining knowledge of this ontological incompletion that emerges as the indiscernible (unknown) of the situation is constitutive of truth. An evaluation can be put forth to determine the indeterminate, and if this evaluation proves capable of spurring further investigation, then there will be a process that, for Badiou, is constitutive of truth. A truth, at bottom, is a process in the Real (*IT*, p. 61).

The second framework is a bit more difficult to grasp, given that it is not reducible to the systematic ordering of multiplicity that typifies set theory. It is that something must occur, or grip and seize subjects, in order to make the jump from ontology to truth possible. While this, I have argued, has not been duly integrated into the trajectory of *Being and Event*, it is from an inquiry into a theory of the subject gripped by an event that Badiou embarked upon philosophy, at least in his work following 1968. Badiou is nothing if not a philosopher of commitment to a cause, and the move to set theory at the time of *Being and Event* signals, I believe, an attempt to provide a rational horizon in which subjective action can be thought in tandem with philosophy. Or rather, the mathematical foundation of *Being and Event* provides an effective safeguard that prevents subject action from lapsing into the pursuit of change for its own sake. What makes Badiou's novelty what it is, then, is that it does more than simply proliferate being in multiple and diverse forms. Rather, it produces something that changes the way in which human beings think in a particular situation, in and through the truths that effectively transform it. Whether or not these truths change the manner in which we do philosophy, however, seems to be a subsidiary question.

Thus, there is some variance in Badiou's definition of philosophy. On the one hand, there is the assumption that there are no such things as philosophical events; events occur locally in particular situations. On the other hand, it seems that if philosophy is forced to respond to particular innovations that have occurred (Marx and Freud for the definition of the subject, Cantor for the definition of being, Cohen for truth), then there would appear to be something akin to events in a philosophical sense. I don't think that Badiou would disallow that, but it is nonetheless pertinent to ask what distinguishes these events from others (say, Schoenberg or Mallarmé for art) that may have little impact on philosophy. In this respect, philosophy appears to be a condition subject to change and rupture like the others, given the fact that the categories of the subject, being and truth are defined through conditions that were made possible within a fairly recent history of human thought.

The above problematic is founded upon a distinction between the possible effects of thought. That is, thought can either produce effects in particular situations (for which it is applicable to experience), or it can transform itself (for which Badiou's project is wholly rational). The former type of change would concern local instantiations of truth, while the latter is engaged in those innovations that have transformed philosophy. There is obviously a need for such a distinction, but it is not without its difficulties. Philosophy has been defined by Badiou as a thinking that oversees the possible coexistence of various truths.[4] It is because philosophy holds an external relation to those conditions in which truth occurs that it avoids the pitfalls of auto-affection that pervade post-phenomenological philosophy.

By this, I mean the belief that philosophy is, in itself, a sufficient medium for thought that does not depend upon other delimited fields of inquiry (such as the sciences) in order to operate. Philosophy does not think itself. If anything, it thinks mathematics. The difficulty, however, occurs when we move from the question, 'What is philosophy?' to the quasi-Heideggerian question, 'What is thought?' Badiou's mathematical ontology has, obviously, transformed the question from determining thought as substance (such that thinking would be defined by consciousness, ontological certainty, or a transcendental framework of cognitive faculties) into one that conceives thought as a capacity. Thought is capable of innovation insofar as it produces truths. For philosophy to oversee the compossibility of such truths in and through what occurs in science, art and politics, one would certainly have to concede that thought does indeed think itself in its specialist fields. But when innovation itself transforms philosophy, decisions are being made that don't simply change the way in which thinking occurs in par-

---

4. 'Philosophy does not pronounce truth but its conjuncture, that is, the thinkable conjunction of truth'. *MP*, p. 38.

ticular fields, but in which thinking occurs in general. And this, I believe, leads Badiou back into a framework of auto-affection in which thought is forced to think itself in and through philosophy.

We can see the difficulty that occurs when we philosophically interrogate Badiou's declaration that mathematics is ontology. The most common question, particularly from phenomenologists, is *why* anyone should accept this to be the case. Badiou's response has tended in two directions. On the one hand, he has been prone to suggesting that being is multiplicity, and that set theory offers the most rigorous means for speaking about that multiplicity. Or, he has suggested that the statement effectively hinges upon a decision from which, presumably, novelty and innovation will follow. In neither instance is there an external reserve of being against which mathematics can be effectively measured. This is largely in keeping with his definition of ontology (for which there is no meta-ontology) and his definition of truth (which is not a correspondence theory). Such a response is quite different from the kind of determinate results that are produced in the sciences. A biologist can study a living organism and produce determinate results about any number of factors that determine its life-cycle. It is less certain if the same biologist would be able to answer the more general question of what life is—and for the most part, such questioning would be highly unnecessary in order to do biology.

Yet Badiou makes the very general question of being and truth necessary for his philosophy. Insofar as this is the case, thinking philosophically requires an engagement with indeterminate fields of inquiry (that is, being and truth) that, perhaps by necessity, will produce indeterminate results. That is, it is hard to argue that mathematics is ontology apart from the fact that it is a determinate system for ordering multiplicity. The decision for set theory as ontology is to yield a determinate, scientific character from something that is far too broad a category for the sciences (ontology). On the other hand, infinity and multiplicity are equally as elusive as the question of being, and this has not stopped many mathematicians from speaking about transfinite infinities in a determinate manner. In this respect, Badiou's meta-ontological decision of set theory is founded upon a possible relation that exists between the inconsistency of infinity as a mathematical domain and the generality of a metaphysics of being. If mathematicians have been able to establish order out of transfinite infinities, then it might be possible to renew a metaphysical project of being on the basis of an order that mathematics provides.

In this respect, addressing the problem of multiplicity (that is, the difficulty of knowing whether multiplicity has an order) as a philosophical problem assumes that there is a possible connection between the generality of what mathematics studies and the generality of being as a question of metaphysics. This may very well be a legitimate approach, given that the domains that qualify the natural sciences (say, the living world for biology, the non-living world for physics) are less clearly definable when we ask what life or nature are in themselves. As I said before, the life of a particular organism is easier to determine than life in general.

But it is no less true that an individual set or ordinal number may be easier to define or determine than multiplicity in general. Badiou's decision for mathematics as ontology is meta-ontological, even if its ultimate ontological criterion is the axiomatic assertion that nothing exists.

While there may be a possible connection between mathematics and philosophy, it is on the basis of philosophy that such a connection is made: there is no third party that oversees the possible connections between the two in the way that philosophy oversees possible connections between art and politics. Philosophy purports to think science in a way that science can't. In this respect, Badiou's philosophy oversees both itself and other disciplines. On the other hand, it is on the basis of a mathematical (if not scientific) ontology that philosophy thinks particular situations, and on the basis of post-Cantorian set theory that philosophy has been able to conceive of truth that can hold for scientific, if not artistic, situations. In this respect, a scientific ontology thinks scientific situations. As Badiou writes, 'there is a philosophical discussion between set theory as a mathematical creation and set theory as an ontological thinking. Science doesn't organize that discussion. This is the reason why philosophy is necessary' (*IT*, p. 184). Perhaps surprisingly, the relation that philosophy may hold to other disciplines is not altogether different from Deleuze's reflections on his own system:

> Every philosophy must achieve its own manner of speaking about the arts and sciences, as though it established alliances with them. It is very difficult, since philosophy obviously cannot claim the least superiority, but also creates and expounds its own concepts only in relation to what it can grasp of scientific functions and artistic constructions. [...]. Philosophy cannot be undertaken independently of science or art. It is in this sense that we tried to constitute a philosophical concept from the mathematical function of differen*t*iation and the biological function of differen*c*iation, in asking whether there was not a statable relation between these two concepts which could not appear at the level of their respective objects. Art, science and philosophy seemed to us to be caught up in mobile relations in which each is obliged to respond to the other, but by its own means.[5]

Now, in contrast to Badiou, Deleuze places philosophy alongside science and art: it does not seem to occupy a relation that oversees the two. On the other hand, it seems to be Deleuze's precise point that possible connections can be established between disparate fields (mathematics and biology) on the basis of a philosophical question of difference. In effect, Deleuze has organized the question of novelty around two concepts (difference and repetition) that are adequate to the propensity of both thought and life to produce itself anew. Something new can occur in philosophy in the same way that something new can occur in art and science according to an ability of thought to differentiate and repeat itself. A philosophy that does this will be adequate to a novelty that exceeds it. Badiou, in contrast, has organized (or more accurately, founded) his philosophy upon incon-

---

5. Deleuze, *Difference and Repetition*, p. xvi.

sistent being and truth in a way that both separates philosophy from the activity that produces novelty, at the same time that it is only on the basis of philosophy that being and truth can form a system. In effect, the competing philosophies of Deleuze and Badiou are internally organized as philosophies around concepts that make possible connections and yield results that have varying degrees of determination. This would comprise the conditions under which their philosophies are distinguished as methodologies.

But it is an altogether different question if the distinctions between the opposing systems of Badiou and Deleuze result from decisions that take an entirely different set of criteria as their basis. It can certainly be one thing to make different decisions about what philosophy is, but if the decisions depend upon a widely different set of criteria, then the comparisons and contrasts between the two systems seem tangential, if not random. Deleuze and Badiou appear connected insofar as their philosophies are organized around the general problems of novelty and multiplicity, on the one hand, and the relation that philosophy holds with other disciplines, on the other. This would account for what I call the internal coherence of their systems, the manner in which they are organized as systematic philosophies. However, there are principles that may inform the decisions for the internal coherence of either thinker's system that are radically peripheral to either system. I am referring here to the various problems around which their philosophies are organized. If we are to compare Deleuze and Badiou as philosophers of the new, we must accept that the qualifications for exactly what constitutes the new may not be the same for both thinkers, and for reasons that are not strictly philosophical.

Change and novelty, in and of themselves, occur independently of philosophy: organisms evolve, innovations occur. This is true for both Deleuze and Badiou. But the primary difference between Deleuze and Badiou is that the former thinker has ascribed the possibility for novelty to an impersonal power that could just as readily apply to animals or non-living entities. Badiou, in contrast, restricts change and innovation to what human beings can do. Although it is easy to typify Deleuze as the more 'organic' of the two philosophers (insofar as personal power, for Deleuze, is essentially self-organizing), it is nonetheless true that Badiou relies upon a biological distinction between humans and animals that cannot be derived from a mathematical ontology.

Let us now examine the way I have characterized (if not caricatured) Deleuze as a philosopher. Bergson's philosophy installed a metaphysics of change as the foundation that, through philosophy, made Darwin's theory of evolution possible. Transferring that metaphysics onto Deleuze's system is largely consistent with the manner in which Badiou reads Deleuze, whereby the virtual as power is coextensive with actualization, or individuation organized through difference and repetition. Various sciences and arts are organized in a similar manner—such as certain evolutionary theories that account for the capacity of an organism to evolve.[6] The

---

6. See De Landa, *Intensive Science and Virtual Philosophy*, pp. 57-8.

one thing that is unique to philosophy is that it produces concepts of difference and repetition: the virtual, lines of flight, divergent series, disjunctive syntheses. One could say Badiou approached a similar problem by using a different set of criteria. This contrast between Deleuze and Badiou concerns the principles of internal organization that each thinker uses to do philosophy: to produce an argument for the superiority of one philosophy over another, one would have to base one's argument upon principles that are external to the systems of either thinker, and thus, in a sense, external to philosophy itself. The only alternative to such an option would be to conclude, with Badiou, that he and Deleuze are two philosophers whose systems are simply incompatible with one another, and thus, in a sense, not comparable. Despite the manifestly critical tone of Badiou's monograph on Deleuze, the reader gets the sense that that the latter option is Badiou's own.

If an effective comparison is to be made between these thinkers, it may have to be on the bases of principles that are *meta*-philosophical—that is, principles that could just as readily have been produced in the sciences, politics and arts. The distinction at hand, then, is one between a metaphysics of change and a metaphysics of truth. While Badiou has argued that Deleuze supports his metaphysics of change through an ontologization of the virtual (a submission of thought to a renewed concept of the One (*CB*, p.11)), this seems cogent only insofar as ontology is taken to be central to Deleuze's system: certainly, there is a whole, but this only becomes a complete totality, a One, when it is ontologized, filled out. And this belief in the centrality of ontology to Deleuze's system appears to be a move that Badiou alone makes. That is, if being is taken to be a pre-given substance, then the whole as being will be a complete totality. If, on the contrary, being is taken as a capacity—to be—then this will fail, not unlike Badiou's inconsistency, to be exhausted in the open whole through which change occurs. And this, most crucially, is because Deleuze replaces the category of truth with that of time, which alone is the true mark of change. If truth is its own criteria for Badiou, then time appears to be something that is the measure of itself. In this respect, the system we use to measure time is simply an abstraction from the actual change that occurs and endures in time itself.

As Badiou observes, for Deleuze truth is analogical or equivocal, while ideas or concepts are absolutely univocal (*CB*, p. 55). Truth, in short, presupposes a division within the univocity of being that Deleuze would resolutely refuse to admit into his system. In a classical—non-Badiouian—sense, truth takes actual beings and refers them not to their virtual power, but to the possibility that they realize as cases of truth. Truth is what makes that ontological division. For Deleuze, then, truth is essentially restrictive and negative: the actualization of a possibility is the negation of a contingent possibility over and against others. The statement, 'A is the case', is the realization of the possibility that A could be the case, as well as a negation of the possibility that A could *not* be the case.[7] In contrast, to affirm

---

7. See Gilles Deleuze, *Cinema 2: The Time-Image*, trans. Hugh Tomlinson and Robert Galeta, Minneapolis, University of Minnesota Press, 1989, p. 130.

the virtual as virtual, one does not depart from actualization as a case of truth at the expense of false cases that are not actualized. For that matter, the Platonic separation between truth and knowledge (that Deleuze rejects and Badiou resolutely maintains) presupposes truth as a point of transcendence to the multiplicity of knowledges and opinions that circulate in any given situation. Not only does this effect a categorical division in being in and through a qualitative separation between truth and knowledge, it also entails that this division be doubled by a second distinction between the one as point of transcendence (truth) and the multiple (knowledge), which a Deleuzian ontology refuses (*CB*, p. 56).

Now, the unique advantage of this refusal of a point of transcendence is that there doesn't seem to be a distinct difference between what a philosopher does and what constitutes artistic and scientific practice. The concepts that are operative in philosophy can function just as readily in other fields, given that a model of physics can employ principles of difference, repetition and qualitative change to yield determinate results. It is an altogether different question if this is operative in Badiou's philosophy. Certainly, an ontology of inconsistent multiplicity can be *applicable* to multiple situations, but is truth the same for an artist in the same way as it is for Paul Cohen as a mathematician? The difficulty here is that Badiou has taken a notion of truth and defined it through a mathematically given model. If this model of truth is to hold for other situations, we have two options. Either Cohen's generic model of set theory furnishes a model for political or artistic truths in an analogical fashion, or we would have to say that Schoenberg is doing the same thing as Paul Cohen, but with a lesser degree of clarity. Either way, we are left with a philosophical definition of truth that may be highly compelling in principle but increasingly obscure when applied to experience. In this respect, the Deleuzian point that truth requires a hierarchy seems quite valid: philosophy provides a model of truth that has applicability to other situations, but does so only with the provision that either truth in art is similar to, or like, what Paul Cohen attempted in 1963, or it is the same thing that Cohen attempted, only less subject to formal rules of constructibility.

The problem is not really that Badiou has made a decision for truth per se (after all, novelty needs to be qualified); it is rather that it loses precision once it becomes a question of particular truths. And we are left with the very general question as to why Badiou even calls this truth at all. From the perspective of the problem of novelty, the Deleuzian refusal of truth as a category seems highly compelling.

This problem is augmented by the fact that Badiou founds his philosophy upon being and truth—a move that places his philosophy in dialogue with a history of Western philosophy that is not exclusively concerned with novelty at all. Indeed, many people approaching Badiou's work for the first time may scarcely notice that novelty is posed as a problem.[8] This is not an altogether illegitimate

---

8. In other words, much of the attention focused on Badiou's work can be spent assessing his ontology over and against other thinkers such as Heidegger, Spinoza, Hegel, Aristotle and so forth. Indeed, much in this area already has been done. The same approach could be taken with Badiou's theory

approach to what Badiou is doing: he does, in many respects, want to be seen as a philosopher in the tradition of Spinoza, Hegel and Heidegger—as someone who radically revamped metaphysics as a project. As such, an interrogation of what Badiou is doing with being and truth will extend well beyond a comparison with Deleuze on the question of novelty.

What has become apparent, then, is the split nature of the project I set for myself in this book. I initially set up a problem of the conditions under which the new can occur, and attempted to expose how Badiou could offer a model of truth that is separate from any principle of the continuity of change at the same time that it maintains a category of truth. Given, however, that Badiou's system maintains classical categories, it was necessary to explain how Badiou's theses of being and truth hold up against the scrutiny of the history of philosophy—in other words, it was necessary to explain Badiou's philosophy in detail so as to hold it up to other great thinkers of being and truth. This problematic may be entirely separate from the original problem. In other words, what makes Badiou interesting as a philosopher may be different from what makes his philosophy interesting from the problem of novelty. In contrast, a thinker of the new may not necessarily be concerned with classical categories at all—Deleuze himself did not have 'a taste' for truth, any more than he considered ontology to be an important category (*CB*, p. 56). This is not necessarily to say that a philosophy founded on classical categories is less adept at approaching the problematic of novelty than that of 'non-classical' thinkers (Foucault, for example); it is rather that those classical categories may be judged according to a set of criteria that is not exclusively concerned with the problem of novelty. And so, if Badiou is to argue that mathematics is ontology and the truth is post-eventar, he must furnish a means for saying why that is the case.

We have already encountered two particular problems with Badiou's theory of truth. The first is that the criteria according to which we judge something to be new may be different from the criteria we use to judge it to be true. Novelty is something that is more directly felt at the level of the situation, rather than the situation's being-qua-being. Second, as I mentioned, in comparison to Deleuze, it becomes problematic to speak of truths in political and artistic situations without falling either into analogy or a version of truth that is increasingly obscure once it is actualized in existing situations. In this respect, Deleuze's philosophy seems to offer a less problematic account for the new, given that it is not mired down in the problematic of truth. On the other hand, even this interrogation of Badiou's system does little to resolve the decision as to which of the two philosophers offers a 'superior' account of, or orientation to, the new. And this is because the above two difficulties are philosophical problems in general, and the analogical nature of Badiou's theory of truth would still be a problem even if his philosophy was not concerned with the problem of novelty. At bottom, what we lack is a for-

---

of truth—only Etienne Balibar seems to have unpacked this problematic alongside thinkers such as Foucault, Canguilhem and Tarski.

mal criterion for determining novelty except for having established a tautological equivalence with truth. And if this is the case, then simply interrogating the systems of either thinker is unlikely to yield a decisive answer to the problematic at hand. We are at an impasse.

I. Beyond the World: Why Novelty?

In an earlier chapter, I put forward the theory that the primary existence of the void—insofar as it was, ontologically, indiscernible being—was enabling of change. In subsequent sections, this came to be fleshed out as a theory of the void as an inconsistent multiplicity that can assume novel forms in and through the production of truths. What we think and determine in the pursuit, or production of truth, is the void that is peripheral to experience. While various assumptions could be made about such an approach, it rests upon the belief that if being is interrogated to its limits, one simply encounters nothing. There is no being beyond its material instantiation that provides a support or principle for how it comes to be organized in various situations that comprise the world. The ultimate ontological support of the world is nothing.[9] It is nonetheless true that there is a world that human subjects encounter and are often forced to make decisions about. Or rather, according to both Badiou and Deleuze, there are worlds that are populated by singularities, multiplicities and 'events' that come to be organized through various trajectories. It is something of an open question whether Badiou's philosophy has any applicability for experience. Even Hegel, who probably is closest to Badiou in departing from the supposed equivalence of being and nothing, notes that the starting point for philosophy is experience.[10]

I will attempt to answer this question by first looking at the applicability of Deleuze to experience. In so doing, I will attempt to resolve the conflict that I have set up between these two thinkers. It is essentially a question of the constitution of the world. In his second book on cinema, Deleuze wrote that 'we no longer believe in this world. We do not even believe in the events which happen to us, love, death, as if they only half concerned us' (*Cinema 2*, p. 171). Deleuze, not surprisingly, had a Spinozist take on this problem: it is not a question of transforming the world, or imagining alternative worlds, but of *believing* that human subjects are part of the world. In this respect, the world as an object of knowledge is less problematic than the relation of the subject to the world, a relation that exists as an article of faith. Belief in the world is an affirmation of the univocity of being—a fact Badiou picks up on quite well in his writings on Deleuze. The world is not constituted through categorical divisions between possibility and actuality, good and bad, that could lead one either to accept or reject it. Faith in the world, then, is an affirmation of the world as it is, and not a knowledge of the world according to a categorical distribution of being.

---

9. In this respect, Peter Hallward is quite correct to qualify Badiou as an ontological atheist.
10. Hegel, *Science of Logic*, p. 16.

This typifies, I believe, a problem particular to the work of the late Deleuze, namely, how the subject can be conceived as a singular expression of the multiplicity of the world. This question is essentially no different from that of the constitution of a world in general, given that the later Deleuze takes the interiority of the subject to be no different from the interiority that constitutes the world as a closed whole. If we separate the question of the existence of the world from that of the forces that populate and constitute it, we are left with nothing other than a pure outside, a multiplicity of force. What allows for the transformation of this outside (as a fundamentally open multiplicity) into a world (a closed whole) is the constitution of a limit that is immanent to force, or the outside, itself. And this limit is not structurally imposed from without, but is the end-result of a densification of the outside—the point at which an inside is determined through the outside. To give the most rudimentary of examples from Deleuze's monograph on Foucault: thought thinks the indiscernibility of what falls outside normative society (say, criminality, madness, deviant sexuality), but only insofar as the various discourses that come to be produced about this outside serve a purpose for the constitution of that society. The various disjunctions that are constitutive of force and power are themselves what trace a limit to the outside and fold that multiplicity of discourse back onto the interiority of a world. Multiplicity, in constituting itself as multiplicity, also organizes itself into an organic whole. Such a process of erecting a limit to the outside was furthermore constitutive of Deleuze's definition of the subject: the subject is the thought that gives a 'worldly' status to the multiplicity of the outside.

The quandary I enter into with this conception is not the usual one typically encountered in Badiou's reading of Deleuze (that is, the conventional accusations of the metaphysics of the One). It is rather the problematic notion of the subject as that which both constitutes and expresses the world from its unique perspective. This is the case even while the subject is what extracts the truly novel character from the multiplicity that is this world's outside. In other words, the subject is that point at which the world and the new are both constituted, or expressed. Furthermore, the limits to self-constitution that define that trajectory are no less determinant for the whole as well. This is what a fold is: it is the point at which the outside creates an interiority that is both subjective and constitutive of an objective world.

It is this conflation of novelty and world that I take issue with. Deleuze views force as a means by which the constitution of the world is an end. At the same time that force inhabits and produces change in the world, it is furthermore productive of the limits that constitute this world as this world. Change, in such a conception, is inseparable from the whole. And, in a second move, it appears that any understanding of the force, or differential relations, that are constitutive of this world amounts to a neutralization of the difference that animates force itself. What makes perceptions of the world unique (their individuation) depends upon a more general tendency of being to be expressed and actualized differentially. For example, the colour green may appear to be distinct from surrounding colours, but may itself be the general, residual effect of differential relations among heterogeneous 'parts' of blue and yellow (to take a not altogether scientific explanation that Deleuze gives in *The Fold*[11]). What is distinct on one level (the colour green) may be generality on another (a relation external to the differential relations that constitute that colour). Deleuze's comment that we can say that everything is unique at the same time that everything is ordinary is thus telling (*The Fold*, p. 91). Or, to use the simpler (but probably more scientific) example of weight training that Rorty introduced earlier, the change in a person's musculature, and with that, the differentiations that are perceptible through perceived definition in one's muscles, may be the residual effect of a long-term process of differential contractions of various muscle groups that have occurred over a long period of time. Change and novelty are the by-products of a general procedure of becoming that could hold for almost all of experience.

From this perspective, it appears that Deleuze lacks a formal criterion for qualifying novelty apart from a general assumption that all being undergoes a trajectory of change. As a thinker of the univocity of being, Deleuze cannot make any ontological qualification of novelty. His option, then, is to make being an actualization of the virtual and a virtualization of the actual. On the one hand, we could define the virtual as a tendency towards change that exists independently of the actual beings that undergo transformation (say, the conversion of the earth's surface into sand, the conversion of that sand into glass, the conversion of glass into a wine bottle). In this respect, virtuality is a residual effect of a set of assumptions about the transformation that actual beings undergo. On the other hand, if being cannot be distributed in some hylomorphic fashion into fixed categories that subsume matter (say, bottles, sand, rocks, etc.), it is only through the virtual that we can understand how an actual manifestation of rocks, bottles and sand are points in a more general trajectory of being that is the virtual. This would assume that the virtual provides the true metaphysical basis for change, and that actual beings are simply instantiations of a greater tendency of being. This makes the question of novelty difficult, for we are left to conclude either that everything is subject to change on behalf of some inherent tendency in the virtual, or that thought is the criterion of novelty insofar as it thinks the difference that is proper to being's manifestation, thus wresting a novel character from the generality of change. That is, the only way to get us out of the impasse of conflating the unique with the ordinary (and thus the new with the commonplace) is from the position of the differential relations that extract the novel character from the ordinary. The difficulty with this approach is that novelty becomes little more than a problem of perspective, a subjective problem.

As I have mentioned, in Deleuze's philosophy, the same set of phenomena could be considered under the auspices of generality or habit, or of repetition. That is, there is no inherent reason why philosophy must be organized around difference and repetition. For example, one could flush a toilet hundreds of times

---

11. Deleuze, *The Fold: Leibniz and the Baroque*, p. 90.

a year and view it each time as a general habit that yields little potential for novelty. On the other hand, an individual could decide to tape record the flushing of a toilet and thus make out of a general everyday gesture a work of art—as Yoko Ono did in 1971. Something new, difference, has been extracted from the generality of a habit in such a way that exhibits a truly creative potential. The problem is not simply that not everyone will agree that this constitutes truly novel or interesting art. It is rather that what Deleuze takes to be new (the repetition of difference) could just as readily, from another perspective, be taken to be the ordinary (the generality of the same). The only formal criteria that distinguishes one from the other is that of the contemplative mind that sees difference and repetition as opposed to sameness and generality. This is not to place a subject at the centre of a Deleuzian world—subjects are no more nor less topologized than the singularities of the outside. Rather, it is that thought, for Deleuze, is disjunctive, while being is univocally neutral. It is from the disjunctive operations of thought—its ability to constitute differential relations within a given field—that novelty is constituted.

Earlier I argued that there is a problem with the lack of a formal criteria for novelty in Deleuze. One could either view the new through the various differenciations of being at local levels—the new would be what is repeated differently—or one could maintain that change is possible only through the whole, and is thus extrinsic to any singular manifestation of the whole at a given point. There is the whole, on the one hand, through which change is possible, and then there is the multiplicity of differences that give form to that whole through their worldly expression. To resolve the difficulty of novelty at an ontological level of having to decide between the one and the multiple is to pose a false problem: the whole is constituted in and through the differences that mobilize it. The differences in question, as I have already mentioned, are discerned at various levels in which the whole is expressed. As we saw, to take only one example, the phenomenological intuition of the colour green as different from its surroundings may be the very general, residual effect of differential syntheses between blue and yellow 'inconspicuous perceptions' (*The Fold*, p. 88). Everything that is differentiated—and, by extension, novel—presupposes a continuity of such differentiation into which its individual character is neutralized. The virtual is a pure differentiation that is, in itself, undifferentiated. This is not a circular definition of how the new is constituted,[12] but rather the whole that makes change, differentiation and novelty possible is itself indifferent to the distinctions and formal criteria that would be necessary for determining if something new can or does occur.

Now, not only does the continuity of the virtual allow for the best possible differentiations among actualized beings (in the sense that everything presupposes the virtual as its ground), the formal distinctions that make actualizations what they are allow for a continuity that is proper to the virtual (whereby the maxim

---

12. On the contrary, it is Badiou who is more prone to such criticism insofar as he proposes that events are constituted by subjects at the same time that subjects constitute events.

of the Leibnizian Deleuze that 'everything happens' finds its necessary support in the differentiated thing). There is no formal criteria for the new in Deleuze precisely insofar as the conditions under which the new can occur are simply common to all being. Badiou, one could object, is essentially no different, given that a mathematical ontology founded upon the void is just as univocal as Deleuze's metaphysics of the virtual. Badiou appears to be at an even bigger disadvantage in this respect insofar as he does not make difference a central category in his work. The point, then, is that one cannot make an argument for the superiority of either thinker's take on novelty on ontological grounds alone. For Deleuze, a given field of phenomena is, in and of itself, ontologically neutral: a philosopher who looks at a multiplicity of animals, for example, may see generality and sameness just as readily as they see difference and repetition. And for Badiou, when situations are considered ontologically, all one needs is a mechanism of multiplicity that is organized according to unifying principles of order. That is, relations between elements in a situation are calculated through an external system of reference. And this makes any contrast between Badiou and Deleuze on behalf of a comparative approach to two philosophies almost impossible. On the one hand, you could maintain that the internal organization of one thinker's position provides no means with which to assess the problems of the other, lest one lapse into the 'misreadings' that have typified Badiou's monograph on Deleuze. On the other hand, once properly interrogated, their systems are remarkably similar: both are certainly concerned with problems of novelty and multiplicity. And even if one were then to distinguish their definitions of multiplicity (say, through a distinction between discrete and continuous multiplicities; actual versus potential infinities, etc.), one would find that both thinkers frequently employ both concepts. Badiou's event is discrete and punctual at the same time that the real numbers are everywhere dense; Deleuze presupposes the indivisibility of movement at the same time that he organizes his multiplicities around singular points. And if this is the case, then Badiou and Deleuze are either doing the same thing or there is a non-philosophical criterion at hand that can resolve the foregoing problematic.

At bottom, Deleuze is a philosopher of the world: to have faith in the world is a principle that is entirely consistent with the criterion for immanence that Deleuze sets for his system. Belief in the world is tantamount to a realization that one is part of the world, that there is not a being that is external to thought, a world whose existence can be doubted or subtracted from knowledge. The conception of the subject that emerged in the work of the later Deleuze was precisely on par with this tendency, for he did not define the subject as a single point of clarity which can then provide a synthetic unity out of the multiplicity that constitutes experience. The primacy of faith over knowledge restores the subject to being constituted from the same multiplicity that makes up the world. The task for thought, then, is to be adequate to the same power that gives rise and birth to the world—the limits that constitute the world fold back to constitute the subject as the expression of the world. Neither the world nor novelty are problems for

Deleuze: they simply are. The problems for which Deleuze became famous in *Difference and Repetition* are problems not because they presuppose a dialectical resolution, but rather because their problematic structure is difference itself—a difference that gives rise to novel forms of life. What Deleuze deems problems, then, are not really problems at all, but rather the conditions that give rise to philosophical thought and the world as it is.

Deleuze's connection of a problem to the world provides the meta-philosophical criterion to readily distinguish him from Badiou. If virtuality proposes a set of relations that are problems, the actualization of the virtual is a solution that presupposes the problem as its ground. This move in Deleuze makes the world a solution to an underlying, virtual problem. In this respect, Badiou is quite correct to view Deleuze as a philosopher of the world. But he is also correct to criticize him on this ground—for if there is one thing that Badiou sees as being problematic for philosophy, it is the world itself. The world is hostile to thought; by extension, any philosophy that orients itself around the existence of a world will be limited in its capacity. Badiou's question is, how it is possible to do philosophy in the present age—not simply within the morass of a trivial postmodern philosophy at which his philosophy ostensibly takes aim, but rather in a world that is hostile to transformative thought? The modernity of Badiou's thought is that the twentieth century has borne witness to a violent and fragile world, for which the two philosophical responses have either been a dystopian dread of the idea of progress and the future (which Badiou, incorrectly, characterizes as nihilism), or a return to the ethics and human rights that typify liberal economies and their representative democracies. The choice here is between a repudiation of the world, or a regulative thought that governs imperfections of the world. Nowhere is the question raised of thought's ability to transform the world. And this, I would argue, is because both ethics or 'nihilism' depart from the existence of the world, however problematic it is.

I have avoided bringing in details of Badiou's political orientation as a philosopher, but it is patently obvious that, in the last instance, politics, art and science have a global marketplace as their ultimate condition of possibility. This, at bottom, is the ultimate condition that constitutes the world—its possible subsumption under the economic conditions set to it by the world market: science can only proceed when funded by pharmaceutical companies and military states, political decisions can be made only when they stabilize the economy, art has value so long as it brings profit. In this respect, it's quite easy to say what the conditions of possibility are for the emergence of the new: capital, a monetary system for ordering and regulating lived, temporal experience.[13] Deleuze and Badiou are in agreement that capital has opened thought onto a world of a pure, unbound multiplicity of elements that is organized in a haphazard manner: subject to vari-

---

13. As Badiou states in an interview with Peter Hallward: 'every proposition that directly concerns the economy can be assimilated by capital. This is so by definition, since capital is indifferent to the qualitative configuration of things. So long as it can be transformed or aligned in terms of market value, everything's fine'. Badiou, *Ethics*, p. 106.

ous territorializations and deterritorializations (or, in Badiou's less ostentatious terms, formal regroupings) that effectively undo the social bond. What becomes a territory for Israel is statelessness for the Palestinian people, which can be re-territorialized under the banner of 'terrorism', 'occupied/disputed' territory, etc. Curiously, global capital becomes the historical medium of the world in which we do philosophy (insofar as no two beings are related to each other apart from the computations of capital), at the same time that philosophy has not begun to think 'on level terms' with capital, of the politics of a world unleashed and unbound in the computation of multiplicity. If contemporary capitalism operates without borders in calculating a multiplicity of elements that populate the world (people, goods, communication networks, local economies), it becomes a pertinent question whether capitalism is grounded upon an inconsistency that is separate from its own powers of computation. The indiscernible in capital would be capital itself: the dense network of figures and calculations that project a future of profit as the determining ground for action in the present. Capital, in this respect, subsumes not only the world, but the possible conditions under which thought proceeds without limits.

In making the question of novelty a modern problem, it would be difficult to overlook the fact that novelty and innovation are cornerstones of capitalist production. Capital has certainly been successful at coming up with new modalities of existence: not simply the commodities it produces, but its organization of the world around a single market, its subsumption of the entire world under the monetary count of capital, finds itself ever more decentralized and dispersed.[14] Everything, so we're told, is new under capital. If Badiou has organized his philosophy around the problem of the rarity of the new, it is because he has made a decision, external to his system itself, to separate thought and action from conditions that have been set to it by the world, and its historical extension in the global marketplace. Badiou may agree with Deleuze that the world needs philosophy, but not because the world is out there to be thought as it is, but to be transformed. There is a multiple-being that is presented under capital and which is regulated by the excess of the state of this multiple being (that is, capital), and this is largely how we experience the world devoid of any principle of unity.

When I stated in an earlier chapter that 'the void alone enables creation', in no way did I mean that the void itself is a creative potential on par with a Deleuzian virtual. And, given the fact that the void is also the primary name of being—an ontological cornerstone to Badiou's system—I was always in danger of running the risk of tying the advent of novelty to existence alone. What I hope the preceding chapters have made clear is that it is necessary to make a detour through properly human activity—the capacity for thinking truth and instituting events—in order for there to be novelty proper. It is an odd challenge facing a minimalist metaphysics that one can have both ontology and a theory of the new. For an ontology founded upon nothing would presume that existence can follow

---

14. See Hardt and Negri, *Empire*.

from non-existence, at the same time as it assumes that something can happen on the basis of nothing (that 'something', Badiou's event, being nothing more than a subjective ability to respond to the existence of the inconsistent nothingness that is being). But to say that 'nothing' enables novelty leaves one searching for a formal criterion for that novelty. On the one hand, we have the problem of resolving Badiou's philosophy with philosophy in general (which would require a fairly strong argument as to why mathematics is ontology); on the other hand, there is the more particular question as to the possible conditions for something new to occur.

My task has been to unravel possible answers to these questions through this comparative exposition of Badiou's philosophy. Regarding the former set of problems, I argued that existence is its own criterion: something exists because it is in its nature to do so. In that sense, there is no ground outside the existence of instantiated, or presented, beings that can provide a foundation for thinking existence. What Badiou has effectively done is to have incorporated that nothing into ontology itself: being and nothing are the same. Badiou could perhaps find himself in a bit of a dispute with mathematicians on this count, since it is debatable whether set theory can provide a foundation for mathematics in general (given that there is more than one set theory). In this case, it would be very difficult to say how it could be a foundation for a philosophy. Badiou's move to make set theory an ontological foundation for a system of philosophy will probably, in the future, be met with resistance by philosophers of mathematics. It is still something of an open question in his native France. But the objections to thinking set theory as a foundation remain unresolved so long as we take foundation in a closed sense of the term. Set theory is notorious for giving birth to problems it could not resolve—primarily Russell's paradox (a response to Frege, not Cantor) and the undecidability of the continuum hypothesis and axiom of choice. Cohen's elaboration of the matter only led to the development of non-Cantorian set theories. My argument is that set theory initially posed a problem of infinities which both axiomatic systems and generic set theory sought to resolve. We can understand set theory as ontology only if we assume ontology to be a problem for which there have been various historical resolutions. In this sense, set theory is an ontological foundation not in a stable sense of providing a foundation that yields determinate results, but in the sense that it poses a problem (of the existence of an infinity irreducible to any principle of totality) that provides an impetus for thought. And this problem that set theory set up at its outset runs directly counter to the existence of a closed totality—a world or universe. The existence of nothing, the fact that we can think on its basis, frees philosophy from conditions that the world sets for it.

Let us return to the example of Zeno's paradox, which was set up in the opening chapter precisely as a denial of the possibility of change. The philosophical flaws of Zeno's original conclusions were that change, or movement, itself could not be conflated with the time that measures it (this time being broken up into indivisible, discrete segments). In such a conception, time would be an abstract, mathematical system much like set theory: it is composed of discrete units (for the purposes of simplicity, seconds, let us say) which form larger collections (minutes, hours, days, weeks, etc.). Although time can be applicable to external states of affairs that are changing, it is itself an abstract system that, in itself, always stays the same (that is, it is a continuous succession of discrete units). At best, time is nothing but the measurement of a movement or change that occurs externally to it. As is well known, Bergson responded to such a predicament by separating the question of time from that of the systems in which it is measured: time itself is change, the system we use to measure it being a mere abstraction that fails to grasp the change that is inherent to the living and non-living world. Like Deleuze's ontology, the Bergsonian virtual is founded upon a metaphysics of change that abstract, scientific thinking fails to grasp.

What we are faced with, then, is a separation of change from the means with which we can assess it. In so doing, we separate the question of change from anything that thought is capable of accomplishing. Badiou's unique contribution to the debate is to have left questions of bodies or arrows out of the picture entirely: thought does not need to look for conditions external to it in order to effect change; it can look at its internal conditions of possibility as they are given in the formal system with which we understand time. That is, Badiou is not interested in moving arrows or bodies, but in the fact that human beings have a concept of time in and through a formal mathematical system of organized multiplicity. Time is nothing but an abstract, formal system of formalized multiplicity that happens to coincide with lived experience. Capital, it could be argued, is a method of computation that proceeds in much the same way. Capital and time, in this respect, are variants on set theory. But it is not the fact that mathematics can establish normative or regulative models for thought that makes these philosophically significant. What the historical advent of set theory proposed was an existence of multiple infinities as a problem for thought, from which a complete overhaul of twentieth-century mathematics followed. If we can then call set theory a foundation for mathematics, it is because it sets up various problems (of the infinitely large, non-denumerable, non-constructible) on which thought can proceed. And because such a system has not departed from its applicability to the world (non-denumerable infinities are not possible objects of experience), it fundamentally frees thought from the limits set to it by experience.

What Badiou has effectively done, then, is to have separated the question of novelty—which is, after all, a category of experience—from the conditions that have been set to it by experience. The advantage of such an approach—so I have argued—is that it effectively frees thought from the various limit conditions that experience sets it (say, the limitations of capital, human finitude, language, etc). But it seems that it is not enough to have a formal system that could work to produce change and innovation in and through the production of truth—it also has to account for the very real possibility of change occurring under these conditions. And it seems the only way that Badiou's philosophy can effectively do this is by falling into an analogy between the ontology and truths of set theory, and the being of real situations and their historical transformations. That is, what is both intriguing and frustrating about Badiou's philosophy is that, however many examples he gives of truth procedures (the Paris commune, the French Revolution, the struggle with the *sans-papiers* in modern France), one always gets the sense that these are not real *events*, but potential sites in which there could be events. At best, they indicate the possibility of the realization of potential transformation, even if, ultimately, it is still an open question whether political events have actually occurred. Ever. Philosophy is not a description of truth procedures that have occurred, but rather a call to action for truth procedures to occur. Whether or not there has ever been a true event is therefore beside the point: it is simply enough to know that there can be events insofar as we are capable of thinking nothing.

And this is what makes Badiou's thought what it is: the very fact that political struggles have ended in failures, the very fact that the world we have created for ourselves is devoid of truth and value does not mean that people should abandon their struggles to produce truth in and through art, science, politics and love. If philosophy confines itself to the conditions that are set to it by experience, it is of course inevitable that it will fall prey to either a postmodern, moribund cynicism or an ethical regulation of a smooth-running state of affairs. The first repudiates any hope of thinking that a different world is possible, while the latter position consigns itself to preserving the status quo of mediocrity that defines the world today (few could credibly argue that medical ethics, business ethics and multinational governing bodies as 'ethical' commissions have improved the standards of living for the majority of the world in the latter half of the twentieth century). It is only by radically separating itself from the world—so radically, in fact, that the question of a philosophical application of thought onto the world becomes an afterthought of sorts—that philosophy becomes an imperative to try out through militant activity. While a reader might bemoan the fact that Badiou's philosophy makes no practical concessions to experience—so much so that it may just as readily not exist—they would be missing the point that the way philosophy becomes experience is not through a reflection upon the world, but through human activity that effectively transforms it.

Bibliography

Books by Badiou

BE *Being and Event*, trans. Oliver Feltham, London, Continuum, 2005.

CB *Deleuze: The Clamor of Being*, trans. Louise Burchill, Minneapolis, University of Minnesota Press, 2000.

CS *Conditions*, Paris, Seuil, 1992.

CT *Court traité d'ontologie transitoire*, Paris, Seuil, 1998.

EE *L'être et l'événement*, Paris, Seuil, 1988.

Ethics *Ethics: An Essay on the Understanding of Evil*, trans. Peter Hallward, London, Verso, 2001.

IT *Infinite Thought: Truth and the Return to Philosophy*, ed. and trans. Justin Clemens and Oliver Feltham, London, Continuum, 2003

LM *Logiques des mondes: L'être et l'événement 2*, Paris, Seuil, 2006.

MP *Manifesto for Philosophy*, trans. Norman Madarasz, Albany, State University of New York Press, 1999.

NN *Le Nombre et les nombres*, Paris, Seuil, 1990.

SP *Saint Paul: The Foundation of Universalism*, trans. Ray Brassier, Stanford, Stanford University Press, 2003.

TS *Théorie du sujet*, Paris, Seuil, 1982.

TW *Theoretical Writings*, trans. Ray Brassier andß Alberto Toscano, London, Continuum Books, 2004.

Articles by Badiou

'Marque et manque: à propos du zero', *Cahiers pour l'analyse*, vol. 10, 1969, pp. 150-73.
'L'ontologie implicite de Spinoza', in Myriam Revault d'Allones (ed.) *Spinoza: puissance et ontology*, Paris, Kimé, 1994.
'Metaphysics and the Critique of Metaphysics', trans. Alberto Toscano, *Pli: Warwick Journal of Philosophy*, no. 10, 2000, pp. 174-90.
'Of Life as a Name of Being, or, Deleuze's Vitalist Ontology', *Pli: Warwick Journal of Philosophy*, no. 10, 2000.
'The Ethic of Truths: Construction and Potency', trans. Thelma Sowley, *Pli: Warwick*

Journal of Philosophy, no. 12, 2001, pp. 245-55.
'Being by Numbers: Interview Alain Badiou', *Artforum*, vol. 33, no. 2, 1994, pp. 84-90.
'Politics and Philosophy', in *Ethics: An Essay on the Understanding of Evil*, trans. Peter Hallward, London, Verso, 2001.

Other Works Cited

Althusser, Louis, *For Marx*, trans. Ben Brewster, London, Verso, 1996.
Aristotle, *Physics*, trans. Robin Waterfield, Oxford, Oxford, 1996.
Bergson, Henri, *Matter and Memory*, trans. Nancy M. Paul and W. Scott Palmer, New York, Zone Books, 1990.
Brassier, Ray, 'Stellar Void or Cosmic Animal? Badiou and Deleuze', *Pli: Warwick Journal of Philosophy*, no. 10, 2000, pp. 200-216.
Butler, Judith, 'Competing Universalities', in Judith Butler, Ernesto Laclau, and Slavoj Žižek (eds.), *Contingency, Hegemony, Universality*, London, Verso, 2000, pp. 136-81.
Butler, Judith, Ernesto Laclau and Slavoj Žižek, *Contingency, Hegemony, Universality*, London, Verso, 2000.
Copjec, Joan, *Read My Desire: Lacan Against the Historicists*, Cambridge, MIT Press, 1994.
Copjec, Joan, *Imagine There's No Woman: Ethics and Sublimation*, Cambridge, MIT Press, 2002.
Cunningham, Conor, *A Genealogy of Nihilism: Philosophies of Nothing and the Difference of Theology*, London, Routledge, 2002.
Dauben, Joseph Warren, *Georg Cantor*, Princeton, Princeton University Press, 1979.
De Landa, Manuel, *Intensive Science and Virtual Philosophy*, London, Continuum, 2002.
Deleuze, Gilles, *Cinema 1: The Movement Image*, trans. Hugh Tomlinson and Barbara Habberjam, Minneapolis, University of Minnesota Press, 1986.
Deleuze, Gilles, *Cinema 2: The Time-Image*, trans. Hugh Tomlinson and Robert Galeta, Minneapolis, University of Minnesota Press, 1989.
Deleuze, Gilles, *Bergsonism*, trans. Hugh Tomlinson and Barbara Habberjam, New York, Zone Books, 1991.
Deleuze, Gilles, *Expressionism in Philosophy: Spinoza*, trans. Martin Joughin, New York, Zone Books, 1991.
Deleuze, Gilles, *The Fold: Leibniz and the Baroque*, trans. Tom Conley, Minneapolis, University of Minnesota Press, 1992.
Deleuze, Gilles, *Difference and Repetition*, trans. Paul Patton, New York, Columbia University Press, 1994.
Deleuze, Gilles, *Spinoza: Practical Philosophy*, trans. Robert Hurley, San Francisco, City Lights, 1998.
Deleuze, Gilles, *The Logic of Sense*, Constantin V. Boundas (ed.), trans. Mark Lester with Charles Stivale, London, Continuum, 2001.
Deleuze, Gilles and Félix Guattari, *What is Philosophy?*, trans. Hugh Tomlinson and Graham Burchell, New York, Verso, 1994.
Deleuze, Gilles and Claire Parnet, *Dialogues*, trans. Hugh Tomlinson and Barbara Habberjam, New York, Columbia, 1987.

Dummett, Michael, 'Can Analytical Philosophy be Systematic?' in Kenneth Baynes, James Bohman, and Thomas McCarthy (eds.), *After Philosophy: End or Transformation?*, Cambridge, MIT Press, 1987, pp. 189-215.
Fink, Bruce, 'Alain Badiou', *UMBR(a)*, no. 1, 1996, pp. 11-12.
Foucault, Michel, 'Questions of Method: An Interview with Michel Foucault', in Kenneth Baynes, James Bohman, and Thomas McCarthy (eds.), *After Philosophy: End or Transformation?*, Cambridge, MIT Press, 1987, pp. 100-17.
Foucault, Michel, *The Archaeology of Knowledge*, trans. A.M. Sheridan Smith, London, Routledge, 1989.
Freud, Sigmund, 'Civilization and its Discontents', in Albert Dickson (ed.), *Civilization, Society and Religion*, trans. James Strachey, vol. XII Penguin Freud Library, London, Penguin, 1991, pp. 243-340.
Hacking, Ian, *The Taming of Chance*, Cambridge, Cambridge University Press, 1990.
Hallward, Peter, 'Generic Sovereignty: The Philosophy of Alain Badiou', *Angelaki*, vol. 3, no. 3, 1998, pp. 87-111.
Hardt, Michael and Antonio Negri, *Empire*, Cambridge, Harvard University Press, 2001.
Hegel, G. W. F., *Science of Logic*, trans. A.V. Miller, London, Allen and Unwin, 1969.
Heidegger, Martin, *Basic Writings: From Being and Time (1927) to The Task of Thinking (1964)*, David Farrell Krell (ed.), Revised & Expanded ed., San Francisco, Harper & Row, 1993.
Heidegger, Martin, 'On the Essence of Truth', in David Farrell Krell (ed.), *Basic Writings: From Being and Time (1927) to The Task of Thinking (1964)*, Revised & Expanded ed., San Francisco, Harper & Row, 1993.
Kaplan, Robert, *The Nothing That Is: A Natural History of Zero*, Oxford, Oxford University Press, 1999.
Lacan, Jacques, *The Four Fundamental Concepts of Psychoanalysis*, Jacques-Alain Miller (ed.), trans. Alan Sheridan, New York, Norton, 1981.
Lacan, Jacques, 'Kant avec Sade', trans. James Swenson, *October*, vol. 51, 1989, pp. 55-104.
Lacan, Jacques, *The Ethics of Psychoanalysis, 1959-1960*, Jacques-Alain Miller (ed.), trans. Dennis Porter, New York, Norton, 1992.
Lacan, Jacques, *On Feminine Sexuality: The Limits of Love and Knowledge - The Seminar of Jacques Lacan, Book XX, Encore*, Jacques-Alain Miller (ed.), trans. Bruce Fink, New York, Norton, 1998.
Lavine, Shaughan, *Understanding the Infinite*, Cambridge, Mass., Harvard University Press, 1994.
Macherey, Pierre, 'The Problem of the Attributes', in Warren Montag and Ted Stolze (eds.), *The New Spinoza*, Minneapolis, University of Minnesota Press, 1997, pp. 65-96.
Miller, Jacques-Alain, 'Suture (Elements of the Logic of the Signifier)', *Screen*, vol. 18, no. 4, 1977-8, pp. 24-34.
Plato, *The Republic*, trans. Desmond Lee, New York, Penguin Books, 1974.
Rorty, Richard, *Consequences of Pragmatism: Essays, 1972-1980*, Minneapolis, University of Minnesota Press, 1982.
Rose, Jacqueline, 'We are all afraid, but of what exactly?' *The Guardian*, 20 March

2003.

Seife, Charles, *Zero: The Biography of a Dangerous Idea*, New York, Penguin, 2000.

Shapiro, Stewart, *Thinking About Mathematics: The Philosophy of Mathematics*, Oxford, Oxford University Press, 2000.

Simont, Juliette, 'Le Pur et l'impur (Sur deux questions de l'histoire de la philosophie dans L'être et l'événement)', *Le Temps Modernes*, no. 526, 1990, pp. 27-60.

Spinoza, Benedictus de, *The Collected Works of Spinoza*, ed. and trans. Edwin Curley, Princeton, Princeton University Press, 1985.

Tiles, Mary, *The Philosophy of Set Theory: An Historical Introduction to Cantor's Paradise*, Oxford, Blackwell, 1989.

van Heijenoort, Jean (ed.), *From Frege to Gödel: A Source Book in Mathematical Logic, 1879-1931*, Cambridge, Harvard University Press, 1967.

von Neumann, John, 'An Axiomatization of Set Theory', in Jean van Heijenoort (ed.), *From Frege to Gödel: A Source Book in Mathematical Logic, 1879-1931*, Cambridge, Harvard University Press, 1967, pp. 393-413.

von Neumann, John, 'On the Introduction of Transfinite Numbers', in Jean van Heijenoort (ed.), *From Frege to Gödel: A Source Book in Mathematical Logic, 1879-1931*, Cambridge, Harvard University Press, 1967, pp. 346-54.

Žižek, Slavoj, The Ticklish Subject: The Absent Centre of Political Ontology, London, Verso, 1999.

Zupančič, Alenka, 'The Splendor of Creation: Kant, Lacan, Nietzsche', *Umbr(a): A Journal of the Unconscious*, no. 1, 1999, pp. 35-42.

Zupančič, Alenka, *Ethics of the Real: Kant, Lacan*, London, Verso, 2000.

Index

Althusser, Louis 107, 129-30
Aristotle: 1, 15-17, 29, 137 n8, 152;
    Physics, 15-16
Badiou, Alain:
    Being and Event, 3-4, 8, 11-12, 14, 22, 23, 26, 29-35, 40, 47-49, 51-52, 56-59, 64, 66, 72-73, 75-76, 82, 85, 88, 96-98, 101-103, 107-108, 111, 127-128, 130-131, 136-38, 151;
    Conditions, 13 n25, 87, 119, 151;
    Court traité, 37-39, 151;
    Deleuze, Clamor of Being, 7 n18, 8 n19, 23, 27, 41, 136-138, 151;
    Ethics, 15n32, 23, 90n25, 100 n8, 102-103, 129-130, 144 n13, 151;
    Infinite Thought, 129 n2, 131, 134, 151;
    Logiques des mondes, 88 n20, 151;
    Manifesto for Philosophy, 3 n4, 73, 81, 114, 132n4, 151;
    Number and Numbers, 12 n24, 15, 22 n41, 46-7, 49 n12, 51, 55-7, 65, 67, 151;
    Theoretical Writings, 88 n20, 151;
    Théorie du Sujet, 98, 106, 116 n25, 151;
    Saint Paul, 10, 23, 115 n22, 151;
    'Being By Numbers', 7n1, 87 n19, 151;
    'Marque et Manque', 107, 151;
    'Metaphysics and the Critique of Metaphysics', 74 n6, 151;

'The Ethic of Truths', 73 n2, 77 n11, 151
Balibar, Etienne 138
Beckett, Samuel 113
Berg, Alban 10
Bergson, Henri 5 n13, 6, 15-18, 29, 127, 135, 147, 152
Bosteels, Bruno 72, 98 n4
Brassier, Ray 8n20, 40, 152
Butler, Judith 80 n14, 105-6, 152
Caesar, Julius 14
Canguilhem Georges, 138
Cantor, Georg 8 n19, 10-11, 13, 15, 41, 47-48, 50, 52-7, 71, 78, 82, 84, 95, 97-8, 104, 126-27, 131-32, 134, 146, 152, 154
Clemens, Justin 129, 151
Cohen, Paul 10, 12, 56, 72, 78, 83-4, 95, 98, 104, 132, 137, 146
Copjec, Joan 17 n37, 98 n5, 110 n16, 152
Critchley, Simon 72
Cunningham, Connor 97, 99, 152
Darwin, Charles 126-27, 130, 135
Dauben, John Warren 47 n7, 53 n19, 152
de Landa, Manuel 7 n17, 18, 19 n40, 135 n6, 152
Deleuze, Gilles: 1-8, 13-15, 17-21, 23, 27, 29-33, 37-41, 62, 66, 92, 98, 104, 127, 129, 134-145, 147,

151-2;
Bergsonism, 5 n13;
Cinema 1, 6, *152*;
Cinema 2, *136 n7*, *139*, *152*;
Dialogues, *1 n1*, *2 n3*;
Difference and Repetition,*3 n5*, *4 n8 and 9*, *5 n10-12*, *134 n5*, *144*, *152*;
Expressionism in Philosophy, 27 n1, 30 n5 and 6, 31 n7, 32 n8, 33 n9, 36 n12-14, 37 n15, 38 n19, 41 n25, *152*;
The Fold, *14 n28 and 29*, *141-42*, *152*;
Logic of Sense, *3 n5*, *152*;
Spinoza, *40 n20*, *152*;
Thousand Plateaus, 27;
What is Philosophy? *2 n2*, *13 n27*, *152*
Descartes, René, 9, 25, 28 n2, 31, 130
Duchamp, Marcel 114
Dummett, Michael 73 n3, 152
Einstein, Albert 78
Euclid 62, 78
Feltham, Oliver 129, 151
Fink, Bruce 9n21, 14, 153
Foucault, Michel 21, 45, 68, 88-9, 90-2, 101, 129, 138, 140, 153
Fraenkel, Abraham 12, 49, 57, 131
Frege, Gottlob 49-51, 56-7, 74, 99, 106-7, 146, 154
Freud, Sigmund 4, 10, 89, 113, 114, 119, 126, 130, 132, 153
Galileo, Galilei 77
Gauss, Carl Friedrich 78
Gödel, Kurt 13 n26, 51-2, 56, 78, 99 n7, 107, 154
Guattari, Felix 2, 13, 127, 152
Hacking, Ian 45-6, 153
Hallward, Peter 90, 96, 139 n9, 144 n13, 153
Hardt, Michael 103 n11, 145 n14, 153
Hegel, G.W.F: 1, 25-6, 37, 49, 52, 60-1, 67, 97, 101, 106, 130, 137 n8, 138-39, 153;
Science of Logic, *52*, *61 n27*, *67*, *139 n10*
Heidegger, Martin 9, 49, 71, 73, 75-6,

119, 126-27, 129, 132 n8, 138, 153
Husserl, Edmund 126-27, 130
Joughin, Martin 41
Kant, Immanuel 13, 60-1, 67, 91, 101, 112 n17, 113 n19, 115 n23, 153-54
Kierkegaard, Søren 119
Kuhn, Thomas 68
Lacan, Jacques: 9, 10, 17 n37, 35, 49, 80 n14, 91-2, 96-8, 101, 104-21, 129, 130, 153;
Encore, *9*, *17 n37*, *92 n28*;
Sem. VII, *112 n18*, *121 n28*;
Laclau, Ernesto 80 n14, 106 n13, 152
Lavine, Shaughan 11 n23, 53 n19, 54 n22, 56 n24, 153
Le Pen, Jean-Marie 65
Leibniz, Gottfried Wilhelm 9, 14 n28, 14n30, 50, 143, 152
Lenin, Vladimir Ilyich 10
Leonardo, da Vinci 114
Lizzitsky El, 114
Lyotard, Jean-Francois 129
Macherey, Pierre 37-8, 153
Mallarmé, Stéphane 113, 132
Marx, Karl 9-10, 46, 126, 130, 132, 152
Michelangelo 114
Miller, Jacques-Alain 98, 106n14, 107, 153
Nancy, Jean-Luc 129
Negri, Antonio 103n11, 145 n14, 153
Ono, Yoko 142
Pessoa, Fernando 113
Picasso, Pablo 114
Plato 1, 9-10, 29, 52, 73-4, 75 n7, 127, 137, 153
Quine, W. V. 62
Riemann, Georg Friedrich Bernhard 62, 78
Rorty, Richard 74 n5, 141, 153
Rose, Jacqueline 118 n27, 153
Rousseau, Jean-Jacques 9
Russell, Bertrand 49, 50-1, 56, 57-8,

74, 78, 91 n27, 121, 146
Schoenberg, Arnold 10, 113, 116, 132, 137
Sedofsky, L. 71 n1, 87 n19
Seife, Charles 17 n39, 52 n16, 53 n20, 153
Shakespeare, William 114
Shapiro, Stewart, 47 n5, 47 n6, 86 n18, 154
Simont, Juliette 34, 154
Smith, Daniel 41 n25
Spinoza, Benedictus de 6 n16, 26-30, 32-42, 47, 60, 64, 98, 137-38, 151-54
Stockhausen, Karlheinz 10
Tarski, Alfred 138
Tiles, Mary 13 n26, 16 n35, 41 n24, 82 n16, 154
Von Neumann, John 10, 49, 52 n17, 55, 58 n26, 78, 99, 154
Weber, Carl Maria von 10
Zeno 15-18, 67, 78, 146
Zermelo, Ernst 10, 12, 49, 51, 78, 131
Žižek, Slavoj 72, 80n14, 97-8, 106 n13, 115, 117, 152, 154
Zupančič, Alenka 112, 113 n19, 154

Printed in the United Kingdom
by Lightning Source UK Ltd.
131456UK00001B/26/P